GODLESS

GODLESS

THE
CHURCH
OF
LIBERALISM

ANN
COULTER

RANDOM HOUSE
LARGE PRINT

Published in the United States of America
by Random House Large Print in association
with Crown Forum, New York.
Distributed by Random House, Inc., New York.

Library of Congress Cataloging-in-Publication Data
Coulter, Ann H.
Godless : the church of liberalism / by Ann
Coulter. — 1st large print ed.
p. cm.
ISBN-13: 978-0-7393-2633-6
ISBN-10: 0-7393-2633-3
1. Liberalism—United States. 2. United
States—Politics and government—1989–
3. Large type books. I. Title.
JC574.2.U6C667 2006
320.51'30973—dc22
2006013355

www.randomlargeprint.com

FIRST LARGE PRINT EDITION

10 9 8 7 6 5 4 3 2 1

This Large Print edition published in accord
with the standards of the N.A.V.H.

For George

Contents

GODLESS

1 ON THE SEVENTH DAY, GOD RESTED AND LIBERALS SCHEMED

> They exchanged the truth of God for the lie, and worshiped and served the creation rather than the Creator. . . . Therefore, God gave them up to passions of dishonor; for their females exchanged the natural use for that which is contrary to nature.
> **—Romans 1:25–26**

iberals love to boast that they are not "religious," which is what one would expect to hear from the state-sanctioned religion. Of course liberalism is a religion. It has its own cosmology, its own miracles, its own beliefs in the supernatural, its own churches, its own high priests, its own saints, its own total worldview, and its own explanation of the existence of the universe. In other words, liberalism con-

tains all the attributes of what is generally known as "religion."

Under the guise of not favoring religion, liberals favor one cosmology over another and demand total indoctrination into theirs. The state religion of liberalism demands obeisance (to the National Organization for Women), tithing (to teachers' unions), reverence (for abortion), and formulaic imprecations ("Bush lied, kids died!" "Keep your laws off my body!" "Arms for hostages!"). Everyone is taxed to support indoctrination into the state religion through the public schools, where innocent children are taught a specific belief system, rather than, say, math.

Liberal doctrines are less scientifically provable than the story of Noah's ark, but their belief system is taught as fact in government schools, while the Biblical belief system is banned from government schools by law. As a matter of faith, liberals believe: Darwinism is a fact, people are born gay, child-molesters can be rehabilitated, recycling is a virtue, and chastity is not. If people are born gay, why hasn't Darwinism weeded out people who don't reproduce? (For that, we need a theory of survival of the most fabulous.) And if gays can't change, why do liberals think child-molesters can? Pedophilia is a sexual preference. If they're born that way, instead of rehabilitation, how about keeping them locked up? Why must children be taught that recycling is the only answer? Why aren't we teaching children "safe littering"?

We aren't allowed to ask. Believers in the liberal faith might turn violent—much like the practitioners of Islam, the Religion of Peace, who ransacked Danish embassies worldwide because a Danish newspaper published cartoons of Mohammed. This is something else that can't be taught in government schools: Muslims' predilection for violence. On the first anniversary of the 9/11 attack, the National Education Association's instruction materials exhorted teachers, "Do not suggest that any group is responsible" for the attack of 9/11.[1]

If a Martian landed in America and set out to determine the nation's official state religion, he would have to conclude it is liberalism, while Christianity and Judaism are prohibited by law. And not just in Cambridge, Massachusetts, where it's actually on the books, but throughout the land. This is a country in which taxpayers are forced to subsidize "artistic" exhibits of aborted fetuses, crucifixes in urine, and gay pornography. Meanwhile, it's unconstitutional to display a Nativity scene at Christmas or the Ten Commandments on government property if the purpose is to promote monotheistic religion. Nearly half the members of the Supreme Court—the ones generally known as "liberals"—are itching to ban the references to God on our coins and in the Pledge of Allegiance. They resisted in 2004 on procedural grounds only because it was an election year.

The absence of a divinity makes liberals' belief system no less religious. Liberals define **religion** as only those belief systems that subscribe to the notion of a divine being in order to dismiss other religions as mere religion and theirs as something greater. Shintoism and Buddhism have no Creator God either, and they are considered religions. Curiously, those are two of the most popular religions among leftists—at least until 9/11, when Islam became all the rage.

Liberalism is a comprehensive belief system denying the Christian* belief in man's immortal soul. Their religion holds that there is nothing sacred about human consciousness. It's just an accident no more significant than our possession of opposable thumbs. They deny what we know about ourselves: that we are moral beings in God's image. Without this fundamental understanding of man's place in the world, we risk being lured into misguided pursuits, including

---

* Throughout this book, I often refer to Christians and Christianity because I am a Christian and I have a fairly good idea of what they believe, but the term is intended to include anyone who subscribes to the Bible of the God of Abraham, including Jews and others.

bestiality, slavery, and PETA membership. Liberals swoon in pagan admiration of Mother Earth, mystified and overawed by her power. They deny the Biblical idea of dominion and progress, the most ringing affirmation of which is the United States of America.

Although they are Druids, liberals masquerade as rationalists, adopting a sneering tone of scientific sophistication, which is a little like being condescended to by a tarot card reader. Liberals hate science and react badly to it. They will literally run from the room, light-headed and nauseated, when told of data that might suggest that the sexes have different abilities in math and science. They repudiate science when it contradicts their pagan beliefs—that the AIDS virus doesn't discriminate, that there is no such thing as IQ, that nuclear power is dangerous and scary, or that breast implants cause disease. Liberals use the word **science** exactly as they use the word **constitutional.** Both words are nothing more or less than a general statement of liberal approval, having nothing to do with either science or the Constitution. (Thus, for example, the following sentence makes sense to liberals: **President Clinton saved the Constitution by repeatedly ejaculating on a fat Jewish girl in the Oval Office.**)

The core of the Judeo-Christian tradition says that we are utterly and distinctly apart from other species. We have dominion over the plants and the animals on Earth. God gave it to us, it's ours—as stated succinctly in the book of Genesis. Liberals would sooner trust the stewardship of the Earth to Shetland ponies and dung beetles. All their pseudoscience supports an alternative religion that says we are an insignificant part of nature. Environmentalists want mass infanticide, zero population growth, reduced standards of living, and vegetarianism. The core of environmentalism is that they hate mankind.

Everything liberals believe is in elegant opposition to basic Biblical precepts.

- Our religion says that human progress proceeds from the spark of divinity in the human soul; their religion holds that human progress is achieved through sex and death.
- We believe in invention and creation; they catalogue with stupefaction the current state of our diminishing resources and tell us to stop consuming.
- We say humans stand apart from the world and our charge is Planet Earth; they say we are part of the world, and our hubristic use of nature is sinful.
- We say humans are in God's image; they say we are no different morally from the apes.

- We believe in populating the Earth until there's standing room only and then colonizing Mars; they believe humans are in the twilight of their existence.

Our book is Genesis. Their book is Rachel Carson's **Silent Spring,** the original environmental hoax. Carson brainwashed an entire generation into imagining a world without birds, killed by DDT. Because of liberals' druidical religious beliefs, they won't allow us to save Africans dying in droves of malaria with DDT because DDT might hurt the birds. A few years after oil drilling began in Prudhoe Bay, Alaska, a saboteur set off an explosion blowing a hole in the pipeline and releasing an estimated 550,000 gallons of oil.[2] It was one of the most devastating environmental disasters in recent history. Six weeks later, all the birds were back. Birds are like rats—you couldn't get rid of them if you tried.

The various weeds and vermin liberals are always trying to save are no more distinguishable than individual styles of rap music. The massive Dickey-Lincoln Dam, a $227 million hydroelectric project proposed on upper St. John River in Maine, was halted by the discovery of the Furbish lousewort, a plant previously believed to be extinct. Liberals didn't even know this plant still existed, but suddenly they were seized with affection for it. They had been missing it all that time! (Granted, the rediscovery of the Furbish louse-wort has improved the lives of every man, woman, and child in America in ways too numer-ous to count, but even so . . .) Liberals are more upset when a tree is chopped down than when a child is aborted. Even if one rates an unborn child less than a full-blown person, doesn't the unborn child rate slightly higher than vegetation?

Liberals are constantly warning us that man is overloading the environment to the detriment of the plants. Howard Dean left the Episcopal Church—which is barely even a church—because his church, in Montpelier, Vermont, would not cede land for a bike path. Environ-mentally friendly exercise was more important than tending to the human soul. That's all you need to know about the Democrats. Blessed be the peacemakers who create a diverse, nonsexist working environment in paperless offices.

Suspiciously, the Democrats' idea of an energy policy never involves the creation of new energy. They want solar power, wind power, barley power. How about creating a new source of en-ergy? Nuclear reactors do that with no risk of funding Arab terrorists or—more repellent to liberals—Big Oil Companies. But in a spasm of left-wing insanity in the seventies, nuclear power was curtailed in this country. Japan has nuclear power, France has nuclear power—almost all modern countries have nuclear power. But we had Jane Fonda in the movie **The China Syndrome.** Liberals are very picky about their admiration for Western Europe.

Now it turns out even Chernobyl wasn't as bad as people thought. In a feat of Soviet engineering, the Chernobyl nuclear power plant in Ukraine exploded in 1986, sending chunks of the reactor core flying into nearby farms and igniting a fire at the reactor that burned for ten days. It was the worst nuclear disaster in history—**finally** giving us a nuclear power plant that killed more people than died in Teddy Kennedy's car. But as the **New York Times** reported in September 2005, "Nearly 20 years after the huge accident at the Chernobyl nuclear power plant in Ukraine, a new scientific report has found that its aftereffects on health and the environment have not proved as dire as scientists had predicted." Instead of tens of thousands of cancer deaths from acute radiation exposure, there were 4,000. Only 50 deaths were directly attributable to the explosion. There has been no increase in leukemia, birth defects, or fertility problems in the surrounding area.[3]

And, I mention again, this was in the Soviet

Union. Soviet engineers couldn't make Jell-O. They'd show up at the World's Fair and stare at a flush toilet like it was a rocket ship. They turned half of Germany into an inefficient manufacturing center. Do you know how hard that is? It's like botching a train wreck. Of course the Soviets screwed up nuclear power!

Instead of taking the environmentalist hamstrings off the muscular American economy—so we can split atoms, drill, mine, and strip—the Democrats want to preside over our state-managed descent into hell. Liberals want us to live like Swedes, with their genial, mediocre lives, ratcheting back our expectations, practicing fuel austerity, and sitting by the fire in a cardigan sweater like Jimmy Carter. If one posits that we have a fixed amount of energy and have to start rationing it, then we are dying as a species. The theory of vegetarianism is that Americans consume "too much" energy. It takes a lot of energy to grow corn to feed animals to feed us—so why don't we become a bunch of grazing farmyard animals ourselves? We can eat grass and share our energy with the birds! Environmentalists' energy plan is the repudiation of America and Christian destiny, which is Jet Skis, steak on the electric grill, hot showers, and night skiing.

Perennially irritating to environmentalists is

mankind's single greatest invention: the flush toilet. You knew it had to happen. Apostles of "dry toilets" insist that we "have to get beyond flush-and-forget technology," as it was put by Sim Van der Ryn, founder of the Ecological Design Institute. Flush-and-forget abortions are one thing, but this is solid human waste we're talking about! Apparently, we need to spend more time thinking about our excrement. Van der Ryn explained that the goal was "to deal with one's own waste as close to the source as possible"[4]—precisely the opposite of what humans have wanted to do with their excrement since the beginning of time. Nonflush toilets were first introduced in America—well, originally by the Indians—but then again in the sixties by a Rockefeller scion who promoted a "dry toilet" called the Clivus Multrum. They pop up again every few years but, oddly enough, never seem to catch on. Dry toilets are like the metric system of human waste disposal.

In 1995, the **New York Times** was enthusiastically reporting on the move away from mankind's greatest invention by homeowners "fed up with overdevelopment, contaminated ground water, and overflowing septic tanks"—but evidently not fed up with living on top of their own excrement. These homeowners were creating environmentally friendly ways to keep their excrement close to them. They created miniature wetlands in their backyards, solar toilets, or composting toilets. Only recently have advocates of nonflush toilets begun to recognize their product's central shortcoming, which is the natural human aversion to the "routine emptying of excrement from the toilets."[5] Instead of the organic method of living in your own excrement, most people prefer the inorganic method of flushing it away from themselves. Consequently, the federal government has done the next best thing for the official state religion, which is to make it a felony to replace a 1.3-gallon toilet bowl with an old-fashioned 7-gallon toilet bowl—or as we call it, "a working toilet."

The whole purpose of living in your own excrement is to save . . . water. Water. Liberals are worried we're going to run out of something that literally falls from the sky. Here's an idea: Just wait. It will rain. Every possible personal use of water combined—steam baths, swimming pools, showers, toilets, and kitchen sinks—amounts to less than 10 percent of all water usage. Agricultural use accounts for about 70 percent of water usage and industrial use more than 20 percent. But again in 2003, the Greens were calling flush toilets "an environmental disaster."[6] They want us to go to the bathroom outdoors because, you know, we're animals. **Question: Are liberals**

clueless about waste management? Answer: Do bears crap in the woods?

Liberals have fervently believed that humans are a blight on the Earth since Thomas Malthus penned "An Essay on the Principle of Population" in 1798. Like the flushless toilet, it's an idea that won't die. In the 1970s, Paul Ehrlich wrote the best-selling book **The Population Bomb,** predicting global famine and warning that entire nations would cease to exist by the end of the twentieth century—among them, England. "[I]t is now too late," he wrote, "to take action to save many of those people." In 2001—despite the perplexing persistent existence of England—the Sierra Club listed Ehrlich's **Population Bomb** as among its books recommended by Sierra readers. How many trees had to be chopped down to make the paper for all those copies of **The Population Bomb**?

Liberals beatify health, no-smoking, camping, non–fossil-fuel travel, organic foods—all while creating exotic new diseases in pursuit of polymorphous perversity. Don't be confused by your capacity for reason! We're just apes. A chief ingredient of the liberal religion is the bestialization of humanity. So on one hand, we have to give up SUVs, snowmobiles, and indoor plumbing, but on the other hand, at least we get the funky bestial behavior. (Including actual bestiality—keep reading!) They believe in the coarse physical appropriation of women by men—hookups, trophy wives, strip clubs. Through movies, magazines, and TV, liberals promote a cult of idealized beauty that is so extreme as to be unimaginable. We must listen to Hollywood airheads like Julia Roberts and George Clooney because they are beautiful. Today's worship of physical perfection is more grotesque than Hitler's notion of the Aryan.

Ugly feminists—or as the **New York Times** describes them, "by the standards of the time, unlovely"[7]—impotently rail against "sexist men" and "sexual harassment" while simultaneously promoting the view that sex has no sacred purpose, it's just for fun. Sex must be dissociated from the idea of raising children, liberated from the transmission of humanity. It's a natural function that should carry no more moral consequence than drinking a glass of water, as their demiurge Lenin said. It's in our genes, and therefore it cannot be immoral. We're beasts. Let's rock!

Toward the goal of divorcing sex from reproduction, liberals will lie about anything. In **Griswold v. Connecticut** (1965), the Supreme Court discovered a constitutional right for married couples to buy contraceptives, premised on the Court's assertion that marriage is a "sacred" institution, protected by "a Right to Privacy older than the Bill of Rights itself." Within a decade, Justice William Brennan would dump the married stuff and extend the right to contraceptives to unmarried people. In a classic boneheaded, factless, legislative pronunciamento, in **Eisenstadt v. Baird** (March 22, 1972), Brennan wrote, "It is inconceivable that the need for health controls varies with the purpose for which the contraceptive is to be used when the physical act in all cases is one and the same." Ten years later, the **New York Times** named AIDS in a May 11, 1982, article headlined "New Homosexual Disorder Worries Health Officials."

A year after **Eisenstadt,** the malleable "right to privacy" metastasized from a right to contraception for married couples to a right to destroy human life in **Roe v. Wade.** What about the poor little tyke's privacy? The question misses the point. "Constitutional right" means "Whatever Liberals Want." Society cannot legislate what goes on "in the bedroom." But if we can't legislate what goes on in the bedroom, why can't I hide money from the IRS under my mattress?

The cult of liberalism is preposterously fixated on youth—all the while devaluing life at the end, by demanding a "right to die." Richard Lamm, the Democratic governor of Colorado, famously said in 1984, "We've got a duty to die and get out of the way with all of our machines and artificial hearts and everything else like that and let the other society, our kids, build a reasonable life."**8** How about you first, Dick?

Instead of seeking wisdom, liberals desire to be seen as clever by being counterintuitive, crazy, and outré. They have an irreducible fascination with barbarism and will defend anything hateful—Tookie, Mumia, Saddam Hussein, Hedda Nussbaum, abortion, the North American Man/Boy Love Association, **New York Times** columnist Frank Rich. If Hitler hadn't turned against their beloved Stalin, liberals would have stuck by him, too. Liberals defend unreason against reason and then call themselves rationalists. They are too important to be bothered by the things that frighten middle-class people worried about the equity in their homes. The truly pathetic liberals are the ones who aren't rich but ape the belief structure of fabulously wealthy Hollywood leftists anyway. Like the bums who stood outside restaurants during the Depression with toothpicks in their mouths, they seem not to realize that the crucial part of being rich is that you have money, not attitudes.

The whole panoply of nutty things liberals believe flows from their belief that man is just another animal. (And not just Kanye West—they're talking about all men.) Only their core rejection of God can explain the bewildering array of liberal positions: We must save Tookie Williams, while slaughtering the unborn. We must eat natural foods, but the right to acquire disease in casual hookups is a holy ritual. We must halt human development so that the Furbish lousewort can be fruitful and multiply, but humans are multiplying too much and threatening the biosphere of the Furbish lousewort. Women are no different from men, but we need a library of laws and codes to protect women from sexual harassment. As Chesterson said, where we once had a few big rules, now we need an encyclopedia of little rules.9

Usually zealots can't make money doing insane things. But liberals have the entire taxpayer-funded "education" apparatus to support them. Public schools are what columnist Joe Sobran calls "liberalism's reproductive system." In lieu of teaching Biblical truth, which—are you sitting down?—used to be the purpose of education, the government schools teach an "amalgam of liberalism, feminism, Darwinism, and the Playboy philosophy." No longer content to ruin their own children, liberals insist on being subsidized by the taxpayer to ruin everyone else's children, too. (Remember the good old days when bums and malcontents would ruin your children for free?)

Among the things the Supreme Court has held

"unconstitutional" are prayer in public schools, moments of silence in public schools (which the Court cleverly recognized as an invidious invitation to engage in "silent prayer"), and displays of the Ten Commandments in public schools. In 1992, the Court ruled it "unconstitutional" for a Reform rabbi to give a nonsectarian invocation at a high school graduation ceremony on the perfectly plausible grounds that Rhode Island was trying to establish Reform Judaism as the official state religion. (Opinion by Justice Anthony Kennedy.) Yes, those scheming Jews have had their eyes on the Ocean State as long as I can remember. Let one Reform rabbi say a prayer in a school there, you might just as well change the state's name to "Jewland."

Even the rare sane rulings from the Supreme Court face massive resistance from the lower courts. Liberal judges feel free to disregard the Supreme Court to achieve the overriding objective of keeping real religion out of government schools. All-important "precedent" matters only when we're talking about **Roe v. Wade,** not rulings on religion.

In a 2001 opinion written by Justice Clarence Thomas, the Court upheld the right of religious groups to participate in after-school activities along with other clubs. It was the second time the High Court had instructed the schools to stop specifically singling out religious groups for discrimination. (One imagines the sound of a rooster crowing if that same court denied the church groups a third time.) Indeed, the case **Good News Club v. Milford Central School** was nearly identical to another case in which the Supreme Court had reversed the exact same court a few years earlier. In his majority opinion, Justice Thomas remarked on the oddity of having to reverse the same court twice on the same issue. Thomas said that while the appellate courts aren't required to cite all the Supreme Court's precedents, they might want to take note of the last time they were reversed on the exact same facts.

Concerned that someone might be reading Leviticus during school hours, Justice David Souter dissented from Thomas's opinion in a hairsplitting exegesis about the precise time classes let out (2:56 P.M.) versus the time the organizers would enter school property (2:30 P.M.). Then again, I suppose arguments about the precise moment something begins have never been liberals' strong suit. At least the 6–3 decision gave us an accurate count of the atheists on the Court, probably as accurate as my dream of giving them all polygraph tests someday. (**Do you believe in a Higher Being?** . . . **No, seriously.**)

Public schools are forbidden from mentioning religion not because of the Constitution, but because public schools are the Left's madrassas. According to Cornell law professor Gary Simson, sex education courses that teach abstinence until marriage are unconstitutional because they violate the Establishment Clause of the First Amendment. Simson says recommending sexual abstinence to teenagers is wrong because it "teaches that this one belief is the only proper one." Liberals used to tell us they were teaching fisting to fourth-graders because "kids are going to have sex anyway!" (Yes, "fisting" is exactly what it sounds like; have a nice day!) Now they've dispensed with that and openly concede that they believe virtue is just one of many equally valid points of view that must be counterbalanced with the argument for promiscuity, group sex, fisting, and other lifestyle choices. At least the crazy Muslims get funding from Saudi Arabia for their madrassas. Liberals force normal Americans to pay for their religious schools.

While any reference to Moses in the schools is strictly prohibited, school authorities can force minors to attend sexually explicit presentations on anal sex and condom use. In 1992, Chelmsford (Massachusetts) High School hired Suzi Landolphi to give a mandatory "AIDS Awareness presentation" to the entire school, apparently designed to reach the one or two human beings on Planet Earth who hadn't heard about AIDS. By her own account, Landolphi is the product of a broken family. She says her mother was an alcoholic who committed suicide, her father physically abused her, and she herself was a chronic bed wetter until age ten. Landolphi was a five-time loser at marriage.[10] So she is definitely the sort of person most parents would want talking to their children about sex. Naturally, the Chelmsford High School administrators realized they had found an Aristotle in their midst.

In her presentation, "Hot, Sexy, and Safer," Landolphi began by telling the teenagers—who were forced by school authorities to be there—"I can't believe how many people came here to listen to someone talk about sex, instead of staying home and having it yourself." In the dry legal language of the complaint later filed by parents of some of the students, Landolphi also "used profane, lewd, and lascivious language to describe body parts and excretory functions," including "eighteen references to orgasms, six references to male genitals, and eight references to female genitals."[11] (And that was just while thanking the school principal for inviting her.) She asked students to show their "orgasm faces" in front of a camera—which would certainly come in handy for any future on-camera careers in the adult film industry. She invited a male student on stage to lick a condom with her. After discussing anal sex,

Landolphi remarked that one would be "in deep sh—." She told one male student he "had a nice butt" and another that his baggy pants were "erection wear." This did not constitute sexual harassment under the law, because, like Bill Clinton, Landolphi supports abortion rights, one may assume. She concluded ninety minutes of this relentless vulgarity by asking a female student to place an oversized condom on the head of a male student and blow it up.

Like most people who enjoy talking to strangers about sex, Miss Landolphi, to put it as charitably as possible, is physically repulsive in appearance. With a presentation that was about as erotic as phone sex with Andrea Dworkin—or actual sex with Andrea Dworkin, come to think of it—Landolphi may have inadvertently promoted abstinence among the student body by generating widespread aversion to the various activities she described. It's no wonder Bible Belt, right-wing Christians get the greatest enjoyment out of sex (another scientific study hated by liberals)[12]—they never have to endure listening to liberals talk about sex.

Parents of Chelmsford students immediately brought suit alleging that by forcing their children to attend Landolphi's presentation without prior notice, the school had violated their privacy right to direct the upbringing of their children.

But the U.S. Court of Appeals for the First Circuit could find no such right in the "living Constitution." The "right to privacy" refers to the right of unmarried couples to obtain contraception. It encompasses the right to kill an unborn baby. It means the right of men to sodomize one another. Where these parents got the idea that "privacy" included their right to keep their children from being forced to make "orgasm faces" in school was anybody's guess.

Tellingly, the federal appeals court also rejected the parents' Free Exercise claim, questioning "whether the Free Exercise Clause even applies to public education."[13] Thus, the court declared a clearly visible Constitutional clause—not buried in the penumbras—officially inapplicable to government schools. (Perhaps what threw them off was the fact that the free exercise of religion—unlike abortion, gay marriage, and sodomy—is specifically mentioned in the Constitution. You can see how that would be confusing.) Allowing parents to interfere with their children's education might impair the state's efforts to indoctrinate children into the official state religion of promiscuity, recycling, and freeing Mumia Abu-Jamal.

Colleges pick up where the public schools leave off, inculcating students in the religion of hating America and hating God. While college professors like the University of Colorado's Ward Churchill act like on-the-edge radicals for calling American bond traders "little Eichmanns," professors are the most cosseted, pussified, subsidized group of people in the U.S. workforce. They have concocted a system to preemptively protect themselves for not doing their jobs, known as "tenure." They make a lot of money, have health plans that would make New York City municipal workers' jaws drop, and work—at most—fifteen hours a week. In theory, the only job requirement of a college professor is to be intelligent, provocative, and open-minded, but their reigning attribute is that they are ignorant, boring, and narrow-minded. These zealous pagans teach the official state religion of liberalism as axiomatic truth.

The stupidest of their students become journalists, churning out illiterate attacks on dissidents from the liberal religion. Within a few weeks of each other in early 2006, both **Rolling Stone** and **Newsweek** magazines displayed their ignorance of Biblical passages cited during interviews. In a **Rolling Stone** interview, Republican senator Sam Brownback criticized countries like Sweden that had legalized gay marriage, quoting the line from Matthew "you shall know them by their fruits." The interviewer, Jeff Sharlet, interpreted Brownback's scriptural quotation as a homophobic slur. Soon gay groups were demanding an apology from the senator.[14] (All I can say to that is: how niggardly of them.)

Meanwhile, **Newsweek** ran an article about the looming danger of evangelicals learning to debate, noting that Jerry Falwell's Liberty University had the number-one debate club in the country. The reporter quoted Falwell saying, "We are training debaters who can perform assault ministry." These evangelicals are scary! **Newsweek** later ran a correction stating: "**Newsweek** misquoted Falwell as referring to 'assault ministry.' In fact, Falwell was referring to 'a salt ministry'—a reference to Matthew 5:13, where Jesus says, 'Ye are the salt of the earth.' We regret the error."[15]

When Al Gore tried to suck up to Christians during the second presidential debate in the 2000 campaign, he utterly mangled Scripture— and not one mainstream media reporter noticed. By way of explaining his nutty environmental beliefs, Gore said, "In my faith tradition, it is written in the book of Matthew, 'Where your heart is, there's your treasure also.' And I believe that we ought to recognize the value to our children and grandchildren of taking steps that preserve the environment in a way that's good for them."

Gore had not merely transformed a core

Christian belief into a Confucian fortune cookie, he had reversed Christian doctrine. The actual Bible—Matthew 6:21—says precisely the opposite of what Gore said, admonishing us to make heaven our only treasure—"For where your treasure is, there will your heart be also."

Not only were Bible illiterates in the media unaware of Gore's faux pas, they actually praised Gore for his brilliant use of Scripture to appeal to the God voters. Writing in **Slate,** William Saletan said Gore scored points in the second debate when he "answered a question about the environment by quoting from the scripture of my 'faith tradition.' The quote—'Where your heart is, there is your treasure also'—had nothing to do with the environment but everything to do with projecting heart and faith."[16] It also had nothing to do with Scripture.

Father Richard John Neuhaus describes being interviewed by a reporter about the pope and referring to the pope by one of his formal titles, "the Bishop of Rome." The reporter responded, "That raises an interesting point. Is it unusual that this pope is also the bishop of Rome?" In another interview, Neuhaus told a reporter that political corruption had "been around ever since that unfortunate afternoon in the garden." This time, the reporter mulled it over before asking, "What garden was that?"[17] In defense of the

American educational system, every single one of these reporters knew how to put on a condom.

In 2003, reporters hounded British prime minister Tony Blair about whether he had prayed with George Bush—as if they were asking whether the world leaders had shot heroin together or shared a hooker. There was so much negative publicity over Blair praying with Bush that Blair's handlers forbade him to attend church with Bush later that year.[18] It's hard to imagine an activity Bush and Blair could have shared that would have been more scandalous, short of taking an SUV to an all-men's club that allowed cigar smoking.

In the book **Under the Banner of Heaven: A Story of Violent Faith,** Jon Krakauer writes of the Bush administration, "This, after all, is a country led by a born-again Christian . . . who characterizes international relations as a biblical clash between forces of good and evil. The highest law officer in the land, Attorney General John Ashcroft, is a dyed-in-the-wool follower of a fundamentalist Christian sect—the Pentecostal Assemblies of God of America . . . and subscribes to a vividly apocalyptic worldview that has much in common with key millenarian beliefs held by the Lafferty brothers and the residents of Colorado City." Yes, it's really those devout Christians we have to keep our eyes on. Who can ever forget all the rioting and bloodshed around the world after hip-hop impresario Kanye West appeared on the cover of **Rolling Stone** magazine as the crucified Jesus?

Krakauer—my guess, not a Christian—is worried about a theocracy based on one born-again Christian in the cabinet of a Christian president and compares Ashcroft to psychopath murderer Dan Lafferty, a member of a radical Mormon sect who brutally murdered a twenty-four-year-old woman and her child. Comparing the attorney general to Lafferty is roughly the equivalent of saying, "Ruth Bader Ginsburg, who belongs to the same religious sect as the Son of Sam . . ."

If liberals are on Red Alert with one born-again Christian in the cabinet of a Christian president, imagine how they would react if there were five. Between 25 and 45 percent of the population calls itself "born-again" or "evangelical" Christian.[19] Jews make up less than 2 percent of the nation's population, and yet Clinton had five in his cabinet. He appointed two to the Supreme Court. Now guess which administration is called a neoconservative conspiracy? Whether Jews or Christians, liberals are always on a witch hunt against people who appear to believe in God.

Incidentally, the country was also allegedly led by an evangelical Christian when Jimmy Carter was president—you know, the kind of evangelical Christian who appears prominently in pornographic magazines while running for president. I guess that 1976 interview with **Playboy** was enough to do penance with liberals for believing in God.

Liberals are constantly accusing Christians of being intolerant and self-righteous, but the most earnest Christian has never approached the preachy intolerance of a liberal who has just discovered a lit cigarette in a nonsmoking section. (Or who has just discovered two born-again Christians in a Republican administration.)

Howard Dean calls the Republican Party "evil." (Somebody better keep an eye on that guy Dean. One of these days he's liable to say something crazy.) In 2005, Representative Nancy Pelosi told Democrats they should vote against the Republican budget "as an act of worship,"[20] which at least is preferable to liberals' usual devotional of offering to perform oral sex on Democrat presidents who keep abortion legal. (Former **Time** magazine White House correspondent Nina Burleigh told the **Washington Post** in 1998, "I'd be happy to give [Clinton oral sex] just to thank him for keeping abortion legal.") Democrats get on their high horses about evil corporations making obscene profits, but try pointing out to them that trial lawyers also make enormous profits suing corporations owned by people who make less than trial lawyers. They think you're just being obtuse for not understanding that trial lawyers are doing God's work. Halliburton helps produce the oil and gasoline that keep us warm, feed us, allow us to travel, power our world, and so on. What do trial lawyers produce again?

The moment self-righteousness takes over, you are dealing with dangerous psychopaths. Liberals are constantly accusing Christians of monumental self-righteousness for daring to engage in free speech or for voting in accordance with their religious beliefs. Compare that with the behavior of practitioners of the liberal religion. Liberals felt entitled to excuse Stalin's murderous regime on the grounds that he was simply trying to build a Communist paradise. Because they passionately believed in Marxism, liberals thought they had a right to lie about being Soviet spies. Yeah, well, some people passionately believe in white supremacy. How about George Clooney making a sympathetic movie about true-believing white supremacists and the evil prosecutors who forced them to name names?

If liberals could cut Stalin slack, there is no behavior they cannot excuse as justified by their passion. A president who was credibly accused of rape and displayed a pervasive pattern of what used to be known as "sexual harassment" was above reproach in liberal eyes. He had saved partial birth abortion! (Thus the charming tributes.) Liberals consider it self-evident that they are being persecuted simply for wanting to do the right thing and always believe their critics' motives are vile and corrupt—which may be why Liberty University routinely kicks their butts in debate.

The people who call Republicans "evil" subscribe to a political platform that essentially consists of breaking the Ten Commandments one by one. They are for adultery, lying about adultery, covetousness, killing the unborn, and stealing from the middle class (the "rich") and giving to teachers and trial lawyers (the "poor"). They create new myths and a new priesthood all to justify a worldview that is the rejection of the Judeo-Christian vision of man's role in the universe. They have more shibboleths than the Old Testament tribe of Gileadites—Halliburton; global warming; antichoice; "Bush lied, kids died!" And they are full of towering, smug, intolerant, self-righteous rage.

If Democrats ever dared speak coherently about what they believe, the American people would lynch them. So they claim to believe in God, much as Paul Begala claims to go "duck hunting" (liberal code for "antiquing"). At the beginning of the 2004 presidential campaign, the Democratic Leadership Council held briefings to teach Democratic candidates how to simulate a belief in God. To ease the Druids into it, the DLC recommended using phrases like "God's green earth." (The DLC also suggested avoiding the use of phrases such as "goddamned, motherf—ing Republicans!") During the primaries, Howard Dean began goading the press to talk about religion but, after claiming the Book of Job was his favorite book in the Bible, was unable to place it in the correct Testament. Regular Talmudic scholars, these Democrats.

Throughout the 2004 campaign, the Democrats were looking for a Democrat who believed in God—a pursuit similar to a woman searching for a boyfriend in a room full of choreographers. The religious outreach coordinator hired by the Democratic National Committee was Brenda Bartella Peterson, who had signed a brief to the Supreme Court advocating the removal of "under God" from the Pledge of Allegiance. Apparently, Madalyn Murray O'Hair was unavailable.

The religion adviser to John Kerry's presidential campaign was Mara Vanderslice. She had previously been the religious outreach coordinator for Howard Dean—an assignment that would have required the patience of Job, whoever the hell he was. Vanderslice had spoken at rallies cosponsored by the radical gay group ACT UP, famous for a protest at St. Patrick's Cathedral at which its members spat the Eucharist on the floor. She had been an organizer of violent protests in Seattle and Washington, D.C., when liberals reacted as any normal person would by smashing Starbucks windows and torching police cars because some bankers had come to town for a meeting. Vanderslice majored in "peace studies" at Earlham College. There she was a member of the Marxist-Leninist group that supported convicted cop killer Mumia Abu-Jamal.[21] That's devoutly religious for a Democrat. In fact, by Democratic standards Vanderslice was a veritable C. S. Lewis.

According to **The Nation** magazine, Vanderslice "cornered" Kate Michelman of NARAL Pro-Choice America at the 2004 Democratic convention (in the proverbial "back alley," one can only hope) to ask Michelman for help "in convincing Catholics that Kerry was really against abortion."[22] ("NARAL" is an acronym for something with "abortion" in the title, but we don't know what because the NARAL webpage won't use the word **abortion**.) Inasmuch as NARAL's raison d'être is to keep abortion legal until the baby is around age thirteen, either Kerry's religion adviser was casually enlisting

NARAL to help lie to the American people or she is even dumber than the average Democrat.

At a church service at the Democratic National Convention held for People of Faith for Kerry (not to be confused with Muslims for Kerry), the church displayed a cloth sign proclaiming: "Lesbians, Gays & Friends at Old South Church" are "Open and Affirming." James Forbes of the Riverside Church in Manhattan delivered the sermon, in which he called for "full employment," "a true livable wage," "universal access to pre-kindergarten and childcare programs," a "progressive tax policy,"[23] and various other items specifically mentioned during the Sermon on the Mount.

And Democrats remain genuinely mystified as to why they didn't win the 2004 election. After the Democrats failed to get a majority of Americans to vote for them in the seventh straight presidential election—since Jimmy Carter won with 50.1 percent of the vote in 1976—liberal minister Jim Wallis leapt into the breach. He proposed to teach the Democrats how to "reframe" their language to make people think they believe in God.[24] **We don't believe this crazy God crap, but let's fake out the American people so we can enact gay marriage and partial birth abortion, and ban God from the Pledge of Allegiance.** His big idea is to redefine Jesus' genuine,

personal, volitional love for the poor as the same
as their impersonal, coercive, compassionless welfare machinery. (Wallis's favorite part of the
Gospel begins, "Blessed are the economically dis-
advantaged in spirit . . .")

The Democrats got off to a good start after the
2004 election when the new head of the Democratic National Committee, Howard Dean, denounced Republicans as "pretty much a white
Christian party." (Even when sneering at
Christians—Christians!—Democrats use blacks
for cover.) To be sure, 80 percent of the Republican Party is white and Christian, slightly higher
than the nation as a whole, which is 70 percent
white and Christian. Democrats cannot conceive
of "hate speech" toward Christians because, in
their eyes, Christians always deserve it.

After lashing out at Christians for no reason,
Dean went on to say the Democrats are "more
welcoming to different folks, because that's the
kind of people we are." In addition to Christians,
whom liberals hate, the Democrats are not particularly welcoming of "folks" who do not believe
it is a Constitutional right to stick a fork in a
baby's head. They are not welcoming to people
who think a human life is more important than a
bird's life. They don't welcome judges who display the Ten Commandments in their court-
rooms. They are not welcoming to people who

believe marriage really is a sacred institution and not just an opportunity to sneak a right to contraception into the Constitution. They are not welcoming to people who think a multiple murderer gang leader like Tookie Williams should be given the death penalty. They are extremely unwelcoming to blacks who stray from the liberal orthodoxy and become Republicans. And David Geffen is distinctly unwelcoming to people who try to walk on the public beach that abuts his house in Malibu.

Democrats revile religion but insist on faking a belief in God in front of the voters claiming to be "spiritual." They can't forthrightly admit they are Druids, so they "reframe" their constant, relentless opposition to every Biblical precept as respect for "science" or the "Constitution"—both of which they hate. Their rage against us is their rage against the Judeo-Christian tradition. I don't particularly care if liberals believe in God. In fact, I would be crestfallen to discover any liberals in heaven. So fine, rage against God, but how about being honest about it? Liberals can believe what they want to believe, but let us not flinch from identifying liberalism as the opposition party to God.

2 THE PASSION OF THE LIBERAL: THOU SHALT NOT PUNISH THE PERP

ssuming you aren't a fetus, the Left's most dangerous religious belief is their adoration of violent criminals. Environmentalists can be dismissed as stupid girls who like birds, but liberals' admiration of dangerous predators is a direct threat to your health. Republicans may not have figured everything out when it comes to controlling crime, but Democrats have figured out nothing. We must maintain constant vigilance over the criminal jus-

tice system, because no matter how often liberals are caught coddling criminals, they always will go right back to it when no one's watching.

Even after the complete failure of liberal policies on crime in the sixties and seventies, and the success of conservative policies on crime beginning in the eighties, liberals are itching to start springing criminals again. Attempts to rehabilitate liberals on this are futile. It's in their DNA. New York mayor Michael Bloomberg, who followed the spectacularly successful mayor Rudy Giuliani, knows the one thing he can't touch is the Giuliani crime policy. So liberals are biding their time, waiting for Bloomberg to be term-limited out of office. By then, the insanity of the Dinkins years will be a distant memory—no memory at all for the recently arrived New Yorkers who moved in after Giuliani made the city safe again. As soon as Bloomberg is out and a Democrat is in, the ACLU will be back again, hamstringing law enforcement, bringing endless police brutality cases, and setting violent predators free. (How does "Mayor Mumia Abu-Jamal" sound to you?)

Liberals believe it is important to never, ever punish criminals because—well, I'm not sure why. They produce a constantly scrolling list of reasons: The perpetrator is too young; the perpetrator is too old; the perpetrator has been rehabil- itated; the perpetrator will not be rehabilitated in prison; similarly situated perpetrators got a dif- ferent sentence; the perpetrator wrote a children's book; the perpetrator was making a statement about society; the perpetrator says he didn't do it (and we're too busy writing him mash notes to look at the evidence); the perpetrator was on cold medication when he raped, murdered, and canni balized a family of four.

Liberals complain about the cruel injustice of disparate sentences, but then they turn around and howl with indignation when legislatures try to implement some degree of consistency by im- posing mandatory minimums. They say over- crowded prisons constitute cruel and unusual punishment, but they always oppose building more prisons. Voters are sternly advised how much new prisons will "cost the taxpayer." When the voters still want to build more prisons any- way, politicians are attacked for "pandering" to voters on crime.

Needless to say, the death penalty is always verboten, except in the narrow case of Enron ex- ecutives or clothing designers who use fur. Liber- als just keep moving fast and talking loudly so you can never nail them on one reason.

Liberals say:

▪ We're the only modern democracy with the death penalty.

I think this should be treated as a selling point: "Come to the United States for the economic opportunity, stay because we fry our Ted Bundys!" Among our many other unique characteristics are these: We're the only modern democracy founded on a belief that all men are created equal; we're the only modern democracy that fought a revolution to redeem that idea and a civil war to prove it; we're the only modern democracy that nearly single-handedly smashed Hitler's Germany and Stalin's Russia; of all modern democracies, we are the wealthiest, most productive, most religious, and most charitable.[1] Do liberals want us to apologize for that, too? While we're at it, I note that we're also the only modern democracy to spurn nuclear power. How about we fire up the Shoreham Nuclear Power Station again and then talk about the death penalty? (Also, incidentally, Japan has the death penalty.)

▪ Innocent men will be executed.

Apparently not. Death penalty opponents would love nothing more than to produce the case of an innocent person who has been executed in this country, but after decades of fanatical research going back more than half a century, they have not been able to find a single one. The last time liberals claimed to have examples of executed men later "proved innocent," attorneys Stephen Markman and Paul Cassell reviewed the cases and found that "proof of innocence" included the word of the executed murderer; any confession by another murderer, no matter how preposterous the claim; defense counsel's bald allegations in opening statements supported by no evidence at trial; and the innocence of a fictional character in a novel that was based on a true crime—even though the author himself repeatedly stated that his book was a work fiction and he believed the real defendant to have been guilty.[2]

▪ **The death penalty does not deter.**

How do liberals know? This is an article of faith, not a statement of empirical fact. If the death penalty doesn't deter murder, how come Michael Moore is still alive and I'm not on death row? In the forties and fifties, before the courts started halting executions on the basis of the judges' personal opposition to the death penalty, murder was rare.[3] As soon as the Supreme Court declared the death penalty "unconstitutional" in 1972, the murder rate soared and has only begun to come down as capital sentences have been gradually reintroduced. Of course the death penalty might deter a little more effectively if the average time spent on death row were not nearly a decade or if death row inmates were not more likely to die of causes other than execution while awaiting their executions. When convicts on death row are dying of old age, we may be a few tweaks short of an effective deterrent.

- ## It is applied unfairly.

This is as opposed to murder and rape, which are distributed among the general population according to a complex formula ensuring fairness and proportionality. Any system of justice that allows compassion, discretion, and leniency will lead to wildly divergent sentences for seemingly similar crimes. For consistency, you want something like the Taliban's Sharia law. Anyone found guilty of homosexuality under Sharia law has a wall dropped on him. End of story.

- ## Capital punishment must be suspended until the exact same percentages of blacks and whites are executed.

What if they don't commit the same number of murders? And how do we compare one murder case with the next? There are all sorts of factors that go into the imposition of the death penalty:

premeditation, multiple murders, the killing of a police officer, torture, accompanying crimes, the background of the defendant, prior record, provocation, acceptance of responsibility, and on and on and on. As it stands, white murderers already receive more death sentences than black murderers[4]—a fact attested to by the current liberal complaint that the death penalty is racist because the system values the lives of white **victims** more than the lives of black **victims.** Murderers, it seems, behave much like the University of Michigan admissions committee and take race into account when choosing their victims. Thus, blacks are more likely to murder blacks and whites are more likely to murder whites. The only way to "value" the lives of black victims more is to start executing more black murderers. No matter what the facts, the death penalty can always be described as "racist": Either we're executing more black murderers than white murderers or we're executing more murderers of whites than of blacks. And so it is, by people who don't care whether or not the death penalty is racist, but simply oppose the death penalty in all cases.

▪ It's a primitive act of retribution.

I'm not sure we need to be lectured on "primitive" behavior by the people who defend abortion on demand and suicide bombers, but eating and bathing are also "primitive" acts. The fact that something has been embraced by many cultures over a long period of time is generally not an argument against its practice. What is "primitive" about being arraigned, formally charged, tried, and convicted by a jury, having that conviction upheld on appeal, and then being executed in a far gentler manner than their victims? Far from primitive, this is the deliberative, sane act of an advanced civilization protecting itself from predators. If anything, modern execution methods are too humane ("Okay, it will only sting for a minute, Mr. Bundy. . . .").

▪ Life in prison spent thinking about the crime is worse than death.

Evidently not to the murderers on death row who regularly fight their executions tooth and nail. But just so we understand: Is the problem here that the death penalty is too humane or not humane enough?

▪ It diminishes us as a society.

Unlike abortion and the president's being serviced by a White House intern, which elevates us as a society.

These aren't just nuts being interviewed by Fox News's Bill O'Reilly. People who believe it's unfair to punish criminals used to be a majority on the Supreme Court. The heyday of liberal activism on the Supreme Court was from 1953 to 1969, with the Warren Court remaking criminal law to benefit criminals. Hundreds of thousands of violent criminals were unleashed on society, where they could commit more rapes and murders. Liberal ideas on crime led like night into day to skyrocketing crime rates in the sixties and seventies. It is impossible to calculate the blood on the hands of Supreme Court justices whose personal view was that it is unfair to punish the guilty. (On the plus side, pervasive outrage over leniency toward criminals gave rise to awesome movies like Charles Bronson's **Death Wish** and Clint Eastwood's **Dirty Harry** movies.)

Soon after liberals got control of the Supreme Court, the death penalty was declared unconstitutional—as were laws against loitering and vagrancy. The Court suddenly discovered a constitutional right to a taxpayer-funded lawyer in the 1963 case **Gideon v. Wainwright.** Today, a foreigner being tried for the murder of his American wife and child can demand that U.S. taxpayers pay for his lawyers and private investigators. As long as everything's paid for, there is no reason for even the manifestly guilty not to waste everyone's time and money on a trial.

In 1961, the Court announced the ever-popular exclusionary rule in **Mapp v. Ohio,** requiring that evidence obtained "illegally" by the police be banned from trial. The exclusionary rule is among the strangest policies ever concocted by the Court: In order to vindicate the right to be free from unreasonable searches and seizures, the criminal goes free. How about punishing the misbehaving policeman? How about docking his pay? Why do random citizens have to be raped, robbed, and murdered because of a policeman's misconduct? This would be like a rule intended to reduce noise during an opera that mandated shooting the soprano whenever anyone in the audience coughed. Although, given the damage the exclusionary rule does to society, it's more like shooting the audience if the soprano coughs.

In a series of cases culminating in **Miranda v. Arizona** (1966), the Warren Court completely eviscerated criminal confessions. Despite the myth of people constantly confessing to crimes they didn't commit—and who among us hasn't copped to a random murder or armed robbery we didn't commit during a moment of weakness?—there are few better methods of distinguishing the guilty from the innocent than a confession. There are some facts only the perpetrator could possibly know, such as where the body is buried. But this tool was taken away from the police, not because of anything in the Constitution but because liberal justices believed confessions caused our system of justice to "suffer morally."

Writing for the majority in **Escobedo v. Illinois** (1964), Justice Arthur Goldberg quoted John Henry Wigmore, dean of Northwestern Law: "As Dean Wigmore so wisely said: '[A]ny system of administration which permits the prosecution to trust habitually to compulsory self-disclosure as a source of proof must itself suffer morally thereby.'"

And so the Court issued a series of opinions that ensured provably guilty criminals would be put back on the streets, rather than allowing our system of justice to "suffer morally." Also in **Escobedo,** the Court held it was unconstitutional to continue to question a suspect the moment he requested a lawyer. In **Massiah v. United States** (1964), the Court held that it was unconstitutional to use informants to investigate a suspect released on bail, because any incriminating statements made to a police informant would be made in the absence of a lawyer. And in

Miranda, the Court held it unconstitutional for the police to question a suspect without first reciting a speech guaranteed to prevent the suspect from confessing.

Ernesto A. Miranda was a rapist who had admitted to kidnapping and rape in a written confession after two hours of questioning by the police. He was convicted of the crimes, but in a 5-to-4 ruling, the Supreme Court threw out the written confession of a rapist because he was not clearly informed of his right to a lawyer before they questioned him. In 1996, NBC News's Tom Brokaw informed his TV audience that Republicans don't care about rape.[5] At least we would have locked up Ernesto Miranda the first time. (He was eventually re-convicted in a retrial.)

At the outset of the Warren Court's campaign to outlaw criminal confessions, Justice Goldberg had proclaimed that confessions were not "reliable"—a position he ascertained not from facts or evidence but from a bald assertion about "the lesson of history" that "a system of criminal law enforcement which comes to depend on the 'confession' will, in the long run, be less reliable and more subject to abuses than a system which depends on extrinsic evidence independently secured through skillful investigation." (I've got a confession to make right here and now: I think Justice Goldberg had a few screws loose.)

If it were reliability the Court was worried about, the confession in **Brewer v. Williams** (1977) should have warmed their hearts. In **Brewer,** a suspected child-murderer, Robert Williams, voluntarily led the police to the body of his murder victim. That's about as reliable as it gets. Williams was being driven in a police car from Davenport, Iowa, where he was apprehended, back to Des Moines, where a little girl, ten-year-old Pamela Powers, had been abducted. Before setting out on the trip, Williams had been warned by three policemen and two lawyers that he had a right not to talk to the police during the drive—pursuant to the full-dress idiocy required by the Supreme Court.

On the drive, one of the detectives said this to Williams:

> I want to give you something to think about while we're traveling down the road. . . . Number one, I want you to observe the weather conditions, it's raining, it's sleeting, it's freezing, driving is very treacherous, visibility is poor, it's going to be dark early this evening. They are predicting several inches of snow for tonight, and I feel that you yourself are the only person that knows

where this little girl's body is, that you yourself have only been there once, and if you
get a snow on top of it you yourself may be
unable to find it. And, since we will be
going right past the area on the way into
Des Moines, I feel that we could stop and
locate the body, that the parents of this little
girl should be entitled to a Christian burial
for the little girl who was snatched away
from them on Christmas [E]ve and murdered. And I feel we should stop and locate
it on the way in rather than waiting until
morning and trying to come back out after a
snow storm and possibly not being able to
find it at all. . . . I do not want you to answer
me. I don't want to discuss it any further.
Just think about it as we're riding down the
road."6

About an hour later, Williams told the police
where he had buried the little girl's body. This
wasn't a question of beating a confession out of
the suspect with a rubber hose. The detectives
had appealed to the last remnants of humanity in
a child-murderer and, amazingly, it had worked.

But the Supreme Court ruled the detective's
magnificent "Christian burial speech" unconstitutional and excluded all evidence that resulted
from it, including the rather crucial fact that

Williams had led the police to the girl's body. Williams, it seems, had been deprived of his constitutional right to counsel. If his lawyer had been in the car with him, Williams would have had no conscience at all and would not have directed the police to the body. Pamela Powers would have rotted by the side of the road, and her parents never would have been able to bury her. But at least we would have avoided a justice system that "suffered morally"!

Liberal justices didn't care whether confessions were "reliable." They just wanted to release child-murderers. Instead of favoring policies that would distinguish the guilty from the innocent, liberals think the guilty deserve as much right as everyone else to go free. The criminal justice system should be like Kurt Vonnegut's short story "Harrison Bergeron," with the courts playing the Handicapper General to ensure that everyone is equal—both the innocent and the guilty. The guilty get a bag of "constitutional rights" so that they are no more likely to be convicted than anyone else.

It wasn't as if no one could predict what was going to happen as a result of all these rulings. Dissenting in **Massiah,** Justice Byron White warned his colleagues that their academic arguments about "whether we should punish, deter, rehabilitate or cure" would allow crime to flourish. He characterized the decision in **Massiah** as discovering a new constitutional right "barring the use of evidence which is relevant, reliable and highly probative of the issue which the trial court has before it—whether the accused committed the act with which he is charged." Justice John Marshall Harlan dissented in **Miranda,** saying the Court was engaging in "dangerous experimentation" with society's criminal laws.

As a result of the Court's experiment, millions of violent predators were unleashed on the public to continue their barbarism. The crime wave of the sixties and seventies can be traced directly to the insanity of the Warren Court era. In the fifties, crime rates were low, but starting right around 1963, crime began to soar. One year after **Miranda,** New York County district attorney Frank Hogan told the Senate Judiciary Committee that confessions in his district alone had fallen from 49 percent to 14 percent solely as a result of the **Miranda** decision. Federal judge and former law professor Paul Cassell has calculated that one decision alone, **Miranda,** has led to the release of about 100,000 violent criminals a year.[7] Instead of hanging their heads in shame and trying to make up for the needless suffering and death inflicted on America by their policies, liberals are proud of releasing violent criminals. In the book **The Warren Court and American Politics,** Lucas A. Powe Jr., a law professor at the University of Texas at Austin, says liberal law professors, of which he is one, have a 'religious and mystical' view of the Warren Court."[8]

Judge David L. Bazelon, a Truman appointee who was chief judge of the D.C. Circuit from 1962 to 1978, didn't wait for the Supreme Court to act before freeing guilty criminals. Punishment, Bazelon said, was "dehumanizing." (And the last thing we'd want to do to animals like Jeffrey Dahmer or John Wayne Gacy is "dehumanize" them.) Bazelon referred to society's "need to punish" as a "primitive urge" based on "vindictiveness" that was "highly irrational." The idea that we should lock criminals up, he said, reflected a "deep childish fear that with any reduction of punishment, multitudes would run amuck."[9] Bazelon believed the criminal is just "like us, only somewhat weaker." Thus, he "needs help if he is going to bring out the good in himself and restrain the bad." The fact that there are criminals is our "social failure," and we are using the criminal as our "scapegoat."[10]

In other words, America's judges were crazier than the criminals they were releasing. Throughout the sixties and seventies, liberal judges behaved like members of the Comintern, issuing new rules based on theories that ignored human nature:

> **But how can Communism work if there are no incentives for workers?**
> Answer: The theory makes it impossible.
> **Okay good, because at first I thought it might not work.**

To cap it all off, in 1967, Lyndon Johnson appointed Ramsey Clark attorney general of the United States. That alone should have been enough to never allow another Democrat in the White House. In fact, that should be its own chapter:

> **Chapter 2.1**
> Under the Democrats, Ramsey Clark was made attorney general of the United States. The end.

Clark, most recently Saddam Hussein's lawyer, immediately imposed a moratorium on the death penalty and halted all new prison construction. Clark believed it was the government's job to rehabilitate violent criminals, not to keep them away from the public. "Prisons," Clark said, "are

usually little more than places to keep people."[11]
Yes—I think that's the idea in a nutshell.

Arthur Shawcross is the two-word explanation
for why normal people prefer locking criminals
up to releasing them, despite the risk we run of
turning them into "scapegoats." In 1972, Shawcross molested and murdered a ten-year-old boy
he had lured into the woods. A few months later,
he raped and murdered an eight-year-old girl. He
was arrested and confessed to the crimes. For reasons that remain mysterious, the charges against
Shawcross for the boy's murder were dropped altogether. Instead, Shawcross pleaded guilty to
manslaughter for the girl's rape and murder and
was sentenced to twenty-five years in prison.

In 1987, after serving only fifteen years in
prison, Shawcross was released by a parole board
chosen by Democratic governor Mario Cuomo.[12]
Despite the conclusion of Cuomo's appointees on
the parole board that Shawcross was ready to become an integral part of society again, society
didn't think so and repeatedly protested having
him in their neighborhoods.

Fortunately for Shawcross, Cuomo's parole
board abjured primitive emotions like vengeance
and retribution and helpfully relocated him to
Rochester, New York—without warning anyone,
not even the police department. The important

thing was to treat Shawcross with dignity and respect. Within two years, Shawcross committed eleven more murders in the Rochester area. He was eventually caught and convicted a second time. This time, he was put away for good—assuming a Democrat never gets into power and sets him loose again.

That's what happened in America when liberals were at the controls. Only in the eighties did the country finally begin to fight its way back from liberal insanity on crime, electing Republican presidents, Republican governors, and Republican legislatures. After owning the Supreme Court lock, stock, and barrel from 1953 to 1973, liberals are now fighting like screaming banshees to preserve the worst of the Warren Court.

Republicans immediately set to work to try to get **Miranda** overturned. President Reagan's sainted attorney general, Ed Meese, assigned a team of lawyers to look into it. Judy Goldberg of the ACLU condemned the campaign against **Miranda,** saying, "Mr. Meese has revealed a profound misunderstanding of what the **Miranda** right is all about." She said Meese and those around him seemed to have the idea that "there's something improper about making people aware of their constitutional rights."[13] Leaving aside the loose meaning of the phrase "constitutional rights" in that sentence, there's also nothing "improper" about having port after dinner, but if my host forgets to serve it, I don't demand that a murderer be unleashed on society. If these are such sacred "constitutional" rights, why are liberals afraid to speak honestly about them?

After twenty years of hard work by Republicans, in 2000, **Miranda** was finally reconsidered by the Supreme Court in a case called **Dickerson v. United States**—where it was upheld on the grounds that the case was now a "precedent." Even Justice William Rehnquist refused to overrule it on grounds of stare decisis. Stare decisis— also known as "what's mine is mine and what's yours is negotiable"—is a ratchet preserving only cases liberals like, while they feel free to completely ignore Supreme Court precedents they don't like. Liberal affection for stare decisis was not much in evidence when they were overruling all those cases dealing with habeas corpus and criminal confessions in the first place. No Democrats seemed to mind when the cases being overruled were **Stanford v. Kentucky** (death penalty for juveniles not unconstitutional) or **Penry v. Johnson** (death penalty for the retarded not unconstitutional) or **Bowers v. Hardwick** (laws against sodomy not unconstitutional). So we got stuck with **Miranda** while liberals wantonly overruled **Stanford, Penry,** and

Bowers—all within fifteen years of the original decision.

Still, though lacking the revolutionary zeal of the Warren Court, the courts have gradually restored at least some common sense in the criminal justice system. As a result of the return to the Republican idea of punishing violent criminals, rather than the Democrat idea of treating violent criminals with kindness and hoping they will repay us with law-abiding behavior, crime rates have plummeted in the past twenty years. Since 1981, most serious crimes have declined dramatically in the United States, while rising or remaining the same in other industrial democracies, such as Australia, Sweden, the Netherlands, and Switzerland—and the rest of those modern democracies that, unlike us, don't have the death penalty. Notably, the rates of conviction and imprisonment increased in America during that time, while declining in the countries that saw an increase in crime. Only when England began to send more criminals to prison in the nineties did their crime rate begin to fall, too.[14]

One group of people has steadfastly ignored the lesson of the sixties and seventies about the release of criminals being linked to more crime. We call them "liberals." Republicans think that after someone has committed a heinous crime, he should be punished and separated from society. Democrats think that after someone commits a brutal crime, our most important objective should be to help him achieve his personhood. The **New York Times** is obsessed with giving convicted felons the right to vote, running dozens of articles and editorials every year: "Stripping convicted felons of the right to vote is a slap at America's democratic ideals."**15** With liberals, the same experiment has to be repeated over and over again.

In a comical episode in 1992, "mainly [Jimmy] Carter appointees" on the Ninth Circuit Court of Appeals, as described in the **National Law Journal**, entered repeated stays of execution in a single night for Robert Alton Harris. Harris had been sentenced to death a decade earlier for kidnapping and murdering two sixteen-year-old boys. He was scheduled to be executed just after midnight on April 21, 1992. But from midnight to 6 A.M., Harris was repeatedly strapped in and out of the gas chamber as "mainly Carter appointees" openly defied the Supreme Court by staying his execution.**16** Evidently no one on the Ninth Circuit noticed that constantly strapping someone into and out of an execution chamber might itself be considered cruel and unusual punishment (although not cruel and unusual enough to suit at least one conservative author). After the Supreme Court was forced to vacate the Ninth Circuit's third stay of the night in the wee hours of the morning, the Supreme Court issued an unusually intemperate order saying there was "no good reason for this abusive delay." This was a ruling so explicit even the Florida Supreme Court might have understood it.

Hours later, Carter-appointed judge Harry Pregerson stunningly defied the Supreme Court a fourth time by entering yet another stay of execution. When liberals act as though they don't know what we mean by "judicial activism," one might point to this as the sort of thing we have in mind. This time, the High Court vacated the stay with an unprecedented order: "[N]o further stays of Robert Alton Harris's execution shall be entered by the federal courts except upon order of this Court." Harris was finally executed at around 6 A.M. on April 21, 1992. The execution would have proceeded with greater alacrity if California had simply relabeled Harris's execution a very late-term abortion.

In 2001, twelve-year-old Lionel Tate savagely murdered six-year-old Tiffany Eunick, a girl his mother was babysitting. Tate kicked, punched, and stomped the little girl for at least five minutes. The beating was so severe that Tiffany's skull was cracked open and her liver split in two. Tate claimed he had been mimicking moves he had seen on professional wrestling on TV, but his own defense experts testified that Tiffany's injuries were not consistent with that story, and the judge called it "inconceivable" that Tiffany's injuries were caused by wrestling moves. After the trial, Tate's new lawyers admitted that the "wrestling defense" was "bogus."

Tate was convicted of first-degree murder by a jury and sentenced to life in prison. Democrats in the state legislature immediately leapt to action and began drafting legislation that would prohibit adult sentences for juvenile offenders like Tate. They needn't have worried—they had Democrat-appointed judges ready to release Tate.

Two years later, a Florida appellate court did release Tate, reducing his sentence for the barbaric murder of a little girl to time served. The original jury had heard the evidence—including the defense's evidence—and had rendered their verdict, knowing it would result in putting an adolescent away for life. But judges who had never heard any of the evidence or laid eyes on Tate thought they knew better. Within a year of Tate's release, he was rearrested for armed robbery of a Domino's Pizza deliveryman, who fortunately ran the moment he saw Tate's gun. If a Democrat judge doesn't release him again, Tate could be well on his way to his own show on

Pacifica Radio—or challenging incumbent Mumia Abu-Jamal in the next New York City mayoral race. The opinion that unleashed a dangerous psychopath on society was written by Judge Barry J. Stone, appointed to the bench by Democrat governor Lawton Chiles. Stone had nothing to worry about: He doesn't deliver Domino's pizza. He always feels perfectly safe at his Pompano Beach home. Releasing dangerous killers has consequences for other people. (For an addendum regarding Lionel Tate's future crimes, please refer to the paperback version of this book, tentatively scheduled for release in Fall 2007.)

No Democrat ever abandoned the Democrats' position on crime more aggressively than Bill Clinton. He rushed back to Arkansas to execute Rickey Ray Rector in the middle of the 1992 presidential campaign. Clinton did everything but pause for a postexecution photo op with the killer's dead body. In his first year in office, Clinton promoted a Democratic "crime bill" to fake out voters and make them think he was against crime. But he never strayed far from the mother ship. Even Mr. Triangulation, "Third Way" Democrat couldn't abandon the basic belief system of his party. As a repeat offender himself, Clinton may have identified with his fellow felons a bit too closely. Consider just three typical Clinton judicial nominees:

One of Clinton's Third Way, centrist choices was Judge H. Lee Sarokin, who had already been appointed to a district court by Jimmy Carter. As district court judge, Sarokin found that a homeless man had a constitutional right to stink up libraries and frighten patrons with his obsessive staring. According to Sarokin, the library's "offensive odor" ban violated the First Amendment apparently because it was a library and there are books in a library, which contain speech, which is protected by the First Amendment. The No-Stinking-the-Place-Up rule also violated "substantive due process" (which doesn't exist), because the odor rule was a "reader-based restriction." And it violated the Equal Protection Clause (which does exist), because the rule had a "disparate impact" on people who refuse to bathe compared with those who bathe regularly. In a rousing conclusion that ought to have gotten him put in a straitjacket rather than elevated to an appellate court, Sarokin wrote that instead of hoping to "shield our eyes and ears from the homeless . . . we should revoke their condition, not their library cards."**17**

A Democratic Senate confirmed Sarokin's appointment to the Third Circuit, and the judge was given greater power to ruin the lives of ordinary Americans. On the Third Circuit Court of Appeals, he overturned the death sentences of two brutal, multiple murderers. William Henry Flamer had fatally stabbed his aunt and uncle a total of 145 times after gaining entry to their home by claiming his grandmother had had a stroke. He confessed to the murders. The other murderer, Billie Bailey, escaped from a work release program and killed an eighty-year-old man and his seventy-three-year-old wife in their farmhouse. Immediately after the murder, he was spotted by a police helicopter running from the farmhouse and was rearrested.

Both men were duly tried, convicted, and sentenced to death, which, on Planet Sane would have ensured their speedy dispatch to a Great Beyond where real punishment awaited them. Instead, both men repeatedly clogged up the state and federal courts with their frivolous appeals, all of which were denied—including three petitions to the U.S. Supreme Court. In none of the appeals did the killers claim they were innocent. But when the murderers' appeals landed on Sarokin's desk, he voted to overturn the capital sentences, an opinion that, mercifully, was in dissent.[18] It was also Sarokin who overturned Rubin "Hurricane" Carter's sentence on the grounds that the prosecution's theory of motive was not supported by the evidence[19]—something that is ordinarily for a jury to decide.

Judge Rosemary Barkett caught Clinton's eye

when she was chief justice of the Florida Supreme Court. (And after the 2000 election, I think we all know what kind of credential that is.) Barkett was described by one of her colleagues on the Florida court as believing murderers were basically good people except for their tendency to sometimes kill people.[20] One such killer was Jacob John Dougan, leader of what he called the "Black Liberation Army," the goal of which was to "indiscriminately kill white people and thus start a revolution and a race war." Dougan killed an eighteen-year-old white hitchhiker, Stephen Anthony Orlando, and then made a tape describing Orlando's murder in gruesome detail, which he mailed to the victim's mother and, this being America, to the media. "I enjoyed every minute of it," Dougan said on the tape. "I loved watching the blood gush from his eyes."

Nearly twenty years after Dougan's conviction, Barkett voted to overturn the killer's death sentence—fortunately, in a dissenting opinion. According to Barkett and her fellow dissenters, Dougan's case was "not simply a homicide case," it was also a "social awareness case." The opinion Barkett joined is worth quoting at some length:

[T]his killing was effectuated to focus attention on a chronic and pervasive illness of racial discrimination and of hurt, sorrow, and rejection. Throughout Dougan's life his resentment to bias and prejudice festered. His impatience for change, for understanding, for reconciliation matured to taking the illogical and drastic action of murder. His frustrations, his anger, and his obsession of injustice overcame reason. The victim was a symbolic representation of the class causing the perceived injustices.

To some extent, [Dougan's] emotions were parallel to that of a spouse disenchanted with marriage, full of discord and disharmony which, because of frustration or rejection, culminate in homicide. We seldom uphold a death penalty involving husbands and wives or lovers, yet the emotions of that hate-love circumstance are somewhat akin to those which existed in this case.

Such a sentence reduction should aid in an understanding and at least a partial reconciliation of the wounds arising from discordant racial relations that have permeated our society. To a large extent, it was this disease of racial bias and discrimination that infect an otherwise honorable person and contributed to the perpetration of the most horrible of crimes. An approval of the death penalty would exacerbate rather than heal

those wounds still affecting a large segment
of our society.

The ruling failed to speculate as to why millions of other black Americans, many of whom
may have also experienced racial discrimination,
chose not to brutally murder white people at random and gash their eyes out. In 1993, when the
Democrats controlled the Senate, Barkett was
confirmed to a seat on the U.S. Court of Appeals
for the Eleventh Circuit in a 61–37 vote.

Frederica A. Massiah-Jackson, of the Philadelphia Common Pleas Court, was known for
shouting obscenities from the bench and identifying undercover policemen in open court. In
1997 Clinton nominated Massiah-Jackson to be
a federal district court judge. Among other notable rulings, she sentenced the brutal rapist of a
ten-year-old girl to the statutory minimum and
apologized to the rapist, saying, "I just don't
think the five to ten years is appropriate in this
case even assuming you were found guilty." She
refused to allow the D.A. to give a pre-sentence
report or victim impact statement, saying, "What
would be the point of that?" After his release, the
defendant was rearrested for raping a nine-year-
old boy.

In another special moment for the Rainbow
Coalition, after being informed that both the de-

fendant and the victim in a rape case had AIDS, Massiah-Jackson said, "Why are we having a trial? We are talking about life expectancy of three years for both of them. What's the difference?" In fact, the victim of the rape did die while Massiah-Jackson's refusal to recuse herself for these statements was tied up in appeals. In the end, Massiah-Jackson sentenced the rapist to one-year probation, allowing him to serve no time for a vicious rape and beating.

Sentencing a defendant who had slashed a woman in the face with a straight razor while stealing her purse, Massiah-Jackson refused to apply a sentence enhancement for use of a deadly weapon. When the D.A. noted that the enhancement was required by sentencing guidelines Massiah-Jackson was presumed to be vaguely familiar with, the centrist judge accused the prosecutor of being "vindictive." Massiah-Jackson was reversed on appeal for ignoring the enhancement.[21]

Indeed, Massiah-Jackson was reversed in a whole slew of criminal cases. But in response to the Judiciary Committee request that she provide a list of her reversals—a pro forma request—she repeatedly claimed she had not been reversed in a single criminal case. After having been caught in this and other lies, largely thanks to Senator John Ashcroft, Massiah-Jackson decided to withdraw her nomination. If Republicans had not won a majority in 1994, Massiah-Jackson would be a federal judge now.

Massiah-Jackson wasn't some random nut nominated by Clinton by accident, like Janet Reno. She was a liberal heroine. The **New York Times** was in high dudgeon when Massiah-Jackson withdrew—and not because Massiah-Jackson had sneered at AIDS victims and rape victims, shouted obscenities from the bench, and outed undercover cops. The **Times** was in a snit because of the "judicial mugging" the Senate had put her through. Massiah-Jackson, the **Times** said, "now returns to the state bench, battered but with her honor intact. Unfortunately, the same cannot be said of the Senate." Indeed, even after all this came out about Massiah-Jackson (despite the encumbrance on getting facts because of the judge's tendency to lie), she was avidly supported for a life-tenured federal judgeship by Philadelphia mayor Edward G. Rendell, top Philadelphia law firms, judges, the NAACP, the Barristers' Association of Philadelphia, the Hispanic Bar Association, the Asian American Bar Association of the Delaware Valley, the Philadelphia Bar Association, and various other now-discredited liberal groups.

The last time the Democrats controlled both houses of Congress and the presidency was during the first two years of the Clinton administration. So we have a pretty good idea of what Democrats think of as a crime-fighting initiative. When Democrats were running the show, their idea for fighting crime was to spend $40 million to set up midnight basketball leagues, $650 million to provide children with "positive attitudes and alternatives to the street life of crime and drugs," and $1.8 billion—**billion**—on the Violence Against Women Act, later declared unconstitutional by the Supreme Court.

Liberals tout the spectacular reduction in crime in the nineties as if criminals were so touched by Bill Clinton's raising taxes on the middle class and establishment of Midnight Basketball Leagues that they decided to abandon their lives of crime and pursue honest lives. This is consistent with liberals' belief—published mostly in journals in Manhattan—that people commit crime because they're angry at "the system," and that if we could just convince them that the system is fair by not putting them in prison, no one would ever commit crime again.

Crime didn't go down in the nineties because of Clinton's idiotic COPS program (Community Oriented Policing Services), which was designed to spend more money on fax machines at rape crisis centers than on new cops. (Despite receiving over $15 million from the federal COPS program, the Atlanta police department, among others, actually reduced the size of its police force between 1994 and 1998.22) The crime rate went down mostly because Republican legislatures built a lot of prisons and because Rudy Giuliani was elected mayor of New York. Needless to say, Democrats ferociously opposed both prison building and Mayor Giuliani.

Whether it is building prisons, mandatory sentencing, three-strikes laws, or the death penalty, if it has to do with punishing criminals, Democrats are against it. Liberals prefer treatment, rehabilitation, alternatives to prison, even creative alternatives to prison—but not prison! That would be "blaming the perpetrator." As a 1993 episode of **60 Minutes** put it, "Building more prisons and jails does not seem to be the answer to high rate of crime in the U.S." Mike Wallace explained: "America has been hit by a crime storm of hurricane proportions, and so there's been an outcry to get even tougher on crime, to send more Americans to prison for longer terms. But does prison work?"23 The answer was an emphatic no, as attested to by the many experts interviewed by CBS News.

The proposition that prison doesn't work is like saying deodorant doesn't work (which college liberals also seem to believe). Of course prison works: It keeps people who commit crimes off the streets because they're in prison. Let's run the numbers: The recidivism rate of armed robbers behind bars is . . . hmmmm, looks like 0 percent!

In addition to the usual pompous idiots touted as "experts" by the mainstream media, Wallace deemed the inmates themselves experts on the efficacy of imprisonment. And who better to debate the merits of punishment than the people being punished?

> WALLACE (**voiceover**): So that $25,000 a year in tax money to keep a prisoner here, what does it buy?
>
> GROUP OF INMATES (**in unison**): Nothing.
> **[Group of Sane Viewers: Yeah, except it keeps you from killing, raping, and robbing us, so there's that.]**
>
> UNIDENTIFIED INMATE #1: We don't even— we don't even get any type of program here.
>
> WALLACE: No program? No work?
>
> INMATES: Nothing.

By "programs," liberals generally have in mind things like the "early release program"—or as I call it, "one-on-one partnering of violent criminals and their future victims." One inmate interviewed on **60 Minutes** warned Wallace, "If prison doesn't offer something, if prison doesn't give some type of way out or some type of future, or some type of life to look for, America is in big trouble." Oddly enough, most Americans were willing to risk the wrath of the **60 Minutes** inmates and keep them behind bars. Between 1995 and 2005, the prison population grew by 30 percent, meaning an additional half million criminals were behind bars,[24] rather than lurking in dark alleys with switchblades. You can well imagine liberals' surprise when the crime rate went down as more criminals were put in prison. The **New York Times** was reduced to running querulous articles with headlines like "Number in Prison Grows Despite Crime Reduction"[25] and "As Crime Rate Drops, the Prison Rate Rises and the Debate Rages."[26]

So liberals turned to their second favorite argument against policies they oppose. (Their first-favorite policy argument is to threaten to kill themselves in back-alley abortions.) To wit, they complained about the burden to the beleaguered taxpayer. As the **Times** put it, "[S]ome of the researchers questioned whether the benefits from the growth of incarceration were worth the cost to taxpayers." Whenever liberals claim to be worried about how much money the government is spending, you know they have some other objection but dare not tell the voters.

All over the country, unbiased, objective newspapers consistently report on prison building solely on the basis of what it will cost the taxpayer. Here are some typical headlines, these from 2005 alone:

PRISON COSTS ARE RUNNING OUT OF CONTROL
Denver Post[27]

REPORT: PRISON COSTS HURTING EDUCATION
Charleston Gazette (West Virginia)[28]

SMALL JAIL, LESS CRIME: SUFFOLK IS SMART TO
REDUCE THE COST OF A NEW JAIL WITH
ALTERNATIVES TO INCARCERATION
Newsday (New York)[29]

PRISONS EAT UP TAX DOLLARS
Wisconsin State Journal (Madison)[30]

MORE SERVING TIME AS TAXPAYERS FOOT BILL
Kansas City Star[31]

How about some newspaper describing an actually useless government program in terms of the cost to taxpayers? What does the federal Department of Education cost? How about the EPA? The Commerce Department? The Bureau of Land Management? Chuck Schumer's office?

An alarmist article in the **New York Times** in 1991 reported that in New Jersey, the Corrections Department "consumes 7 percent of all state spending."[32] (The remainder of the state budget is dedicated to paper for publishing the state's sexual harassment guidelines and payroll expenses for any married governor's gay lovers.) Besides enforcing the law, what other crucial functions does state government have? Keeping marauding predators off the streets is the most basic function of any government. Liberals think the government should be responsible for things like establishing a national "Earth Day," determining how much water we can have in our toilets, and sending mammoth delegations on taxpayer-funded sightseeing trips to Africa because Clinton has just been caught with an intern and needs to shore up his black support. They view keeping killers and rapists off the streets as a crazy luxury for times when government coffers are flush. Democrats aren't worried about the cost of prison; they are worried that if there are more prisons, criminals might be sent there.

The second major factor in reducing crime in the nineties was Rudy Giuliani, Republican mayor of New York City. By pursuing policies that were relentlessly opposed by liberals throughout his tenure in office, Giuliani reduced the murder rate in New York City from about 2,000 murders a year under Democratic mayor David Dinkins to 714 the year Giuliani left office. Giuliani cut the murder rate an astonishing 20 percent his first year in office. Major crimes dropped by 16 percent his first year in office and another 14 percent the next year. (And the amazing thing is that he did all this without midnight basketball, which was replaced by a Giuliani program known as "midnight rounding up of armed suspects.") New York became one of the safest cities in America. The **New York Times** noted the remarkable development in an article headlined "New York City Crime Falls but Just Why Is a Mystery"[33]—which it was, at least to liberals, who spent most of the Giuliani years calling him a fascist.

Lives were saved when Giuliani cut the murder rate—mostly black lives—but liberals weren't praising Giuliani for the miraculous reduction in crime; they were attacking him as a stormtrooper every single year he was in office. But by the end of Giuliani's administration, the Reverend Calvin Butts, liberal pastor of Harlem's Abyssinian Baptist Church, was describing Giuliani as King Josiah of the Bible, who "brought order, peace, the law back to the land." The black minister told the **Times,** "I really think that without Giuliani, we would have been overrun."[34]

Even after Giuliani's triumphant success, liberals demean his accomplishment. Those who won't believe will never believe. They say the crime rate was already falling, as if the drop in the number of murders during the Dinkins administration from 2,154 murders in 1991 to 1,995 murders in 1992 was the equivalent of the Battle of Midway. It was probably a bookkeeping error. Or they attribute the plummeting crime rate under Giuliani to the end of the crack epidemic, the economy, and, most charmingly, the increase in abortions among the "poor" beginning in the seventies. (Just wait until Bill Bennett hears about that!) What's striking about the factors liberals stress is that they never involve catching and punishing criminals. Under no circumstances are we to fall for the canard about the reduction in crime being caused by obvious explanations like enforcing the law, issuing longer sentences, or supporting the police.

Saying the end of the crack epidemic ended the crime wave merely begs the question, What ended the crack epidemic? It's like saying the end of the crime wave ended the crime wave.

And that must have been one hell of an abortion rate in the first half of the century for the nation to have enjoyed such low crime rates up until the sixties. In any event, I believe we're already aborting as many babies as NARAL's Kate Michelman can get her hands on.

The "Clinton economy"—which only became something to brag about sometime after the Republican takeover of Congress in 1994— provably had nothing to do with declining crime rates. Under the "Clinton economy," the crime rate went up in cities all over America— Baltimore, Charlotte, Columbus, Las Vegas, Memphis, Milwaukee, Nashville, Philadelphia, and Phoenix. Contrary to liberal ideas about improving criminals' self-esteem, it turned out that raising the cost of committing crime worked even better. In the midst of a terrible national economy in Clinton's first years in office (the real "Clinton economy"), Giuliani cut crime dramatically in New York City. And of course, New York's economy was booming throughout the eighties, when the crime rate was exploding.

Few opposed Giuliani more aggressively than Bill Clinton. Even before Giuliani took office, Clinton had campaigned against him in ugly racial terms. When Giuliani was running against Dinkins in 1993, Clinton publicly bemoaned the fact that some New Yorkers would not vote for Dinkins solely because he was black. **Not make-believe black, like me,** Clinton added. **You know, black-black.** "Too many of us," Clinton said, "are still too unwilling to vote for people who are different than we are." In case that was too subtle, Clinton added, "[T]his is not as simple as overt racism," but a "deep-seated reluctance we have, against all our better judgment, to reach out across those lines." Then again, maybe it was a deep-seated reluctance to reinstall a mayor under whose watch about 8,000 New Yorkers had been murdered.

Once Giuliani was elected, Clinton opposed him every step of the way, but then he turned around and claimed credit for Giuliani's crime policies. Even the **New York Times** was shocked by Clinton's shamelessness in using crime as a "bragging point" during his 1996 reelection campaign—without once mentioning Giuliani. Giuliani's policies on crime, the **Times** said, would do "as much to re-elect [Clinton] as any Democratic mayor."[35] Thirty-five percent of the reduction in the national crime rate from 1993 to 1995 was attributable solely to the reduction of crime in New York City during Giuliani's first years in office. As the **New York Times** admitted in one of the rare articles during the nineties not calling Giuliani an "authoritarian,"[36] "[W]hile constituting less than 3 percent of the country's population," New York City alone "was responsible for 155,558 of the 432,952 fewer reported crimes over the three years."[37]

But according to Clinton, it was Democratic policies like "community policing" that had caused the massive reductions in crime in the nineties. Campaigning for reelection in 1996, Clinton said, "I'm telling you, folks, we can prevent crime and catch criminals if we have more people serving their communities out there, visible, who know the kids on the streets, who know the neighbors, who know the law-abiding folks."**38** David Dinkins had been a big proponent of "community policing," too. Giuliani jettisoned the policy and reduced the crime rate of the Dinkins era by nearly 70 percent.

Far from crediting Giuliani, Clinton's Justice Department repeatedly investigated the New York City police for alleged civil rights violations—investigations that became suspiciously frequent about the time it appeared that Clinton's wife would be running against Giuliani for Senate. Inasmuch as New York police shot fewer civilians than any other big-city police department, New York was an odd place for the Clinton administration to concentrate its investigative efforts. In Washington, D.C., for example, the police were seven times more likely to shoot civilians than New York police. Washington was also conveniently located in the same city as the U.S. Department of Justice that was sending investigators up to New York.

To this day, Democrats demand that we credit Clinton for the plunging crime rate in the nineties—which did not begin to plunge until Giuliani became mayor of New York. Clinton may have tried to socialize health care, presided over a phony Internet bubble, spurned Sudan when it offered him Osama bin Laden on a silver platter,**39** sold a burial plot in Arlington cemetery to a campaign contributor, engaged in sex romps in the Oval Office, been credibly accused of rape by Juanita Broaddrick, obstructed justice, had his law license suspended and gotten himself permanently disbarred from the U.S. Supreme Court, and pardoned a lot of sleazy crooks in return for political donations on his way out of office—but, we're told, at least he was terrific on crime! Everything Clinton actually did himself was a failure or a felony, so he has to claim credit for the successes of Republicans like Giuliani.

After 9/11, when the Clinton presidency looked even more ridiculous than it did when he was still in office, Clinton convened a group of his former advisers to create a PR strategy to burnish his legacy. (You know, just as Washington, Lincoln, and Reagan did. Great presidents always do this after they leave office, right? Hello? Is there anybody there? Hello?) Prominent among the Clinton flacks' talking points was one about how Clinton cut the crime rate. Campaigning for John Kerry in 2004, Clinton told a Philadelphia audience that when Democrat Ed Rendell had been the mayor, "we worked together to bring down the crime rate. We did it with more cops on the street and assault weapons off the street."**40** According to the **New York Times,** Philadelphia was one of nine major cities where the crime rate went up in the years following the enactment of Clinton's crime bill.[41]

Democrats are not interested in restoring order. They will never abandon their deranged sentimentality about violent criminals. Now it's just a matter of catching them when they forget to lie. Or finding the liberals who don't know they're supposed to lie. On MSNBC's **Hardball,** Chris Matthews asked Richard Goldstein of the **Village Voice:** "In the history of New York, did you have safe streets till Giuliani came along?"

Goldstein said, "Chris, I lived in New York all my life, okay? I was safe, I was safe, I did not see cops pulling down the pants of black kids in the streets. I feel less safe today in New York City than I did twenty years ago. Now, you know, you, you, your class of people did very well under Giuliani. Mazel tov. But a lot of people really suffered under him. The police practices in this city were reprehensible. They were—the federal government called him on this."[42]

It was like watching an interview of an insane person. I can't seem to find any documentation of cops-pulling-down-the-pants-of-black-kids rates under Dinkins versus those rates under Giuliani, so I am unable to address that very important point that Goldstein raised. But we do know that a lot fewer blacks were murdered during the Giuliani years. Indeed, Goldstein was claiming to feel less safe in Giuliani's New York just a few months after the Reverend Butts was comparing Giuliani to King Josiah of the Bible.[43] What does he know? He's just a black man in Harlem.

One by one, a stumped and bewildered panel responded to Goldstein, saying New York sure seemed a lot safer to them:

MATTHEWS: . . . when I go to New York, it's not funny, when I go to New York, it's safe to walk around. . . . I feel a lot better in New York. And I'll tell you something, the subways, everything, has changed about New York. And one guy's responsible for it that I can see. And I'm not loving the guy. I'm just admitting it. Go ahead.

TERRY JEFFREY, **Human Events:** Yes, I'm not a New Yorker; I do visit there. It's stark when you go there how much nicer it is in New York City than it was twenty years ago.

To this, Goldstein said, "Well, you like South Carolina. What do you expect?" What a stunning rhetorical riposte, sir! I say, you've cut me to the quick! The incisive thrust of your logical cutlass has struck me to the bone! Alas, I fear the wound is fatal! Oh, untimely death!

But back to the point—which was it? Was

New York safer before Giuliani or did Goldstein simply prefer it when there were three times as many murders per year and it was less like South Carolina? Or—and this is the theory I'm favoring—is Richard Goldstein of the **Village Voice** mentally retarded?

Most Democrats have at least learned they're supposed to lie about their ideas on crime. Now liberals are forced to sit around thinking, **Can we get away with this?** It is a striking fact that, after Giuliani, in order to be mayor of New York even liberal politicians have to claim to be Republicans. After Giuliani's success, crime control in places like New York City could run on autopilot forevermore—if there were no liberals. But the moment Republicans leave the room, the ACLU will come back in and reset the controls.

While elected Democrats have learned not to have their careers dependent on the good behavior of criminals they release from prison, their constituents are still holding candlelight vigils for every heinous murderer on death row. It is a liberal ritual to turn palpably guilty criminals into causes célèbres. Among the most famous liberal martyrs are executed Soviet spies Ethel and Julius Rosenberg, Soviet spy and convicted perjurer Alger Hiss, the Central Park rapists, gang leader and multiple murderer Tookie Williams, cop killer Mumia Abu-Jamal, violent multiple murderer Rubin "Hurricane" Carter, executed Italian anarchists Sacco and Vanzetti—all provably guilty. With liberals' track record, it may be time to reopen the Scottsboro Boys' case.

Only recently have we learned not only that Sacco and Vanzetti were absolutely guilty of cold-blooded murder—which is no surprise—but also that their liberal defenders knew the truth all along. Their lawyer knew it and cooked up an alibi for them. Phony progressive Upton Sinclair knew it, even as he denounced the American justice system for framing two innocent immigrants because of their unconventional political views.

Nicola Sacco and Bartolomeo Vanzetti were ruthless anarchists who killed a couple of payroll carriers for a Boston shoe factory in 1920 in order to bankroll their bombings of government buildings. After their arrest, they repeatedly lied to investigators. Police found a loaded gun on Sacco that matched the crime weapon, almost literally giving prosecutors a smoking gun. Sacco and Vanzetti were tried by jury and sentenced to death. In the U.S. justice system's typical "rush to justice" fashion, seven years passed between Sacco and Vanzetti's murder spree and their eventual execution. Among the appeals was one you will see whenever liberals start weeping for some criminal: They produced an eleventh-hour "confession" from someone who would face no additional punishment for confessing (in this case, because he was already in prison).

But Sinclair wrote a groaning 750-page tome called **Boston,** a historical novel in the James Frey style, suggesting that Sacco and Vanzetti had been sentenced to die for a crime they didn't commit. According to Sinclair's novel, these two poor immigrants had been framed by the rich and powerful in Boston—despite the fact that their victims were hardly corporate chieftains but payroll carriers, Frederick Parmenter and Alessandro Berardelli, the latter an Italian immigrant himself. Nonetheless, Sinclair insisted it was the social conservatism of the day that led to the convictions of Sacco and Vanzetti simply because they were immigrants with socialist and anarchist views.

Thanks to recently unearthed letters from Sinclair to his lawyer, we now know that Sinclair was aware all along that Sacco and Vanzetti were guilty. He also knew that the only perjured testimony at trial came from the defendants' alibi witnesses. In private letters to his lawyer, Sinclair admitted that while researching his book, he had met with the anarchists' defense attorney in a hotel room and asked for the truth. In Sinclair's own words, the defense lawyer said "the men were guilty," and even told Sinclair "in every detail how he had framed a set of alibis for them."[44]

Facing what he called "the most difficult ethical problem" of his life, Sinclair decided to lie in his book, his moral indignation undimmed. As Sinclair explained in his letters, "It is much better copy as a naive defense of Sacco and Vanzetti because this is what all my foreign readers expect, and they are 90% of my public." (In the article about the Sinclair letters that exposed him as a fraud, the **Los Angeles Times** reporter still insisted on referring to Sinclair as "one of America's most strident truth tellers." It's nice to be a liberal.) In one letter, Sinclair admonishes his lawyer, "This letter is for yourself alone. Stick it away in your safe, and some time in the far distant future the world may know the real truth about the matter."[45] But not while there was money to be made from the America-hating Left.

Sinclair accused Hollywood of "blacklisting" movies about Sacco and Vanzetti, apparently because no one turned his book into a movie. Liberal claims of "blacklisting," like sex tapes, always appear at the ideal time to advance the liberal's career goals. The Internet Movie Database lists seven films made about Sacco and Vanzetti, three made in Hollywood, including a TV movie by Sidney Lumet, which was nominated for four Emmys. The 1971 Italian film **Sacco e Vanzetti**—with music by Joan Baez—was nominated for the Palme d'Or at Cannes. I guess the two payroll carriers murdered in cold blood by Sacco and Vanzetti will have to wait another day for their movie.

Ginned up by liberal frauds like Upton Sinclair, 250,000 protesters marched in Boston the day Sacco and Vanzetti were executed, and another 200,000 engaged in a violent march the day of their funeral. There were protests in Switzerland, Germany, Argentina, England, and Mexico and violent riots in France, where thousands fought with the police in Paris. Liberals would not have this much fun again until the Rosenbergs were executed.

In some cases, it was literally the same people defending Sacco and Vanzetti who would later be defending Soviet spies Julius and Ethel Rosenberg and Alger Hiss. In 1927, Felix Frankfurter—Harvard Law School professor and future character witness for Alger Hiss—wrote a book purporting to exonerate Sacco and Vanzetti, **The Case of Sacco and Vanzetti: A Critical Analysis for Lawyers and Laymen.** Supreme Court Justice William O. Douglas referred to Frankfurter's book as his "bible." Edward R. Murrow championed Sacco and Vanzetti on his **See it Now** broadcasts for CBS News on one of the rare nights he wasn't scoffing at Soviet espionage. Liberals produced books, paintings, songs, even an opera about Sacco and Vanzetti, the last featuring Sacco's aria "The Whole Shoe." In 1977, on the fiftieth anniversary of their executions, Massachusetts governor Michael Dukakis cleared their names and proclaimed August 23, 1977, Nicola Sacco and Bartolomeo Vanzetti Day in Massachusetts.

These preening revolutionaries, secure behind the guns of a civilian police force in a democratic society—and in many cases, doorman buildings, private security forces, bodyguards, and gated communities—make a sport of demanding that the guilty be set free. To do the maximum damage to civil society, liberals love to claim that there is some larger social context to the alleged frame-up, exposing the ugly underbelly of American society—preferably discrimination against minorities. Sacco and Vanzetti were framed because they were poor Italian immigrants. The Rosenbergs were framed because they were Jews. Leonard Peltier was framed because he's an Indian, not because he shot and killed two FBI agents in the seventies.

Poor David Berkowitz (the Son of Sam killer) missed the liberal myth of wild anti-Jewish hysteria in America by about three decades, so there were no liberals to claim that he was innocent.

Timothy McVeigh's Aryan features ensured that no liberals would weep for him. In fact, McVeigh's swift trial and execution illustrate how all death penalty cases might proceed in this country if we could just get rid of the liberals. Today, the favorite liberal template about America's corrupt criminal justice system is that the system is racist. So if you're a cold-blooded murderer, you want to be black to attract white liberals to your cause. (Who values the lives of black victims more now?)

In 2005, when Stanley "Tookie" Williams, a founder of the violent Crips gang, was finally getting the punishment he deserved for four brutal murders he had committed twenty-six years earlier, he nearly surpassed Bill Clinton in popularity with liberals. His life story had been made into a movie, he had been nominated for the Nobel Peace Prize, and the usual array of Hollywood zombies were somberly discussing his "contributions to society." He was like the Lance Armstrong of deranged shotgun killers.

Despite Tookie's overwhelming popularity with white liberals, California governor Arnold Schwarzenegger declined to pardon him, on the grounds that he had killed a lot of people, started one of the most violent gangs in America, and refused to admit his crimes, much less apologize for them. Schwarzenegger's Austria was so disgusted with their native son for refusing to grant Tookie clemency, they immediately stripped Schwarzenegger's name from a mammoth soccer stadium. Austrian politicians began proposing new names for the stadium, such as "Tookie Williams Stadium," "Crips Stadium," or perhaps the elegant "Quadruple Murderdome." (I made up only the last one.)

It's one thing to simply oppose the death penalty in all cases—and I mean **all** cases, including Timothy McVeigh—but with the death row paparazzi, it never ends with that. They develop relationships with the killers, clubs, newsletters, and fanzines. They turn themselves into overeager PR agents, helping ensure that no murderer's philosophical musings will be lost to the world. It is a religious obsession—except, because it's a false religion, there's no joy in it.

Instead of allowing fallen men like Tookie Williams to confess, repent, and ask God for mercy, liberal busybodies rush in and lock the men into a lie, damning their souls forever. They are like a Bizarro-world version of Christian missionaries, promoting eternal damnation. Surrounded by earnest "Innocence Project" groupies, the guilty will never confess, never repent, never get right with God. **No! No! Don't repent! Tell a lie right before you die, Tookie!**

Among the most unusual displays of affection for a killer concerns convicted child-murderer Dennis Dechaine in Maine. The fact that Dechaine is manifestly guilty is not what makes the case unique. What's strange is that Dechaine is white and therefore his conviction permits of no larger indictment of American society. There will be no "Free Dennis" rallies in Paris. His supporters would have preferred a founder of the Crips, but alas, they live in Maine. At least his crime was vile.

The case began in 1988, when Jennifer Henkel returned to her home in Bowdoin, Maine, to find her baby alone and her twelve-year-old babysitter Sarah Cherry missing. Henkel found a notebook and a car repair receipt with Dechaine's name on it in the driveway. While searching for Cherry in the nearby woods, the police came across the very same Dennis Dechaine, who claimed he had been fishing and got lost, but oddly had no fishing pole. (Dechaine was not only one of the world's most depraved criminals but also among the stupidest.) When asked to explain how his notebook and car receipt had turned up in the driveway of the house whence Cherry had apparently been abducted, Dechaine initially denied the papers were his. Realizing that this explanation was preposterous, he said whoever abducted the girl must have stolen the papers from his pickup truck and placed them in the driveway to frame him. But when the truck was later located—near where Cherry's body would be found—it was locked. Further raising suspicions before they found Dechaine's truck, he had tried to hide the keys to his pickup under the car seat of a police cruiser—indicating that Dechaine knew his truck was locked and he had the keys even as he was claiming his papers had been stolen from it.

The tire tracks in the Henkels' driveway were later found to be consistent with Dechaine's pickup.

Still, the police hadn't found Cherry, so they released Dechaine.

Whether or not it is admissible evidence, consider this fact: Before anyone knew what had happened to Cherry—even whether she was still alive—Dechaine's attorney told three government attorneys that Cherry was dead and that the police were looking for her body in the right place.

The police later found Cherry's body where Dechaine's lawyer indicated they would—in the woods where Dechaine had been fishing without a fishing pole. The little girl had been bound and gagged, raped anally and vaginally with sticks that were still protruding from her. She had been stabbed repeatedly in the throat and head, and strangled with a scarf. The rope used to bind Cherry was later demonstrated to be part of the same rope that was found in Dechaine's truck. The knife Dechaine had once kept on his key chain was about the size of Cherry's knife wounds, but after Cherry's murder, it disappeared from the key chain. Various witnesses placed Dechaine, someone dressed like Dechaine, or someone driving a red pickup truck that matched Dechaine's at the Henkel home or walking to and from the woods where Cherry's body was found. Before the police found Dechaine, for example, he had stopped at one couple's home and asked to use their garden hose to wash himself off, which he did while they watched.

When the police picked up Dechaine after finding Cherry's body, Dechaine made a series of confessions. He said, "I can't believe I could do such a thing. The real me is not like that. I know me. I couldn't do anything like that. It must be somebody else inside of me." On three separate occasions throughout his arrest, booking, and arraignment, Dechaine made similar statements to four police officers, often emotional and crying, saying, "Oh my God, it should never have happened. . . . Why did I do this?"

After Dechaine's conviction, aging baby boomers in Maine with peculiar obsessions like camping and establishing a single global currency started a group dedicated to denying his guilt. Along with a few Democrats in the Maine legislature, they insist Dechaine is innocent, based on such arguments as that he is "nice." As one Dechaine supporter explained, "I could never imagine him doing anything like that because he's such a nice guy."[46]

The liberal busybodies supporting child-killer Dechaine now number more than one thousand. They ritualistically engage in ceremonial letter-writing, protesting, petition-circulating, fund-raising, book- and songwriting in tribute to their icon, child-killer Dechaine. (The book that purports to vindicate Dechaine by systematically ignoring all incriminating evidence was written by a former member of the Bureau of Alcohol, Tobacco, and Firearms. Perhaps his next project could be figuring out who killed all those kids at Waco.) They have bake sales and car washes—though a proposal for a no-pole fishing tournament was rejected on the grounds that it was "too soon." They try to enter floats in local parades. There is a website, Trial and Error Dennis, to spread Dechaine's lies on the Internet and draw in more advocates for the child-murderer.

They pore over the evidence like grim devotees of **Court TV,** savoring the jargon and legal minutiae they have not the slightest chance of ever comprehending. There was DNA on Cherry's

fingernails that wasn't Dechaine's! Even if true—
and the claim is questionable because of chain-
of-custody issues—this proves: There was DNA
on Cherry's fingernails that wasn't Dechaine's. It
doesn't prove Dechaine didn't murder Cherry.
The world is fairly bristling with human DNA. If
Cherry bought candy, read a magazine, or played
with friends before arriving at her babysitting job
that day, she might have picked up human DNA
from any number of people. Only in the case of
rape is DNA capable of excluding a suspect—
and even then only if the victim was not sexually
active and there was only a single rapist. In virtually all other cases, DNA can only include suspects; it can't exclude suspects.

And yet a Democrat in the Maine legislature,
Rosaire Paradis, a longtime supporter of Dechaine's,[47] has sponsored a bill that would essentially spring him from prison based on this
utterly meaningless DNA evidence. The Democrat's bill would allow new trials for all convicted
criminals in Maine if their defense lawyers can
produce some DNA from the general vicinity of
the crime scene that does not belong to the convict. Maine already allows a new trial based on
DNA evidence—but only if the DNA is material
to the convict's identity as the perpetrator. Under
Paradis's bill, any DNA from the crime scene
area—"including but not limited to" that found

on any household item—that does not belong to the convict will generally warrant a new trial. This is a get-out-of-jail-free card for all child-molesters and murderers in Maine who, like Dechaine, were convicted many years ago because it is virtually impossible to reconvict defendants in old cases, after witnesses have died or moved out of state and memories have faded. In Dechaine's case, one of the main witnesses against him was his own lawyer, who has since died.

With missionary zeal, the Dennis believers are utterly devoted to a child-killer. They are too busy being impressed with their own virtue to worry about torturing Cherry's parents with endless appeals on behalf of the man who murdered their daughter. The Dennis believers don't care. Self-righteousness is like a drug, creating the warm sensation that you are more moral, more compassionate, more sensitive than anyone else in the universe. Once you've done it, you have to do it again and again and again. Dechaine supporter Peggy Blanchard explained her commitment to Dechaine this way: "It's a gut feeling. I have looked into his eyes. I can tell he's not the man who killed that poor little girl."**48** Really? How about looking into my eyes and telling me tomorrow's winning Lotto numbers? Never mind that Dechaine told his lawyer where her body was buried before the police found it. How about looking into his eyes and saying, "Confess, repent, Jesus loves you?"

Compare the Dennis groupies to ordinary Christian Ashley Smith. In March 2005, Smith was taken at gunpoint at her Duluth, Georgia, home and forced into her apartment by rape suspect Brian Nichols, who had killed four people in the previous forty-eight hours during his escape from an Atlanta courthouse. At some point during her abduction, Smith began reading to Nichols from the Christian book **The Purpose-Driven Life**—in direct violation of his constitutional right never to hear any reference to God, in public or private, for any purpose, ever, ever, ever! (For more on this right, go to the People For the American Way website.) Smith read a paragraph to Nichols about serving God by serving others, and Nichols asked her to read it again. He listened intently and told Smith he was already dead, saying, "Look at my eyes." But Smith looked into his eyes and told him God had a purpose for him, perhaps to minister to other lost souls in prison. Smith read some more, both from the **Purpose** book and from another popular book—the New Testament. (In the Hollywood version, Smith will be reading from the Koran and playing Kanye West CDs.) Nichols told Smith she was "an angel sent from God," calling her "his sister" and himself her "brother in Christ." He said he must have come to Smith's home for a reason—in Smith's words, that "he was lost and God led him right to me to tell him that he had hurt a lot of people." The next morning, Nichols surrendered without incident, an utterly transformed human being.

Most people have trouble seeing the divine spark in people who take our parking spots. Smith could see God's hand in a multiple murderer holding her hostage. By showing Nichols genuine Christian love, Smith turned him from a beast to a fellow sinner, still deserving of punishment, but also of forgiveness. This phenomenon, utterly unknown to liberals, is what's known as a "miracle." That's how a real religion responds to rapists and murderers. In the liberal religion, there is no grace, only lies and death, some of it everlasting.

3 THE MARTYR: WILLIE HORTON

he martyrdom of Willie Horton will go down in history as the beginning of the Democrats' official rejection of democracy. In 1988, the Democratic presidential candidate was Massachusetts governor Michael Dukakis, card-carrying member of the ACLU. He was running against Vice President George Herbert Walker Bush. Most people knew the election was over at the very beginning of the first presidential debate, when 6'2" Bush shook

hands with Dukakis, who claims to be 5′8″ (i.e., around 5′3″). Any remaining doubts were resolved during the second presidential debate, when CNN's Bernie Shaw asked Dukakis, an avid opponent of the death penalty, if he thought he would change his mind about the death penalty if his wife was raped and murdered.

> DUKAKIS **[bloodless, technocratic voice]**: No, I don't, Bernard. And I think you know that I've opposed the death penalty during all of my life. I don't see any evidence that it's a deterrent, and I think there are better and more effective ways to deal with violent crime. We've done so in my own state. And it's one of the reasons why we have had the biggest drop in crime of any industrial state. . . .

> **zzzzzzzzzzzzzzzzzzzzzzzzzzzzzzzzzz [Notice how the Radio Shack model seems eerily to imitate a real human being!]**

But when the inevitable happened and Dukakis did lose the election, Democrats went to work creating a myth that the Bush campaign had won the election with a racist ad campaign about a black criminal named Willie Horton. Apart from what this suggests liberals think of the American people, since that election, without fail, liberals have refused to accept the results of any election that doesn't go their way. Democrats attribute their consistent inability to get a majority of Americans to vote for them to the machinations of evil, conspiratorial forces, such as the Supreme Court or the Diebold corporation—all beginning with the myth of the racist Willie Horton ad.

Liberals have an unparalleled capacity to create a myth when the truth will destroy them. The Willie Horton ad provoked hysteria from the Democrats because Horton's release exposed their obsessive fetish with releasing violent criminals. Horton is like Horst Wessel, the semiretarded stormtrooper whose death in a bar fight with Communists was glorified in a song that became the official Nazi Party anthem. In liberal mythology, Horton is a martyr, but instead of shedding his own blood, he spilled other people's blood. Today the only way you will hear about Horton is as an example of how race is used in an ugly way in American politics. That's the only apparent relevance of Willie Horton.

In fact, Horton is the full explanation for why someone like Michael Dukakis should never be allowed near any government job—although there are ample other reasons. Horton was a career violent criminal who had been convicted for murder and duly sentenced to life in prison without possibility of parole. That should have been the end of the story. But while serving his life sentence, Horton was released on "furlough" by Dukakis. Shocking penology experts at the ACLU, Horton struck again, viciously.

The crime that put Horton in prison—before Dukakis released him—was an act of wanton violence. After robbing a convenience store, Horton sliced up Joey Fournier, the seventeen-year-old kid behind the cash register, stabbing him nineteen times and then stuffing his mutilated body into a garbage can. It wasn't chance-medley, shots fired, and in the confusion someone ended up dead. It would not have made a fun segment on **COPS.** Fournier had already handed over all the money from the cash register when Horton savagely murdered him. This wasn't Horton's first run-in with the law: He had already been convicted of attempted murder in South Carolina for repeatedly stabbing a man.

Horton was duly convicted of first-degree murder and sentenced to life in prison. Dukakis had vetoed the death penalty in Massachusetts, so this was the maximum sentence available. No sane person would have allowed Horton to walk the streets ever again. But under the weekend furlough program lustily promoted by Dukakis, Horton was released from prison. Despite his eleven disciplinary infractions in prison—and the fact that he had committed a brutal murder—Massachusetts prison officials concluded that Horton, I quote, "projects a quiet sense of responsibility." It is a point of pride with liberals that Horton came back from his first nine furloughs—which I believe breaks my old record of eight consecutive furloughs without raping or killing anybody. But then there was that tenth furlough. Horton was released on a 48-hour furlough on June 6, 1986, and he never came back.

On April 3, 1987, Maryland resident Cliff Barnes had just gotten home from work and was getting undressed when Horton burst through the bathroom door with a woman's stocking over his head. He began beating Barnes viciously, pistol-whipping him and screaming obscenities— or, if you prefer, "projecting a loud, obscene sense of responsibility." Fortunately, Barnes was white or at this point Horton almost certainly would have been guilty of a hate crime. Horton then dragged Barnes to the basement and bound and blindfolded him. Over the next several hours, Horton slashed Barnes's torso with a knife dozens of times. He jammed the barrel of a gun into Barnes's eyes and mouth, telling Barnes he planned to hang him and watch him die. As with Horton's murder of Joey Fournier, there was no purpose to these sadistic attacks. Barnes told him where the credit cards were. Horton had broken into the house much earlier in the day; he could have cleaned the place out and left. But Horton had waited for the homeowners to return so he could torture and kill them. The legal mumbo-jumbo for this is "premeditated."

Nearly five hours after Barnes was attacked, his fiancée, Angela Miller, came home, where she was set upon by Horton. He dragged her into the bedroom by the throat, cut her clothes off with a knife, and savagely beat and raped her. Barnes heard it all, gagged and bound in the basement, unable to help her or even let her know he was alive. This is the point at which it is believed that Cliff's support for Michael Dukakis began to erode.

As Horton was raping Miller again a few hours later, Barnes managed to escape—twelve hours after he had first encountered Horton in his bathroom. Bleeding through his shredded clothes, Barnes had to go to four houses before he found anyone who would let him in to call for help. (The people at the first three houses later explained that they mistook him for a violent inmate furloughed by Governor Dukakis.) Back at the house, as soon as Horton realized Barnes was gone, he took off in Barnes's car, leading police on a wild chase before he was finally captured.

Horton was tried and convicted in Maryland. The judge sentencing him refused to send Horton back to Massachusetts, saying, "I'm not prepared to take the chance that Mr. Horton might again be furloughed or otherwise released."

Until the presidential campaign, Dukakis had displayed "F-you" arrogance whenever anyone questioned his precious furlough program. After their ordeal, Cliff Barnes and Angela Miller never heard a peep out of Dukakis, certainly no apology. They tried to meet with him, traveling to Massachusetts—just to talk to him, tell him what they went through, and ask him how someone like Horton could have been released. Dukakis refused to meet with them. He imperiously dismissed their request for a meeting, saying, "I don't see any particular value in meeting with people." (Perhaps they should have broken into the governor's mansion and lain in wait, nylon stockings over their heads, until he came home.) Dukakis actually took the occasion of the Maryland couple coming to see him to reaffirm his support for the furlough program, saying Massachusetts had "the kind of furlough program we should have." The sister of Joey Fournier, Horton's first victim, started a group, Citizens Against an Unsafe Society, to prevent murderers like Horton from being furloughed, but Dukakis refused to even meet with the group and, according to Fournier's sister, fought them "tooth and nail."

When Al Gore raised the issue of the lunatic Massachusetts furlough program during the Democratic primaries in 1988, Dukakis responded, "Al, the difference between you and me is that I have run a criminal justice system and you never have."

Even the Democratic Party knew not to defend the furlough program the way Dukakis had. Instead, during Dukakis's presidential bid, they claimed the furlough program was first enacted under a Republican governor. Needless to say, this was a lie. Yes, **some** furlough program existed under the prior governor, but not one that allowed the release of first-degree murderers. The idea behind prison furloughs was to reintroduce prisoners sentenced to a term of years back into society gradually, before their inevitable release. The problem wasn't furloughs per se; it was furloughs for people like Willie Horton, who were never supposed to take a free breath again. It took the famous Massachusetts Supreme Judicial Court to discover a right to furloughs for first-degree murderers. (The next thing you know, they'll be discovering a right to gay marriage.) After the court extended furloughs to first-degree murderers, the Massachusetts legislature quickly passed a bill prohibiting furloughs for first-degree murderers.

The Greek midget vetoed it. He vetoed it.

Dukakis defended his veto, saying that removing murderers from the furlough program would "cut the heart out of efforts at inmate rehabilitation." (At least he didn't say removing murderers from the furlough program would slash inmate rehabilitation with a knife nineteen times and stuff it into a garbage can after it had turned over all the money.) I mention again: Horton was sentenced to LIFE IN PRISON WITHOUT POSSIBILITY OF PAROLE! He didn't need "rehabilitation," because he wasn't supposed to be released, ever. Only through the specific intervention of Dukakis did the furlough program become a way for liberal politicians to do end runs around a life sentence. This is why we need the death penalty. Without it, you always run the risk that a Democrat will come to power and start releasing all the prisoners sentenced to life in prison.

So it wasn't going to work for the Democrats to keep saying the furlough program was originally signed into law by a Republican governor. It was Governor Michael Dukakis who insisted on furloughing first-degree murderers.

It was only well into the 1988 presidential campaign, after Willie Horton became a major issue—and after 75,000 angry Massachusetts citizens signed a petition to put the furlough policy on the ballot—that the Greek homunculus finally yielded to the legislature's demand that the furlough program be off-limits to first-degree murderers. Forced to sign the bill, Dukakis still said he opposed it: "I don't agree with the House vote."

Releasing Willie Horton is the perfect emblem of liberal idiocy. Michael Dukakis, the Duke of Brookline, bought into the whole liberal catechism on how to deal with criminals, starting with the idea that the government is not supposed to lock up vicious murderers but rather develop programs to help them increase their self-esteem. Horton had been tried, convicted, and sentenced to life in prison. But Dukakis thought Horton should only spend six days a week in prison for committing a mutilation murder of a seventeen-year-old boy in cold blood.

Liberals always claim they want to talk about "issues" in presidential campaigns—I suppose because "character" isn't a good topic for them. Well, the Massachusetts furlough program that released Horton was an issue, as good an issue as you'll ever get. Rarely in politics has an attack ad been so honest. State legislators tried to correct an insane ruling by a crazy liberal court allowing first-degree murderers to be released on furlough. But Dukakis wouldn't let them. And he wanted to be president.

Republicans thought that was a relevant issue.

But the fair, unbiased, objective media were outraged at the Bush campaign for running ads on the furlough of Willie Horton. There were actually two Willie Horton ads, and they are generally conflated. Both were terrific ads. The Bush campaign's Willie Horton ad never showed a picture of Horton, which complicated their sneaky plan to appeal to Americans' nearly hysterical hatred of black people. The only ad to show Horton's face was produced by an independent group that included Horton's victims, Cliff Barnes and Angela Miller. The victims' ad was made on a shoestring budget and was probably seen by about six people in West Virginia. More people have seen Britney Spears's failed reality show than saw the victims' Willie Horton ad. (And a lot fewer people saw the victims' Willie Horton ad than the NAACP's ad during the 2000 campaign assigning responsibility to George Bush for the murder of James Byrd.) No one would have even been aware of this Willie Horton ad but for the Democrats' caterwauling about it. If anything, the Horton ads helped Dukakis by allowing the Democrats to stir up black voters, who might not otherwise have warmed to the Greek geek.

In all, Dukakis had furloughed 82 first-degree murderers, 184 second-degree murderers, and 287 sex offenders.[1] The media ignored this. It was left to Cliff Barnes to investigate the furlough program being unreported by our aggressive watchdog media that shouldn't be required to reveal their sources because they are working in "the public interest." Other murderers furloughed by Dukakis included Donald Robertson and Bradford Boyd. Robertson raped a ninety-three-year-old woman and her seventy-two-year-old daughter and then stamped on their chests so hard that he crushed their internal organs. Despite being sentenced to two consecutive life terms, Robertson was released under Michael Dukakis's furlough program after only eight years in prison. He never came back. Bradford Boyd was serving time for rape when he committed first-degree murder in prison. Still, he was furloughed. While out on furlough, he viciously beat a man, repeatedly raped a woman, and then killed himself. (On the plus side of the ledger, Boyd hasn't committed any crimes since then.) The mainstream media didn't find these stories, Barnes did. They were too busy writing articles about Bush "Slinging Mud on the Low Road to Office,"[2] and "Republicans Riding to Victory on Racism,"[3] and "Bush Tactics Turn Ugly."[4] According to the vast majority of media stories on the 1988 presidential campaign, it was an "ugly" tactic for the Bush campaign to mention the Massachusetts furlough program.

The mainstream media were bristling with defenses of Dukakis's furlough program—in particular, the claim that practically every state had furlough programs just like Massachusetts. On June 24, 1988, the **Washington Post** ran a news story by T. R. Reid titled "Most States Allow Furloughs from Prison; Bush Lashes Dukakis for Stance on Policy That Has Been Adopted by Much of Nation." The article began, "Dukakis' support for the concept of furloughs puts him squarely in the mainstream today among corrections officials from coast to coast." On NBC's **Today** show, Anthony Travisono, then the executive director of the American Correctional Association, said, "Governor Dukakis has taken the rap for something that everybody does." He compared the furlough program to Ivory soap, saying, "It's the decent thing to do. It's like the Ivory soap commercial, which is 99 and 44 one-hundredths percent pure. Occasionally, an inmate lets us all down." Yes, under any criminal justice system, occasionally a drug dealer or armed robber is released and then commits a murder. The only way to avoid that is to lock up all first-time criminals for life—which, come to think of it, was exactly how long Horton was supposed to stay in prison. Also on the **Today** show, Princeton's John DiIulio assured viewers, "Virtually every state in the country has some kind of a furlough program." He said, "Over 30 other states will furlough someone who is a murderer."[5] This still misses the point. Not all murderers are sentenced to life in prison. Horton had been.

No other state in the union would have furloughed a murderer serving a life sentence. The only one that would had a governor who wanted to be president.

But the headlines told a different story:

PRISON EXPERTS SAY BUSH ATTACKS DUKAKIS
UNFAIRLY
Los Angeles Times, October 12, 1988

STUDY SAYS 53,000 GOT PRISON FURLOUGHS IN
'87 AND FEW DID HARM
New York Times, October 12, 1988

SPECIALISTS DEFEND FURLOUGH POLICY:
MASS. PROGRAM SAID TO BE IN MAINSTREAM[6]
(The "mainstream," no less!)
Boston Globe, October 15, 1988

REPORT SAYS PRISON FURLOUGHS WIDESPREAD,
SUCCESSFUL
Associated Press, October 13, 1988

SUCCESS HIGH IN MOST PRISON FURLOUGH CASES
Post-Standard (Syracuse, New York),
October 23, 1988

EXPERTS: BUSH DISTORTS ON FURLOUGHS
Newsday (New York), October 21, 1988

These headlines—typical in the days before the alternative media—were provably false. No other state furloughed murderers ineligible for parole. And you wonder why liberals have lost their minds over Fox News Channel, where it is now possible to hear something other than press releases from the Democratic National Committee.

Eventually, the Dukakis campaign tried counterattacking with a furlough "attack ad" of its own. For weeks on the campaign trail, Dukakis had blatantly engaged in the rhetorical device of preterition—mentioning the murder of Patsy Pedrin while pretending not to mention it. **I would never stoop so low as to talk about my opponent's homosexuality!** Pedrin, a pregnant mother of two, had been murdered by Angel Medrano, a drug dealer furloughed from a federal prison while Bush was vice president. Dukakis raised the subject of Pedrin's murder to suggest that it had resulted from the exact same sort of furlough policy as the one that freed Horton. Over and over again, Dukakis said, "I would never use that kind of human tragedy to accuse the president of being soft on crime."

To make it absolutely clear that he would

"never" exploit a family tragedy like the murder of Patsy Pedrin for political gain, Dukakis's campaign ran commercials about the murder. Dukakis apparently had trouble grasping abstract concepts, like "without possibility of parole" and "never." In the commercial, the narrator accused Bush of "false advertising," saying, "Bush won't talk about this drug pusher—one of his furloughed heroin dealers—who raped and murdered Patsy Pedrin, pregnant mother of two." The commercial showed Pedrin's dead body being carried out of her house in a body bag—something her children must have enjoyed seeing.

Contrary to Dukakis's self-advertisements, his ad did nothing but exploit a family tragedy. In fact, Medrano was not on furlough; he was in a halfway house because he had served his sentence and was about to be released. Until he killed Pedrin, Medrano had no record of violence of any sort, much less murder. The only policy that could conceivably have prevented Pedrin's murder would be life imprisonment for drug dealers. Was Dukakis for that? I don't think so: as Massachusetts governor, he had vetoed mandatory sentences for drug dealers.

Even if the halfway house program had been to blame for Pedrin's murder—which it wasn't—Vice President Bush was not running for president based on his good work on the federal criminal justice system. Dukakis was constantly bragging about his experience running a criminal justice system—including his innovative furlough program.

Since none of their other defenses of Dukakis's furlough program were working, the Democrats reverted to their default argument: they accused Republicans of racism. This was consistent with author Peter Brimelow's definition of a "racist" as "someone who is winning an argument with a liberal." At first, the Democrats didn't realize the Horton ad was racist. Only when nothing else managed to defuse the issue did it suddenly hit them like a ton of bricks: The only reason anyone could possibly object to Horton's release from prison is that **he was black.**

On **This Week with David Brinkley,** Dukakis's running mate, Lloyd Bentsen, allowed that there were "racial elements" to Bush's raising the furlough issue. Representative Richard Gephardt referred to the Bush campaign's Horton ad, saying, "Hitler would have loved these people." Dukakis's former campaign manager, Susan Estrich, said, "There is no stronger metaphor for racial hatred in our country than the black man raping the white woman." Horton wasn't a "metaphor"! He was a real murderer and rapist who had already killed a person before being released from a life sentence by Dukakis, whereupon Horton savagely beat a man and raped a woman. Say, aren't feminists against rape? Wait, let me get my notes. . . . Yes! I have it right here! They **are** against rape. Dukakis aide Donna Brazile said the Bush campaign had used the "oldest racial symbol imaginable," referring to the image of "a black man raping a white woman while her husband watched." Again, this wasn't an "image," it was a real case, and I'm not sure how that image would be improved if it had been a white man raping a woman while her husband watched. As Cliff Barnes said: "It didn't make any difference to me or my wife whether Willie Horton was black."

Years later, the Democrats would forget that it was racist to mention Willie Horton. Al Gore was the first politician to mention Horton, raising his name during a 1988 primary debate with Dukakis. But during the 2000 Democratic primary, when Bill Bradley tried pointing out to Democratic primary voters that Gore was the man who had injected Willie Horton into the 1988 presidential campaign, liberals decided it wasn't racist after all and chose Gore as their presidential candidate.

What some might say is racist is the liberal idea that blacks should be required to defend the worst elements of their race. White people are never put in a position of having to defend white scum.

Timothy McVeigh? Sure, go ahead, kill him!

Jeffrey Dahmer? Kill him!

John Wayne Gacy? Kill him!

Robert Alton Harris? Kill him!

Why do blacks have to support Willie Horton? Who made that rule? It's not as if white people were looking at Horton and saying, This shows what all blacks are like. What white people were saying was: This shows what idiot liberals like Michael Dukakis are like. As Alan Keyes said, when Democrats "look at Willie Horton they see a black man. When I look at him, I see a rapist and a murderer."

The whole mythology of the racist Willie Horton ad is a joke. Even the victims' ad that showed Horton's face would not be deemed racist by anyone who had ever been to our planet. Was this Vermont circa 1780? No! It was Massachusetts in the 1980s. Some criminals in twentieth-century America are black. Meanwhile, the Bush campaign bent over backwards to avoid any acknowledgment of the fact that Horton was black, going to the ridiculous extreme of showing all white people in prison. You could have run that ad past the editorial board of the **New York Times** and the editors would have concluded, No, this ad is not racist. The Bush campaign surely wished that

Horton had been Chinese, Indian, German, Malaysian—an Aleut!—anything but black. But the issue was simply too important to drop just because liberals would call Republicans racist.

The only reason the Democrats cried racism over the Willie Horton ads was that it was one of the greatest campaign issues of all time. The Massachusetts furlough program wasn't an odd, extraneous little issue Dukakis got tagged with unfairly. Dukakis was almost a parody of the Democrats on crime. He had been given repeated opportunities to change course on furloughs— even on the precise issue of Willie Horton's furlough. He could have apologized, met with Cliff Barnes and Angela Miller, signed a bill to deny furloughs to first-degree murderers, or simply refrained from criticizing the bill he finally did sign doing just that. But he wouldn't do it. Dukakis didn't even have someone on his staff to warn him, **Just in case you ever think about running for president, sir, you might want to tone down your gushing about furloughs for first-degree murderers.** Horton was the essence, the heart, the alpha and omega of liberal ideas about crime and punishment, to wit: Release the guilty. Willie Horton showed the American people exactly what was wrong with liberal theories about crime.

But when Dukakis lost, a whole myth had to

be created about the racist Willie Horton ads. Whenever Democrats lose—especially to people as stupid as they say Republicans are—they claim they were cheated somehow. Liberals would spend the next decade trying to persuade Americans that they were bigots who had fallen prey to the ugly racist tactics of the Bush campaign. The transmitter of all liberal idiocy, Michael Moore, summarized what liberals think of Americans in **Bowling for Columbine** when he said, "[W]hether you're a psychotic killer or running for president of the United States, the one thing you can always count on is white America's fear of the black man"—as evidenced by Michael Moore, who has done everything possible to avoid contact with them.

Even before Dukakis lost the 1988 election, liberals were hard at work setting up the argument that Bush won because of the racist Willie Horton ads. At a Republican press conference before the election to discuss Dukakis's record on crime, national defense, and fiscal policy, Bush's spokesmen showed three campaign ads, with Governor John Sununu, Senator Arlen Specter, and former senator John Tower on hand to answer questions. But the reporters only wanted to ask about the unfairness of the Willie Horton ad based on their entire knowledge of the case, which they had gleaned from Dukakis campaign press releases. Here's a sample of press questions about the Horton ad:

> QUESTION: Senator Specter, Democrats suggest—Reverend Jackson said it only a few minutes ago—that the Willie Horton situation and the furlough situation bears the opportunity or the risk to polarize the entire country, and that while the Bush-Quayle team maintains that this is not something to sow the seeds or bring up bad blood, that this is exactly what's going on and it should be stopped. What do you have to say to that?
>
> SEN. SPECTER: Well, as I understand it, Governor Dukakis and his key campaign aides have moved off the issue of racism. . . . Racism just isn't in this issue, just isn't in this campaign. Everybody wants to have security on the streets and in their homes. . . .
>
> QUESTION: Senator Specter, to follow up if you can on this Willie—you didn't show us the Willie Horton spot but you've used it. Don't you think the use of that picture, whether or not it is originally intended, can be seen as a racial overtone to this spot?
>
> SEN. SPECTER: . . . I do not think that is a fair characterization; you can judge for yourself.

But the Bush-Quayle campaign has not depicted race in any way, shape, or form, either as to any culprit from the furlough program, or any victim of such a culprit.

QUESTION: Senator, I experienced stonewalling from the Federal Bureau of Prisons when I asked about furloughs and they withheld totally details on transfer furloughs. Point number 9, here on page 3, says that Angel Medrano is not on furlough. Was he not on a transfer furlough, which is one of the furlough programs of the Federal Bureau of Prisons?

BUSH STAFF: We can do that right now. According to the Bureau of Prisons, Medrano was not on furlough.

QUESTION: Was he escorted?

BUSH STAFF: He was in a—he escaped from a halfway house.

GOV. SUNUNU: There's an important point. What was the charge under which Medrano was being imprisoned?

QUESTION: That's not my point.

BUSH STAFF: It was drugs. He was not imprisoned for murder.

QUESTION: Isn't that the exact same thing? . . .

SEN. SPECTER: No. No. That is not the same thing.[7]

And then there were thirty seconds left for John Tower to answer questions about national defense.

Whatever else voters knew about Willie Horton in 1988, one thing the media didn't want them to know about was his crimes. In the entire Nexis archives for 1988, the only place you will find a detailed description of what Horton did to Cliff Barnes and Angela Miller is in a press conference that Barnes had to hold himself—and where reporters repeatedly asked him if he was a racist. A search for the words "Willie Horton and the Maryland couple" produces 219 documents on Nexis. A search for the words "Willie Horton and Joey Fournier" produces 219 documents. But run the words "Willie Horton and racism," and Nexis tells you, "This search has been interrupted because it will return more than 1,000 documents."

Reporters were more interested in getting Horton's side of the story. So many reporters wanted to interview Horton that he needed an aide to help him field media requests. (Full disclosure: For a brief period in 1989 Willie Horton and I shared the same publicist.) Even Horton knew Dukakis couldn't win—though he did support Dukakis for president. Talking about his attack on the Maryland couple in the same abstract way liberals talk about 9/11, Horton said, "It occurred at the most unopportune time for me and Dukakis."[8]

And yet books have been written on how the media played right into Bush's hands on the Willie Horton matter. Kathleen Hall Jamieson, professor of communication at the Annenberg School for Communication at the University of Pennsylvania, wrote a 3,000-word treatise— which she turned into a book—about how the Bush campaign played the media like a fiddle with the Willie Horton issue, "insinuat[ing] an entire vocabulary about the campaign into press coverage."

For example, Jamieson claims it was a Bush administration dirty trick to get the media to call him "Willie Horton"—she refers to him only as "William Horton." As proof that "Willie" was a cruel invention of the Republicans, Jamieson cites the following facts: "[H]is given name is William, he calls himself William, court records cite him as William, a July 1988 **Reader's Digest** article identifies him as William J. Horton, Jr., and press reports prior to the Republican ad and speech blitz name him 'William.'" I'm pretty sure what really caught people's attention about the Horton case was his rape and torture of Cliff Barnes and Angela Miller while on furlough from a life sentence—and not that his name was "Willie."

In any event, except for the claim about what "he calls himself," these are all restatements of the same manifestly obvious fact: Horton's given name is "William." I assume everyone grasped this without Jamieson's laborious exegesis. Of course prison records referred to Horton as "William," and for that reason, so would early news accounts. That's his legal name. Orenthal James Simpson's court records don't refer to him as "O.J."

Jamieson's only real claim is that Horton called himself "William." First of all, how on earth does she know? Did she interview his cellblock buddies? Do a phone survey of Horton's surviving victims? Unless Horton is an aspiring host for **Queer Eye for the Straight Guy,** it doesn't exactly ring true. "Bill" we might have believed— but "William"? No. In fact, in an interview with liberal columnist Jimmy Breslin the day of Bush's inauguration, Horton refers to himself in the third person as "Willie Horton."

According to Jamieson, another example of the media's pro-Bush bias was the constant reference to "weekend furloughs." Jamieson indignantly reports that Horton was actually released on a 48-hour furlough that began on a Friday, "which means he should have returned to prison while most of us were still enjoying what we usually define as a weekend." No doubt most Americans would have approved of the furloughs had they realized that. What was invidious about the "weekend furloughs" phrase, Jameison said, was that "weekend is a time for recreation and leisure. This association suggests that the assault and rapes were leisure activities for the prisoners." In fact, of course, the prisoners spent their furloughs reading the **New York Times,** having brunch, and taking in a Woody Allen movie at the Beekman like everyone else. Again, I think what people had a problem with was the fact that rapists and murderers were being released from prison at all, not whether the furloughs ended on a Sunday or a Monday.

Jamieson was appalled that Bush lackeys over at the **New York Times,** the **Washington Post,** NBC News, CBS, and **MacNeil/Lehrer** used words like **slashed, terrorized,** and **tortured** to describe what Horton did to the Maryland couple. Such words, she said, "are not the words usually used by reporters to characterize crime" (especially when they're describing counterfeiting, bribery, and fraud cases). Compared with a detailed accounting of what Horton actually did to the Maryland couple, words like **terrorized** and **tortured** are sweet euphemisms, like saying "Hitler subdued the Sudetenland." Apparently,

Jamieson thinks reporters should have said Horton "interviewed," "met with," or "chatted with" the Maryland couple.

Most peculiar coming from a good progressive like Jamieson, she was indignant that reporters did not stress the fact that at the time of the attack, Barnes and Miller were living in sin! According to Jamieson, only pro-Bush bias in the press could explain why reporters did not muddy up the victims by pointing out that the couple only married sometime after Horton's attack. She even provided a list of the worst offenders.

This was the same press that used some variation of the word **racist** nearly ten times more (295) than Cliff Barnes's name (30) in news stories about Willie Horton in 1988. While Jamieson was indignant about news stories that referred to a 48-hour furlough that began on Friday as a "weekend furlough," she seemed to miss media lies that fell more within the accepted definition of **lie,** such as that Dukakis inherited the furlough program from a Republican governor or that other states had the same furlough program.

In a rash act of journalism, the **Lawrence Eagle-Tribune,** the newspaper in the town where Joey Fournier had been murdered, ran a major series on Dukakis's furlough program. Unaware that good reporting consists of writing about Jeff Gannon week after week (see Frank Rich) or calling Bush "Bushie" (Maureen Dowd), the reporters produced nearly 200 factual articles about the Massachusetts furlough program. The **Eagle-Tribune**'s coverage was widely credited with ending furloughs in Massachusetts for first-degree murderers. Even the Pulitzer committee broke a long-standing tradition of ignoring good journalism and awarded the newspaper a Pulitzer Prize for the series.

Journalism professors attacked the series as the "journalistic version of a lynching," in the words of Bruce Porter, a professor at Columbia's Graduate School of Journalism. There were sleazy maneuvers available to the reporters that they did not use! As an example of the slipshod reporting, Porter noted that "the paper never mentioned that furlough programs had been created in 1972 under a Republican governor, Francis Sargent, or that first-degree murderers were ruled eligible for it by the Massachusetts Supreme Judicial Court in 1973." For failing to reprint Dukakis campaign press releases, the **Eagle-Tribune** had committed "outrageous errors"—or as normal people would say, it was "bristling with facts."

The liberal hysteria on Willie Horton was so intense that the lead author of the Pulitzer Prize–winning series disavowed the prize. Susan Forrest, now a reporter with **New York Newsday,** said she was "ashamed" of her work on Massachusetts's furlough program. She added that when the prize was announced, "there was a party and I didn't even go. Deep down I never felt I deserved it." I'm sure Comrade Stalin will give her a fair trial.

The Democrats ran a man for president who had released a violent lunatic from prison despite a life sentence. But instead of Republicans raising Willie Horton constantly to say, **This is the same Democratic Party that released Willie Horton,** it's Republicans who are supposed to be embarrassed by Willie Horton. The reporter who wrote a Pulitzer Prize–winning series on the Massachusetts furloughs leading to a change in the law retracted her work. The rewriting of history was complete.

4 THE HOLIEST SACRAMENT: ABORTION

o liberal cause is defended with more dishonesty than abortion. No matter what else they pretend to care about from time to time— undermining national security, aiding terrorists, oppressing the middle class, freeing violent criminals—the single most important item on the Democrats' agenda is abortion. Indeed, abortion is the one issue the Democratic Party is willing to go to war over—except in the Muslim world, which is jam-packed with

prohibitions on abortion, because going to war against a Muslim nation might also serve America's national security objectives. To a liberal, 2,200 military deaths in the entire course of a war in Iraq is unconscionable, but 1.3 million aborted babies in America every year is something to celebrate.

The Orwellian dishonesty about abortion begins with the Left's utter refusal to use the word **abortion.** It would be as if members of the National Rifle Association refused to use the word **gun.** These "pro-choicers" treat abortion the way Muslims treat Mohammed: It's so sacred, it must not be mentioned. Instead we get a slew of liberal euphemisms for baby-killing: "reproductive freedom," "a woman's right to control her own body," "terminating a pregnancy," "freedom of choice," "a woman's own private medical decision," "a procedure," "access to health care," "family planning," "our bodies, our selves," "choice." Choice is important when it comes to killing babies, but not so much when it comes to whom you hire, whom you associate with, what you think about evolution, how much gas your car consumes, how much water comes out of your bathroom showerhead. . . . The only other practice that was both defended and unspeakable in America like this was slavery. There are three indirect references to slavery in the Constitution, but the words **slave** and **slavery** never appear.

The **New York Times** and the rest of the mainstream media will only refer to partial birth abortion as "what its opponents refer to as partial birth abortion." What do its supporters call it? Casual Fridays? Bean-with-bacon potato-chip dip? Uh . . . Steve? "Partial birth abortion" isn't some meaningless, poll-tested name, like "assault weapon." It's a straightforward legal description of the procedure that is to be prohibited by law. If there were a better name for it, you can be sure the **New York Times** would use it.

The 2003 partial birth abortion ban enacted by the U.S. Congress and signed into law by President Bush defines a "partial birth abortion" as an abortion in which the person performing the abortion

deliberately and intentionally vaginally delivers a living fetus until, in the case of a head-first presentation, the entire fetal head is outside the body of the mother, or, in the case of breech presentation, any part of the fetal trunk past the navel is outside the body of the mother, for the purpose of performing an overt act that the person knows will kill the partially delivered living fetus; and

performs the overt act, other than comple-
tion of delivery, that kills the partially delivered living fetus.

As one can see, actual descriptions of partial
birth abortion do not tend to help the pro-
abortion side. "Partial birth abortion" **is** the
euphemism.

In 1995, **60 Minutes** set out to prove there
was no such thing as "a partial birth abortion."
Ed Bradley asked Colorado abortionist Warren
Hern what the term meant.

> BRADLEY: What is a partial-birth abortion?
>
> DR. HERN: Well, I'm not really sure I know.
>   The—there's no such thing in the medical
>   literature.
>
> BRADLEY: Would most doctors in this coun-
>   try know what a partial . . .
>
> DR. HERN: No, there's no such thing.
>
> BRADLEY: It doesn't exist?
>
> DR. HERN: No.
>
> BRADLEY: So where does this term come
>   from?
>
> DR. HERN: Propaganda term. It's a political
>   term; has no medical meaning.[1]

This is as opposed to precise medical terms,
like **choice** and **back alley abortions.** This is

pure sophistry, along the lines of liberals pretending not to know what **liberal** means. **Battery** and **sexual assault** aren't "medical" terms, either. They're legal terms, descriptions of what the law prohibits. The fact that the medical community has not dignified this particular form of infanticide with a name doesn't mean legislatures can't ban it.

60 Minutes also sought to assure viewers that despite all the hullabaloo about partial birth abortion—whatever the hell that is—such abortions were extremely rare, performed only in extenuating circumstances. You know, like pregnancy. Consider the lunacy of both denying that "partial birth abortions" exist and then discussing the frequency of that nonexistent procedure. Bradley interviewed two women who had had partial birth abortions on horribly deformed babies who could not have lived outside the womb. One woman told Bradley, "In terms of misinformation, the biggest one is that they are—there are thousands and thousands of these abortions being done in the third trimester on normal babies with healthy mothers carrying normal babies. Well, if that's the case, where are they?" Yes, indeed. Why aren't more of these dead babies speaking up?

In a voiceover, Bradley then said that Helen Alvaré, spokeswoman for the National Conference of Catholic Bishops, "wouldn't tell us where they are, but she insists they are there." In fact, Alvaré did better than tell Bradley "where they are": she quoted the man credited with inventing partial birth abortions, Martin Haskell, who told **American Medical News** that 80 percent of the partial birth abortions he performs are "purely elective." At this, Bradley asked Alvaré, "Why is this interview with Dr. Haskell so important?"

Bolstering the claim that partial birth abortions are extremely rare, Bradley insisted, "Of the one and a half million abortions performed every year, only a tiny percentage, somewhere between 600 and 1,000, are performed in the third trimester of pregnancy." To talk only about how many abortions are performed in the "third trimester" is just another way of lying about abortion. It is like talking about only the number of partial birth abortions performed by left-handed abortionists with hairy moles on their faces. The third trimester begins at 26 weeks. Babies can take a breath outside the womb at around 19 weeks. At 14 weeks, they have eyes, ears, hair, toes, fingers, and fingernails. I think what repels most people about partial birth abortions (or "casual Friday") is the fact that that baby is having its brains suctioned out.

A few months after Bradley assured viewers that the nonexistent partial birth abortion occurs only about 600 to 1,000 times per year, the **Record** (Bergen, New Jersey) reported that a single abortion clinic in Englewood, New Jersey, performs about 1,500 partial birth abortions every year on babies 20 to 24 weeks old.[2] Contrary to the claims of the women interviewed by Bradley whose entire expertise was based on having had partial birth abortions themselves, one doctor at the clinic said, "[M]ost are for elective, not medical, reasons: people who didn't realize, or didn't care, how far along they were."

With the pro-choicers, even their talking points are lies. It is a point of honor with the abortion crowd to claim that no one is **for** abortion. As far back as 1978, Cory Richards of Planned Parenthood told **Newsweek** magazine, "Strictly speaking, no one is **for** abortion." Carol Werner of NARAL expanded on the point: "The phrase 'pro-abortion' is totally inaccurate. We are pro-choice. What matters is that the option is there so the woman can exercise it."[3] An op-ed piece in the **Washington Post** in 1989 titled "The Real Issue: Choice" reminded readers, "No one is for abortion."[4]

And a 1991 op-ed in the **Chicago Tribune** argued for a federal law requiring taxpayer money to be spent on abortion counseling, saying, "No one is 'for' abortion. Nonetheless, freedom to terminate an unwanted pregnancy must remain an option precisely because society has not yet made it possible for all pregnancies to be wanted."[5] By 2005, the claim that "no one is for abortion" had to be stated as a cliché, as it was in an article in **Conscience,** a journal for pro-choice Catholics, attacking the bishops for missing this important point: "As stated many times by all prochoice advocates: no one is for abortion, no matter how often and how loudly the bishops and their minions say it. Saying it doesn't make it so, but they haven't figured out anything else to say."[6]

After all their prattle about how no one is **for** abortion, it took about five seconds for Mama Alito, magnificent primogenitress of Supreme Court nominee Samuel Alito, to smoke them out. Speaking of her son, Rose Alito told reporters, "Of course he's against abortion." And then all hell broke lose.

USA Today raised Mama Alito's remark in an editorial demanding "straight answers" from Alito on his views of "the court's established abortion-law jurisprudence" that "keeps the government out of citizens' bedrooms and most intimate decisions."[7] Columnist Ellen Goodman listed as a "telltale" sign about Judge Alito "we know what Alito's 90-year-old mother knows: 'Of course he's against abortion.'" Five Democratic congresswomen, along with Marcia Greenberger, co-president of the National Women's

Law Center, held a press conference to announce their opposition to Alito. In an adorable statement, Representative Jan Schakowsky cited Mrs. Alito's remark and said, "We trust what our mothers say."**8** (It's so cute when the pro-abortion crowd starts citing mothers as moral authority.) But wait a minute! I thought everybody was "against abortion"! What happened to the talking point about how "no one is **for** abortion"? Mrs. Alito put an end to that in a hurry. As Aleksandr Solzhenitsyn said, "Violence does not and cannot flourish by itself; it is inevitably intertwined with lying."

Then there's the canard about a united front of women supporting abortion, while misogynist men try to keep it from us. Feminists have a charming slogan memorialized on buttons sold by the National Organization for Women, and the title of a book: "If men got pregnant, abortion would be a sacrament." Apparently it isn't a sacrament now only because of the overwhelming hatred men have for women. How about this slogan: "If women had to pay for dates, rape would be a sacrament."

It's rather churlish of the NARAL types to complain about men's insufficient support for abortion. Men support abortion more than women do. On the basis of casual observation, single men between the ages of eighteen and thirty are strongly supportive of a woman's right to have irresponsible, casual sex with them. Maybe NARAL should work on getting more women to support abortion before attacking the primary beneficiaries of it, or what we used to call "cads."

Indeed, it's hard to see how abortion could be any more of a sacrament for some men. Bill Clinton sold out nearly every single Democrat special interest group (also his party, his vice president, his advisers, his wife, his daughter, and his family—but that's another story). There was only one issue Clinton was absolutely committed to: killing the unborn. Congress passed bans on partial birth abortion twice in large bipartisan votes. Clinton vetoed the bills both times. This is a man who took polls to decide what he would do for his vacation. He even relied on a "quick show of hands" to decide which woman to hit on during stops on the campaign trail. But in the face of huge majorities opposed to partial birth abortion, Clinton's support for the gruesome procedure was unflagging. Say what you will about the man, at least he knows his base.

Moreover, if women are so pro-abortion, why are virtually all abortionists men? If ever there was a need for a Take Our Daughters to Work Day, it's at the abortion mills. As the male director of a Cleveland abortion clinic explained, women tend not to enjoy doing "abortions over and over for moral reasons." Also, problems arise when the women doctors become pregnant. Not only does a pregnant abortionist tend to "upset the patients," but, he said, "if a woman is carrying a baby, she doesn't like to abort someone else's."[9]

But according to Senator Dianne Feinstein (D-CA), **Roe v. Wade** is critically important because "women all over America have come to depend on it." Leave aside any moral questions about baby-killing—a term I have come to understand baby-killing supporters dislike. At its most majestic, this precious right that women "have come to depend on" is the right to have sex with men they don't want to have children with.

There's a stirring principle! Leave aside the part of this precious constitutional right that involves (1) not allowing Americans to vote on the matter and (2) suctioning brains out of half-born babies. The right to have sex with men you don't want to have children with is not exactly "Give me liberty, or give me death." In the history of the nation, there has never been a political party so ridiculous as today's Democrats. It's as if all the brain-damaged people in America got together and formed a voting bloc.

The Federalists drafted the greatest political philosophy ever written by man and created

the first constitutional republic. The anti-
Federalists—or "pre-Democrats," as I call them—
were formed to oppose the Constitution, which,
to a great extent, remains their position today.
Andrew Jackson, the father of the Democratic
Party, may have had some unpalatable goals,
but at least they were big ideas: wipe out the
Indians, kill off the national bank, and institute
a spoils system. Love him or hate him, he never
said, "I'll be announcing my platform sometime
early next year." The Whigs were formed in opposition to everything Jackson stood for. The
Republican Party emerged from the Whigs
when the Whigs waffled on slavery. (They were
"pro-choice" on slavery.) The Republican Party
was founded expressly as the antislavery party,
which to a great extent remains their position
today. Having won that one, with 600,000 white
men having to die to redeem the principle that
all men are created equal, today's Republican
Party stands for life, limited government, and national defense. And today's Democratic Party
stands for . . . the right of women to have unprotected sex with men they don't especially like.
We're the Blacks-Aren't-Property/Don't-Kill-
Babies Party. They're the Hookup party. (For
people who claim to be so concerned with "privacy," they certainly don't hesitate to make the

sweaty details of their private lives central to the national debate.)

No Republican is so crazily obsessed with any issue as the Democrats are with abortion. During the debate on the bankruptcy bill in 2003 and then again in 2005, Senator Chuck Schumer (NY) introduced an amendment to the bill that would exclude protesters at abortion clinics from bankruptcy protection. That was the Democrats' main objective in a major restructuring of the bankruptcy laws in America: ensure that fines levied against abortion-clinic protesters would not be dischargeable in bankruptcy.

It wasn't even a law vaguely related to children or reproduction, like a health care bill   it was a bankruptcy bill. How maniacally insane do you have to be to bring up abortion in a debate on a bankruptcy bill? How about the Defense appropriation bill? **There must be one abortionist for every thirty men in the field.** This would be like Republicans demanding an amendment to the bankruptcy bill saying you can't discharge money you owe to a gun manufacturer in bankruptcy. The amazing thing is, the abortion amendment to the bankruptcy bill actually was approved by the Senate in 2003 and was only narrowly defeated in the Senate in 2005, by a 53–46 vote.

At the 1992 Democratic National Convention, which nominated Bill Clinton, the Democrats wouldn't even allow a pro-life Democrat governor of a large swing state to speak. Governor Robert Casey was the enormously popular governor of Pennsylvania. But the Democrats wouldn't let him speak because of his pro-life views. You might say the Democrats were running that convention like a plantation—and I think you know what I'm talking about, girlfriend. (Copyright: Hillary Clinton.)

When Senator John Kerry of Massachusetts was the Abortion Party's candidate in the 2004 presidential election, he expressly endorsed taxpayer-funded abortions—amid a stream of reminders that he had been an altar boy and that religion helped lead him "through a war." In the sort of convoluted nonsense Democrats spout whenever the topic is abortion, Kerry said during the second presidential debate, "[Y]ou don't deny a poor person the right to be able to have whatever the Constitution affords them if they can't afford it otherwise." Unless, of course, it's a quality education at a nonpublic school. I have a right to free speech; how about the government buy me a newspaper? Hey! Doesn't the Constitution protect my right to travel in a brand-new Cadillac Escalade? I'll take a red one, please.

After Kerry lost an election in which voters said the most important issue to them was "moral values," suddenly Democratic double-speak on abortion reached epic proportions. Senator Dianne Feinstein began complaining that Republicans were "painting the view of the pro-choice movement as abortion on demand—and nothing can be farther from the truth." One thing that could be farther from the truth is something that's untrue. She seemed to have forgotten that the Democrats' presidential candidate stated loud and clear—in a widely viewed presidential debate, no less—that he was for abortions at any time for any reason, paid for by the taxpayer if necessary. This is also known as "abortion on demand." Former NATO general Wesley Clark was only slightly more explicit than all the other Democratic candidates for president, saying a woman should be free to abort her baby right up until the moment of birth. And consider: Clark might have been the Democrats' presidential candidate if he hadn't been endorsed by Michael Moore.

Another Abortion Party candidate for president in 2004 was Howard Dean, a former medical resident with Planned Parenthood, the largest abortion provider in the United States. During a January 15, 2004, conference call with reporters, Dean, being a raving lunatic, said, "No doctor is going to do an abortion on a live fetus. That doesn't happen. Doctors don't do that. If they do, they'll get their license pulled, as well they should."[10] (Yes, you're reading that correctly.) At the risk of belaboring the obvious, abortions, by definition, are performed on live fetuses; otherwise it's called a "miscarriage." After the election, when Dean was campaigning to be chairman of the Democratic National Committee, he said the Democrats should stop turning their backs on pro-lifers. Doctor Demento said, "I don't have any objection to someone who is pro-life, if they are really dedicated to the welfare of children."[11] Conversely, I suppose, if you are pro-abortion and you hate kids, Dr. Dean would be cool with that, too.

Things were so bad, NARAL Pro-Choice America even decided not to oppose a bill that would require doctors to anesthetize babies being aborted after the twentieth week of pregnancy, called the Unborn Child Pain Awareness Act.[12] Planned Parenthood, however, seems to oppose it still.[13] How deranged would you have to be to oppose such a bill? Evidently the wording of the act contained several unacceptable terms, including **unborn, child, pain,** and **awareness.** The word **act** they were okay with.

The pro-abortion zealots demand that the Democrats swear absolute fealty to their craziest positions, and generally the Democrats are happy to comply. They need the money. In 2004, pro-abortion groups gave over $1.4 million in hard money to candidates for national office—more than twice as much as did pro-life groups. Emily's List is a political fundraising group that gives money only to female candidates who support abortion. In 2004, Emily's List raised $34 million. By comparison, the National Right to Life Committee raised only about $1.7 million.[14]

Showing the raw principle of the modern Democratic Party, among the Democrats who have abandoned pro-life positions to become pro-choice are former president Jimmy Carter, Senator Dick Durbin, former representative Richard Gephardt, Representative Dennis Kucinich, the Reverend Jesse Jackson, and chubby nutcase Al Gore. All but Durbin have run for president. It's easy to imagine a going from being pro-abortion to anti-abortion based on new information—ultrasounds, medical advances, pictures of babies smiling in the womb. But it's hard to see how new information could produce the reverse conversion. Everyone knows it's a terrible thing for a woman who doesn't want to be pregnant to be pregnant. But Al Gore explained his conversion experience, saying he had "talked to a lot of women who taught me about the kinds of circumstances that can come and the kinds of dilemmas that women can face." Only for a Democrat could that constitute new information.

How about **I talked to a lot of plantation owners and I found out they really do need slaves to pick the cotton.**

Still, despite the massive infusions of money, the NARAL ladies keep failing to produce the votes needed to win an election. The problem for the Democrats is that "Give me liberty or give me the right to have unprotected sex" just isn't that inspiring a rallying cry.

Republican presidential candidates win historic landslides when they make abortion a central part of their campaign, as Ronald Reagan did. Democratic candidates have to weasel out of defending abortion by claiming they want to make abortion "safe, legal, and rare" merely to win a plurality. What other basic, constitutional rights do its staunchest advocates urge us to exercise as little as possible? Speech? Free assembly? Not quartering soldiers in our homes?

Not surprisingly, polls have shown that being pro-life was more helpful to politicians than being pro-choice. In a 1996 **Los Angeles Times** poll, 27 percent of respondents said they were more likely to vote for Bush because he was pro-life, but only 18 percent said they were more likely to vote for Al Gore because he was pro-choice.

The Democrats need pro-life votes, but there's the small problem that they won't budge an inch on abortion. So they make crazy arguments for abortion, allowing not the tiniest restriction, while periodically pretending to have qualms about abortion. It's the most amazing spectacle, as if Ronald Reagan were slashing our taxes while talking about what a "sad, tragic choice" it is to cut taxes or giving speeches about how tax cuts should be "safe, legal, and rare." Except that even Reagan didn't have the gusto for cutting taxes that the Democrats have for ending human life. It would be so easy for the Democrats to say, "Okay, we're against partial birth abortion," or "We've changed our mind on parental notification of a minor's abortion." But they can't even say that.

The Democrats' only hope is to lie and pretend they stand for something other than the right of women to have unprotected sex with men they don't like. For example: the right of women not to commit suicide. During the Supreme Court confirmation hearings for John Roberts, Senator Feinstein said, "As a college student at Stanford, I watched the passing of the plate to collect money so a young woman could go to Tijuana for a back-alley abortion. I knew a young woman who killed herself because she was pregnant." I know a man who killed himself because of high taxes.

To find out what Democrats really think

about abortion, you have to read **The American Prospect** or listen to liberal hate radio talking about Republican judicial nominees like Priscilla Owen: **This country cannot have a woman on any federal court if she interpreted a law that says a parent has to be notified of a minor child's abortion to mean that a parent has to be notified of a minor child's abortion. That's like the Nazis! Lock your doors tonight, America!**

One begins to appreciate why Democrats aren't wild about any political system that permits people to vote. Liberals would have no chance of advancing their bizarre policy agenda if Americans were allowed to have a say in the matter. So they manufacture phony "constitutional rights" in which the Constitution always sounds suspiciously similar to the ideological agenda of the ACLU. We know what Democrats **want** to do, but it's suicide for candidates to run on ensuring the right of minor girls to have partial birth abortions paid for by the government without parental notification. This has to be done through the courts.

Abortion is the sacrament and **Roe v. Wade** is Holy Writ. This is why we have to have World War III every time there's an opening on the Supreme Court. As long as **Roe** is the law of the land, elected Democrats can hide behind the

Supreme Court's ruling. They rarely have to cast votes on abortion bills, because the High Court has removed abortion from the democratic process. All the Democrats have to do is smear any Supreme Court nominee who might possibly vote to overturn **Roe** and finally allow Americans to vote on abortion.

Consequently, the single most important job in the universe for the Democrats is a seat on the Senate Judiciary Committee—to protect made-up "constitutional rights" to things like abortion and the right never to have to see Christians praying. No Democrat from a swing state is allowed to sit on that committee. Democrats on the Judiciary Committee from the most liberal states in the nation are in utterly safe seats—Senator Chuck Schumer from New York, Senator Teddy Kennedy from Massachusetts, Senator Richard Durbin from Illinois, Senator Dianne Feinstein from California, Senator Herb Cole from Wisconsin, and Senator Russ Feingold from Wisconsin.

This leads to the astonishing spectacle of Teddy Kennedy, in full-dress sanctimony, getting all high and mighty with Supreme Court candidates as if the nominee had done something heinous like drown a girl and walk away from it because he had diplomatic immunity in the state of Massachusetts. Maybe there's a better committee for Senator Drunkennedy to sit on—one that does not require constant moral grandstanding from the Democrats.

Fortunately for the Democrats, People for the American Way holds the copyright to the words **troubling** and **concerned.** I bet Mary Jo Kopechne was "troubled" and "concerned" about the senator's leaving her trapped in a car under water while he went back to the hotel to create an alibi. It's hard to imagine any group of people— who are American citizens—with less understanding of what Americans are like than People for the American Way. Some would say gun ownership is part of the "American Way," but that's not what they have in mind. They probably thought it was kind of a corny name, but it was the only way people from the Upper West Side of Manhattan and Malibu could push a left-wing agenda on America by stealth. They believe in the most extreme version of abortion rights, the right to an abortion at any stage of the pregnancy, no anesthesia for the baby—just as George Washington and Abraham Lincoln did!

Of course, if most people agreed with People for a Small Slice of the Upper West Side Way, Democrats might have won a majority of votes from the American people more than one time since Lyndon Johnson was president—and that was twenty years ago, when liberals made up

"Watergate" and Jimmy Carter beat the hapless Gerald Ford with 50.1 percent of the vote. For the past decade, Democrats have rarely been able to get Americans even to vote for senators who might confirm judges who support their loony ideas on abortion.

Senator Dianne Feinstein is a great point person for the Democrats on abortion. Unlike Durbin, Kennedy, and Schumer, she's not a hack, she never drowned anyone, and the Anti-Defamation League isn't trying to put her in a lockbox. But most important, Feinstein helps nurture the myth that abortion is a women's issue. Even Feinstein prefers to cite "polls," as if she were just trying to represent the people of her state and abortion wasn't really that big a cause for her personally: "Well, obviously, I come from a state that is 71 percent supportive of **Roe.** The American people are—according to the latest ABC poll—60 percent supportive of **Roe.**"

In a 2000 **Los Angeles Times** poll that surveyed more than 2,000 Americans over several days, 65 percent of respondents said abortions should be illegal after the first trimester. Seventy-two percent of women wanted to make second-trimester abortions illegal, compared with only 58 percent of men. More than half of the respondents said abortion should be illegal in all circumstances or only to protect the life of the mother or in the cases of rape and incest. Fifty-seven percent said they believed abortion was murder. The article describing the poll was bristling with rationalizations from "gender studies" professors who claimed support for abortion was declining because the younger generation had no memory of the terror before **Roe v. Wade.** Yeah, okay, maybe. Or maybe it's that support for all liberal ideas is always at its zenith before people figure out what liberals are talking about. (This is known as "the Howard Dean effect.")

The opinion in **Roe,** written by Justice Harry Blackmun, has gone from being a joke to being the centerpiece of American jurisprudence. Liberals pretend to be shocked that then-judge Clarence Thomas told the Senate Judiciary Committee during his confirmation hearings that he had never debated **Roe.** This is ridiculous—no one debates Harry Blackmun's opinion in **Roe.** It would be humiliating, like discussing the plot of a **Will & Grace** episode.

Roe was so preposterous that Supreme Court clerks referred to it as "Harry's abortion."[15] Harvard law professor—and Watergate special prosecutor—Archibald Cox said of the opinion in **Roe,** "Neither historian, nor layman, nor lawyer will be persuaded that all the prescriptions of Justice Blackmun are part of the Constitution." Stanford Law School dean John Hart Ely

said **Roe** "is not constitutional law and gives almost no sense of an obligation to try to be." Harvard law professor Laurence Tribe has said that
"the substantive judgment on which it rests is
nowhere to be found." Even Ruth Bader Ginsburg has called **Roe** an act of "heavy-handed judicial intervention" and ridiculed the opinion
during her confirmation hearings. A lot of people
who favor abortion criticize the opinion in **Roe.**
But no one who opposes abortion says, "I'm
against abortion, but **Roe** certainly is a well-
argued opinion."

The idea that law students sit around discussing the subtle legal reasoning in **Roe v. Wade**
is absurd. No one talks about the "legal analysis"
in **Roe,** because there is none. Liberals wanted
abortion, so they discovered a right to it. And yet
Thomas is endlessly attacked for responding to
Senator Patrick Leahy's question during the confirmation hearings about whether he had ever
"debated" **Roe,** by saying, "Only, I guess, Senator, in the fact in the most general sense, that
other individuals express concerns one way or the
other and you listen and try to be thoughtful."
Patricia Ireland of the National Organization for
Women justified her organization's defense of
President Clinton's sexual harassment after having opposed Clarence Thomas on the grounds
that Thomas had "told an absolutely unbelievable

story of saying that he had never even discussed **Roe v. Wade.**"[16]

Michael Kinsley was still blathering in 2005 about Thomas's "outright fib"—even "perjury"—to denounce the idea of Thomas being nominated to chief justice.[17] Kinsley sneers at the claim of Thomas's supporters that "he didn't commit perjury because he testified only that he had never 'debated' **Roe,** not that he had never 'discussed' it." I'll take "discussed" for 10. There's no there there—there's nothing to talk about in **Roe.** Denounce, laugh at, ridicule, attack—yes. Discuss—no.

For people who pin their hopes and dreams on a right invented out of whole cloth in **Roe v. Wade,** liberals are real sticklers about what the Bible says. In 2005, the **New York Times** triumphantly announced that the word **abortion** is not mentioned anywhere in the Bible. Marshaling its evidence, the **Times** noted that in the index to the Bible, one can find "how many times Jesus talked about the poor (at least a dozen), or what the Apostle Paul wrote about grace (a lot)." But those seeking instruction on abortion "will not find the word at all."[18] It doesn't have words like **child rape** either, but that doesn't mean Christianity is ambiguous on the subject.

Incidentally, another text that doesn't have the

word **abortion** in it is the U.S. Constitution. It doesn't even have the word **privacy.** Would that liberals would be as literal when reading a constitution that sets forth specific enumerated rights as when reading the Bible! Liberals are incapable of extrapolating anything about abortion from commands like "Thou shalt not kill." But they unmistakably see a right to abortion hidden in the Privileges or Immunities Clause.

Liberals can't win on abortion in a frank discussion, so they come up with a series of feints, euphemisms, and stalking horses to promote their most sacred belief. They raise procedural blockades to conservative judges, preferring to put the American people to sleep with long exegeses on the history of the filibuster rather than clearly explaining that what they mean by "out of the mainstream" is: "opposes abortion when a girl can't fit into her prom dress."

After the 2004 election, the Democrats took secret polls and determined that they could not defeat Bush's judicial nominees on ideological grounds.[19] The Democrats' own polls showed that referring to Republican judicial nominees as radical right-wing Republicans was "the least effective approach."[20] It wasn't the conservative judges whose viewpoints were radical, it was the American people's! Suddenly nothing made sense anymore to liberals who learned about the world from reading the op-ed page of the **New York Times.**

Abortion fanatics know they can't fly under their own flag. So the Democrats use the blacks to front for the feminists. Whenever you see a Democrat getting all worked up about some egregious violation of "civil rights," I promise you, he's not talking about discrimination against a black person. Democrats don't care about race discrimination: They are the party of race discrimination! George Wallace, Bull Connor, Bob Byrd—all Democrats! What Democrats mean by "civil rights" is the civil right of a woman not to inform her husband she's aborting his baby; the civil right of a minor to have an abortion without notifying her parents; the civil right of a woman to plunge a fork into the head of a child as it struggles through the birth canal because it has a cleft lip. That's "civil rights." Before we jettison the "living Constitution," how about inventing a constitutional right not to hear Democrats invoke the phrase "civil rights" when what they mean is "abortion"?

The vicious smearing of Judge Robert Bork, Reagan's nominee to the Supreme Court in 1987, was the Democrats' first open admission that they can't win on abortion in an open fight. Even Democrats knew they couldn't scare people by telling them Bork believed in terrible things like parental notification before a minor has an abortion. **America to Democrats: So do we.** Instead, they had to make ugly allegations that Bork was an evil bigot who would bring back "segregated lunch counters," in Senator Drunkennedy's famous phrase. Bork had filed briefs in major civil rights cases and had won the respect of people like Justice Thurgood Marshall. Marshall told **Legal Times** reporter Stuart Taylor, "I think he'd have been a credit to this Court." Marshall complained to Taylor that Bork had gotten "a bum deal," and had been "tarred unfairly as an enemy of black people."[21] Democrats didn't care that they were smearing a defender of blacks' civil rights: The right to destroy human life was at stake!

Democrats were stymied in their use of the race card to protect abortion rights when President George Bush (41) nominated Clarence Thomas to the Supreme Court the next year. The feminists had to call in Anita Hill for a last-minute Hail Mary smear of Thomas as a sexual harasser. To preserve the right of women to have sex with men whose babies they don't want to carry, the Democrats nearly derailed the appointment of the second black justice ever to sit on the highest court in the land. That's their commitment to "civil rights." Hill was believed to be lying by two-thirds of the public. Liberals rewarded her with fawning profiles and a "Woman of the Year" award from **Glamour** magazine.

But the most outrageous example of the Democrats' using blacks to front for abortion rights was their ugly racial attack on Judge Charles Pickering. What the Democrats did to Pickering tells you all you need to know about how they use black Americans to protect abortion rights. As a young prosecutor in the sixties, Pickering worked closely with the FBI to go after the Ku Klux Klan in Mississippi. In 1966, he testified against Klan member Sam Bowers, on trial for murdering civil rights activist Vernon Damer. After testifying, Pickering and his family needed FBI protection. The Klan later claimed credit for defeating Pickering when he ran for the state legislature. Unlike all the Democratic members of the Judiciary Committee who would later accuse Pickering of racism, he sent his children to the Mississippi public schools, where it was fairly certain they would run into black people.

Pickering's real crime was that he was "antichoice." In 1976, he chaired the subcommittee of the Republican Party's Platform Committee, calling for a constitutional amendment to overturn **Roe v. Wade.** As a state senator he voted to support a human life amendment to the Constitution. And as the president of the Mississippi

Baptist Convention, Pickering presided over a meeting where the convention adopted a resolution calling for legislation to outlaw abortion. His most virulent opponents were People for the American Way, NARAL, the National Women's Law Center, and the Alliance for Justice. NARAL President Kate Michelman declared that Pickering "has an open hostility to a woman's right to choose."[22]

The feminists wanted abortion on demand, so blacks in Mississippi were told to take a back seat. The Democrats used their Goebbels big-lie tactics to claim Judge Pickering had lowered the sentence of a cross-burner because he hates blacks. It didn't take a lot of investigation to get the real story—even **60 Minutes** did it.

Pickering's objection to the sentence in the cross-burning case was simply that a wildly disproportionate sentence was being requested for the least culpable defendant. The government struck a deal with two of the cross-burners, letting them off with misdemeanor convictions and no prison time. During the proceedings, it became apparent that the government had made deals with the wrong men—including the ringleader of the attack, who had a criminal record and had once shot a gun into the cross-burning victims' home. After letting two defendants off with a wrist slap, the Department of Justice wanted the third defendant—a simpleton who had stupidly gone along with the others—sentenced to **seven and a half years** in prison. There are child-molesters and murderers who serve less time. Eventually, the Clinton Department of Justice agreed with Pickering and requested a sentence of two years in prison. But the Democrats later seized on this case to accuse Pickering of being soft on cross-burners.

Black Mississippians who knew Judge Pickering and had nothing to gain by defending him refused to go along with the smearing of the judge. On **60 Minutes** Charles Evers, brother of murdered civil rights leader Medgar Evers and a Pickering supporter, engaged in this exchange with the head of a local branch of the NAACP that was opposing Pickering:

> CHARLES EVERS: You know, maybe you don't know, you know that Charles Pickering is a man who helped us to break the Ku Klux Klan. Did you know that?
>
> CLARENCE MCGEE: I heard that statement made.
>
> EVERS: I mean, I know that. Do you know that?
>
> MCGEE: I don't know that.
>
> EVERS: I know that. Do you know about the young black man that was accused of rob-

bing the young white woman. You know about that?

MCGEE: Nope.

EVERS: So Charles Pickering took the case. Came to trial and won the case and the young man became free.

MCGEE: I don't know about that.

EVERS: But did you also know that Charles Pickering is the man who helped integrate his churches. You know about that?

MCGEE: No.

EVERS: Well, you don't know a thing about Charles Pickering.[23]

As **60 Minutes** reported, Judge Pickering "enjoys strong support from the many blacks who know him. In his hometown of Laurel, four of the five black city council members say they back him, because of all he's done to improve race relations. And many black attorneys who practice before him say Pickering is fair and first-rate."[24] The Democrats' attack on Judge Pickering was nothing but a kiss-ass, spineless, contemptible suck-up to feminists on abortion.

The day before Kerry won the Democrats' Best Fake Patriot contest in Iowa, he was on ABC's **This Week with George Stephanopoulos,** calling Judge Pickering "a cross-burning defending judge."[25] It had been 24 hours since

Kerry had sucked up to the feminists, so he had to get that out of the way by blackening Judge Pickering's name on national TV. While Kerry endlessly bragged about his undaunted valor in Vietnam, it would have been nice if he had ever shown one ounce of courage by standing up to the feminists.

The Democrats will sell out blacks, blue-collar workers, Catholics, Hispanics, and the elderly. But they will never cross NARAL. The most important thing isn't the little guy, the poor, the voiceless, civil rights, or the "other America." The most important value to liberals is destroying human life.

When a political party seeking votes from the American people views nothing as more sacred than ending human life, it has more to worry about than the risks of casual sex. Republicans aren't even sending in their A-team anymore— and the Democrats still can't win. The Democrats are being routed on every issue—gun control, national security, gay marriage, taxes, crime. The abortion ladies are the only ones still to be thrown off the boat. Republicans have won the battle of ideas on abortion, and now it's just a matter of time before the Supreme Court over- turns **Roe** and allows Americans to vote. The death of **Roe** is going to be like the death of the Soviet Union, and not only because both events make liberals sad. **Roe** is already dead, we're just waiting for the official proclamation. Liberals think they can demand a ruling from the Supreme Court that will take all risk out of trysting sex. But the High Court can't do that any more than penicillin can. Liberals seem not to realize their real complaint is with a Lawmaker whose judgment cannot be appealed.

5 LIBERALS' DOCTRINE OF INFALLIBILITY: SOBBING HYSTERICAL WOMEN

iberals are perennially enraged that Republicans are allowed to talk back. For years, this wasn't a problem, because, in Lenin's immortal words, they had seized the telegraph office. There were only three TV stations, three major newspapers, and a handful of national magazines, all run by liberals. But at least since Rush Limbaugh got a microphone, liberals haven't been able to make arguments in a vacuum. The Left's long-running mono-

logue had become a dialogue, and they didn't like it one bit. So now they constantly try to re-create a world where they can hurl slander and treason without anyone arguing back. They needed a doctrine of infallibility.

The appearance of Fox News Channel nearly drove liberals berserk: they were supposed to control 100 percent of news dissemination. When conservatives used to criticize the media, liberals always acted perplexed and indignant at the idea that a TV station could have a political bias. Then Fox News came along, and to listen to liberals, you'd think we were living in a police state. Fox News isn't even particularly conservative, though it is recognizably American. I believe the one verified atrocity committed by Fox News was the wearing of American flag lapel pins by some anchors after 9/11. Assuming—against all evidence—that Fox News is every bit as conservative as CBS is liberal, it is still just a small beachhead in a universe of liberal-speak. But the mere existence of one solitary network that doesn't toe the party line has driven the Left insane. Liberals have made documentaries attacking Fox News, written books denouncing Fox News, screamed about "lying liars" on Fox News, and established websites to document the cruel deceptions of Fox News.

The result of all this glandular hysteria is: The

five top-rated cable news shows are all on Fox News. Bill O'Reilly has more than 3 million viewers a night, while CNN viewers are measured in the hundreds of thousands and MSNBC by the occasional show of hands. Still, the establishment news shows on ABC and NBC have more than 10 million viewers apiece—yet another tribute to the overwhelming power of inertia. Even the fake news on CBS has more than 7 million viewers. Brit Hume gets a lousy million viewers and liberals think it's fascism in America.

Inconsolable over the death of the old media, liberals told us that the nation was being torn apart by "angry voices," "polarizing rhetoric," "angry white men," "the politics of division." They said the nation has never been so divided, forgetting the somewhat polarized era America experienced between 1861 and 1865. Then people remembered the sweetness and light we got from liberals during, say, Watergate or the Bork hearings, when they had total control of the media. Liberals' idea of harmony is: Democrats win everything all the time and no one else can talk.

Next Democrats tried explaining that they were being shellacked by the superior media savvy and rhetorical skills of Republicans—like that silver-tongued devil George W. Bush. They said their ideas were too complex to fit on a bumper sticker. This is crazy. "I [heart] partial birth abortion" fits quite easily. They said they just needed to retool their message, formulate winning sound bites, and talk about "God's green Earth" and maybe Democrats wouldn't keep frightening people. But the retooling didn't work. It turned out it really was the Democrats' message that Americans hated.

Finally, the Democrats hit on an ingenious strategy: They would choose only messengers whom we're not allowed to reply to. That's why all Democratic spokesmen these days are sobbing, hysterical women. You can't respond to them because that would be questioning the authenticity of their suffering. Liberals haven't changed the message, just the messenger. All the most prominent liberal spokesmen are people with "absolute moral authority"—Democrats with a dead husband, a dead child, a wife who works at the CIA, a war record, a terminal illness, or as a last resort, being on a first-name basis with Nelson Mandela. Like Oprah during Sweeps Week, liberals have come to rely exclusively on people with sad stories to improve their Q rating. They've become the "Lifetime" TV network of political parties. Liberals prey on people at a time of extreme emotional vulnerability and offer them fame and fortune to be that month's purveyor of hate. Victory goes to the most hysterical.

One way or another, the Bush administration was heartless for responding whenever it was attacked. It was cruel to respond to Cindy Sheehan, whose son died in Iraq, leading Cindy to become a rabid anti-war protester. Sheehan called Bush "the biggest terrorist in the world," a "fuhrer," an "evil maniac," and a "filth-spewer." But according to liberals, no one was allowed to sound a note of dissent—because Sheehan lost a son in Iraq. It was treason to respond to Joe Wilson, who accused the Bush administration of lying about the case for war with Iraq based on Wilson's trip to Niger. Wilson called Bush a "liar" and Cheney a "lying son of a bitch."[1] But no one could say Wilson's alleged expertise was based on a nepotistic junket he was sent on because his wife worked at the CIA.

Maureen Dowd of the **New York Times** made the point plainly by comparing Sheehan to Joe Wilson, saying, "The Bush team tried to discredit 'Mom' [Sheehan] by pointing reporters to an old article in which she sounded kinder to W. If only her husband were an undercover C.I.A. operative, the Bushies could out him." One wonders how exposing anything about Cindy could discredit her more than the poor imbecile's own words have.

In addition to Sheehan and Wilson, over the last few years the Democrats have used:

- a grieving Carolyn McCarthy, whose husband was murdered by a lunatic on the Long Island Rail Road, to lobby for gun control
- a paralyzed, dying Christopher Reeve to argue for embryonic stem-cell research
- a gaggle of weeping widows to blame President Bush for 9/11
- a disabled Vietnam veteran, Max Cleland, to attack the Iraq war and call Bush, Cheney, and every other human who ever disagreed with him a "chicken hawk"
- a rare Democratic Purple Heart recipient, Congressman John Murtha, to argue for surrender in Iraq

In all these cases, Democrats took the position that the spokesperson immunized the message from criticism, no matter how vicious or insane it was. Former **New Republic** editor and gay marriage advocate Andrew Sullivan brandished the openly gay chaplain to New York City's firemen, who himself died at the World Trade Center on 9/11, in his ongoing, nonstop argument for gay priests. The chaplain died on 9/11, therefore the pope should back off.

Democrats will even use our own people against us! After Democrats claimed Barry Goldwater was clinically insane when he was the Republican candidate for president, as soon as he went senile and started attacking the "religious right," he became a conservative oracle for the media. Reagan aide James Brady was respected by liberals only after he was shot in the head by John Hinckley and became a spokesman for gun control groups. Back when Nancy Reagan was consulting an astrologer about Reagan's schedule after he was shot by Hinckley, liberals denounced her as a nut controlling the White House with a Ouija board. But after Reagan died of Alzheimer's disease and Nancy expressed support for embryonic stem-cell research, liberals anointed her Seer of Technology. I can't think of a single example of conservatives doing this. Far from trying to prevent liberals from responding, we enjoy watching liberals try to mount a counterargument—especially in the case of Cindy Sheehan, with that weird disconnect between the viciousness of her comments and her itsy-bitsy, squeaky voice.

After 9/11, four housewives from New Jersey whose husbands died in the attack on the World Trade Center became media heroes for blaming their husbands' deaths on George Bush and demanding a commission to investigate why Bush didn't stop the attacks. Led by all-purpose scold Kristen Breitweiser, the four widows came to be known as "the Jersey Girls." (Original adorable name: "Just Four Moms from New Jersey.") The Jersey Girls weren't interested in national honor, they were interested in a lawsuit. They first came together to complain that the $1.6 million average settlement to be paid to 9/11 victims' families by the government was not large enough.

After getting their payments jacked up, the weeping widows took to the airwaves to denounce George Bush, apparently for not beaming himself through space from Florida to New York and throwing himself in front of the second building at the World Trade Center. These self-obsessed women seemed genuinely unaware that 9/11 was an attack on our nation and acted as if the terrorist attacks happened only to them. The whole nation was wounded, all of our lives reduced. But they believed the entire country was required to marinate in their exquisite personal agony. Apparently, denouncing Bush was an important part of their closure process. These broads are millionaires, lionized on TV and in articles about them, reveling in their status as celebrities and stalked by grief-arazzis. I've never seen people enjoying their husbands' deaths so much.

The increasingly rabid widows demanded a commission to investigate why the FAA didn't realize, when it first received word about a "hijack-ing," that this was part of a monstrous terrorist attack involving four commercial planes about to be turned into cruise missiles. On **Donahue,** Breitweiser said, "I'd like to know how our Pentagon, which is the home of our Defense Department, was hit an hour and 45 minutes after the air traffic controllers knew that they had airliners up that were hijacked. I don't understand how that's possible."2 It wasn't even an hour and 45 minutes between the first plane taking off from Logan Airport and the third plane crashing into the Pentagon.

American Airlines Flight 11 took off at 7:59 A.M., so obviously nobody knew at 7:59 that any planes were off-course, much less about to attack the nation. Air traffic controllers in Boston first notified higher-ups that Flight 11 had been hijacked at 8:25. That plane crashed into the World Trade Center at 8:46—with F-15 fighter jets in hot pursuit. At 8:47 A.M., the FAA first received notice that United Airlines Flight 175 out of Boston was behaving abnormally. Minutes later, unbeknownst to the FAA, American Airlines Flight 77 was hijacked and diverted toward the Pentagon. At 9:03, Flight 175 crashed into the second World Trade Center building, at which point we knew the nation was under attack. Even after it was clear that an attack was under way, there was no way of knowing which of the thousands of other planes in U.S. airspace at the time, if any, was going to crash next, much less where such a crash might occur. The FAA grounded all domestic flights at 9:26 A.M., and at 9:37 A.M. American Airlines Flight 77 crashed into the Pentagon.[3]

The 9/11 Commission became the Jersey Girls' pet project. Breitweiser said, "We simply wanted to know why our husbands were killed," and "why they went to work one day and didn't come back."[4] Oddly enough, "swarthy Muslim beasts flew planes into our skyscrapers" did not appear to be one of the possible answers. They demanded a commission to investigate—much as wives of the dead at Pearl Harbor demanded commissions to investigate FDR throughout World War II.

We're already paying the salaries of 535 members of a standing bipartisan commission, which is called "the U.S. Congress." But by establishing an "independent" commission, the Democrats were able to ensure a whitewash of Clinton's utter incompetence, cowardice, and capitulation to enemy regimes whose princes might be rich enough to write checks to the Clinton presidential library, during the eight years leading up to 9/11.

The commission consisted of five members

chosen by congressional Democrats, four members chosen by congressional Republicans, and the chairman chosen by President Bush. While the Republicans picked gutless moderate Republicans like Slade Gorton and Thomas Kean, Democrats named liberal attack dogs like Richard Ben-Veniste, a former Watergate prosecutor who testified in defense of perjury and obstruction of justice during Clinton's impeachment hearings, and Jamie Gorelick, Clinton's deputy attorney general and the chief architect of the policies that prevented the FBI from unraveling the 9/11 plot before it happened. That's "bipartisan" in Washington.

This would be like a commission on henhouse management with the Republicans carefully choosing well-credentialed hens and the Democrats sending in bloodthirsty foxes. During the commission's "investigation," Clinton's former national security adviser, Sandy Berger, was caught secreting Clinton-era documents out of the National Archives by stuffing them in his pants and socks. Leave it to a Clinton lackey like Berger to turn a probe of the worst terrorist attack in history into an episode of **Get Smart.** Sandy Burglar later pleaded guilty and was sentenced to community service and ordered to pay more than $50,000.

The Democrats treated the 9/11 Commission as one more battlefield in their ongoing war with Republicans, while bewildered Republicans looked on helplessly. For Democrats, everything is political—Coretta Scott King's funeral, Paul Wellstone's memorial, a Dixie Chicks concert. They will turn a major national disaster like a hurricane breaking the levees in New Orleans into a political football. Republicans demanded that President Richard Nixon resign for one lie; Democrats went to war to defend President Clinton for a mountain of lies and felonies, with not one Democrat voting to remove Clinton from office. Even the Supreme Court was shocked by this: In a breathtaking rebuke, not a single justice attended Clinton's next State of the Union address, not even the justices Clinton had appointed. Speaking of which: When a Democrat is in the White House, Republican senators vote by huge majorities to confirm extreme left-wing lawyers to the Supreme Court, such as former ACLU lawyer Ruth Bader Ginsburg. When a Republican is president, Democratic senators turn every Supreme Court nomination—even lower court appointments—into Armageddon.

Conforming to pattern, when a commission was convened to investigate intelligence failures that preceded 9/11, Republicans mistakenly imagined that the purpose of the commission was to investigate intelligence failures, not to be a partisan game for the Democrats to rewrite history.

The only valuable information about government failures leading to 9/11 has come out in the press, not the commission report.

The "Clinton Whitewash Commission" covered up a classified military data-mining project known as "Able Danger," for example. The Able Danger intelligence operation was said to have identified Mohamed Atta, the leader of the 9/11 attack, and perhaps three other hijackers, more than a year before the attack—in other words, back when you-know-who was president. The commission completely ignored this stunning information, almost as if they were trying to cover something up.

When the media got wind of Able Danger, long after the commission had completed its report, the Democratic co-chairman of the commission, Lee Hamilton, denied that they had heard anything about Able Danger. "The 9/11 commission," Hamilton said, "did not learn of any U.S. government knowledge prior to 9/11 of surveillance of Mohamed Atta or of his cell. Had we learned of it obviously it would've been a major focus of our investigation."[5] A day or two later, Hamilton changed his story, admitting the commission had been told about Able Danger, but claimed they didn't mention it in their report because it was not "historically significant."[6] (This time the word **obviously** was conspicuously absent from his prepared statement.)

Able Danger wasn't "historically significant" in the sense that the intelligence gathered by this operation did not stop the 9/11 attack. It could not have prevented the attack, because the information produced by Able Danger was destroyed by the Clinton administration.[7] So on Hamilton's theory, the only way for Able Danger to have been "historically significant" is if the intelligence had prevented the attack, in which case there would have been no need for a 9/11 Commission. I think that's what the Commission was supposed to be looking for.

The commission report was also short on information about the policy instituted by Clinton's deputy attorney general, Jamie Gorelick—which is odd, since she was sitting right there on the commission, thanks to the Democrats. Gorelick had specifically prohibited intelligence agents from telling law enforcement agents about suspected terrorists in the country. Gorelick issued guidelines that—according to the words she wrote—"go beyond what is legally required." She said she erected the wall in order to be absolutely sure that any intelligence information gathered would be admissible at a later crim-

inal trial. As terrorism prosecutor Andrew Mc-
Carthy says: "The object of a rational counterter-
rorism approach is to **prevent** mass murder from
happening in the first place, not to improve your
litigating posture for the indictment you return
after thousands of people have been slaughtered."
Apart from the Great Wall of China, the wall sep-
arating intelligence gathering from law enforcement is the only man-made structure on earth
visible to space aliens.

Back when Clinton was protecting the nation
with the able assistance of his deputy attorney
general, Jamie Gorelick, prosecutors and FBI
agents were screaming from the rooftops that
Gorelick's "wall" of separation between intelligence and law enforcement would lead to dead
Americans. Mary Jo White, the Clinton-
appointed U.S. attorney for the Southern District of New York, wrote a letter directly to
Gorelick, warning, "The single biggest mistake
we can make in attempting to combat terrorism
is to insulate the criminal side of the house from
the intelligence side of the house, unless such in-
sulation is absolutely necessary." White continued, "Excessive conservatism . . . can have deadly
results." The commission received a copy of this
letter to Gorelick, but curiously did not see fit to
include it in the final report.

Then–Attorney General John Ashcroft told

the commission that the wall had prevented FBI agents from even being told 9/11 hijackers Nawaf Alhazmi and Khalid Almihdhar were in the country until weeks before the attack. So 3,000 Americans are dead, but we can all rest easy: Nawaf's and Khalid's constitutional rights had been secured the day they flew a plane into the Pentagon. Ashcroft read a letter from an FBI agent to headquarters, angrily remarking that the Gorelick guidelines were giving "the most protection" to Osama bin Laden. FBI headquarters responded, "We're all frustrated with this issue. These are the rules. [The FBI's National Security Law Unit] does not make them up. But somebody did make these rules. Somebody built this wall."

And the somebody who built the wall was a 9/11 commissioner chosen by the Democrats. Apart from the Wright brothers' invention of the airplane itself, no single innovation was more responsible for the 9/11 attacks than Gorelick's decision to put up this wall. And yet Gorelick was never called upon to explain why department guidelines ever should have gone beyond what the (literally) suicidal law required. The 9/11 Commission report barely mentioned the wall. Perhaps it, too, was deemed "historically insignificant." Instead of calling Gorelick as a witness, the 9/11 Commission wasted the time of current administration officials in the middle of a war, demanding that they testify to well-known events.

The 9/11 Commission was a scam and a fraud, the sole purpose of which was to cover up the disasters of the Clinton administration and distract the nation's leaders during wartime. Not only did the Jersey Girls claim credit for this Clinton whitewash machine, they spent most of the hearings denouncing the Bush administration for not stopping the 9/11 attack from the weak position handed it by the Clinton administation. Specific policies of the Clinton administration were all but designed to ensure that the 9/11 attacks could not be stopped. "Just Four Moms from New Jersey" were satisfied knowing that Clinton felt their pain. That was all that mattered.

In an interview with Deborah Norville about Condoleezza Rice's testimony before the 9/11 Commission, Jersey Girl Breitweiser complained: "[R]eally, she spent the day just saying that, 'No, I didn't do anything wrong. No one asked me to do this. How would I know?'" In the same interview, Jersey Girl Patty Casazza demanded to know why Rice didn't stop the attack on the basis of the now-famous August 6 "PDB," or Presidential Daily Briefing. Casazza said the August PDB "certainly stated that Osama bin Laden was all set to do an attack on the homeland here in the United States," and "with that information, I don't know how you wouldn't have, you know, put up a better defense."[8]

If this PDB was so important, why has the media shied away from printing it? The **New York Times** never had room, just one day, to print the entire PDB? All you ever hear about is the title: "Bin Laden Determined to Strike in U.S." (Midwest Girl Determined to Succeed in Hollywood.) In fact, the full PDB is a Cliffs Notes history lesson on al Qaeda. It reads like a homework assignment that should have been done earlier but wasn't and instead got quickly cobbled together at midnight by hitting the encyclopedia: "[Bin Laden] prepares operations years in advance and is not deterred by setbacks."[9] And there you have it! The entire 9/11 plot!

Indeed, all the information about bin Laden in the August PDB comes from the nineties. Not one fact in the PDB is more recent than 1999. Thus, for example, the memo recites these facts:

- "Bin Ladin [**sic**] since 1997 has wanted to conduct terrorist attacks in the U.S."
- "The millennium plotting in Canada in 1999 may have been part of Bin Ladin's

first serious attempt to implement a terrorist strike in the U.S."

- "Two al-Qaeda members found guilty in the conspiracy to bomb our Embassies in East Africa were U.S. citizens and a senior EIJ (Egyptian Islamic Jihad) member lived in California in the mid-1990's."[10]

While the PDB had a lot of old news about bin Laden, it didn't have much to say about his future plans. Even if the memo's stale information had been recast in the form of urgent warnings—rather than as factual data from a boring book report—the PDB did not predict one single fact about the 9/11 attack. There is nothing in the memo that could possibly have prevented 9/11.

The four statements in the PDB hinting at al Qaeda's future operations were these:

"CIA and the FBI are investigating a call to our Embassy in UAE in May saying that a group of Bin Ladin supporters was in the U.S. planning attack with explosives."

The 9/11 attack did not involve explosives.

"We have not been able to corroborate some of the more sensational threat reporting, such as that from a [redacted] service in 1998 saying that Bin Ladin wanted to hijack a U.S. aircraft to gain the release of 'Blind Shaykh' 'Umar 'adb at-Rahman and other U.S.-held extremists.'"

The 9/11 attack was not an attempt to ransom the Blind Sheik or any other Muslim terrorists, which would have required taking live hostages, not just killing a lot of people by crashing the planes.

"FBI information since that time indicates patterns of suspicious activity in the country consistent with preparations for hijackings or other types of attacks, including recent surveillance of federal buildings in New York."

The 9/11 attack did not target any federal buildings in New York.

"A clandestine source said in 1998 that a Bin Ladin cell in New York was recruiting Muslim-American youth for attacks."

None of the nineteen hijackers were youths recruited from a bin Laden cell in New York.

If the entire federal government had gone on Red Alert in response to the August 6 PDB, FBI agents would have been rousting suspected terrorists in Queens and looking for swarthy men in U-Haul trucks outside the federal courthouse in New York. In theory, they might also have instituted racial profiling at airport security, which would have prevented both the hostage-taking mentioned in the August PDB and the actual

9/11 attack. Liberals won't let us do this after 9/11; they certainly wouldn't have let us do it before 9/11.

So besides a general historical review of al Qaeda (noun, Arabic for "the base," terrorist group formed in 1980s that seeks to attack the U.S.) based on information known since at least 1999, the few bits of information about future attacks contained nothing of relevance to the actual attack.

Why didn't the media ever see fit to reveal the full text of the August 6 PDB? It's not as if this memo wasn't being used to bash the administration. The media deliberately prevented Americans from seeing the memo in order to attack Condoleezza Rice for saying the document contained only "historical information"—which it did.

Of course, there were clues about what the famous PDB contained. When Richard Ben-Veniste interrogated Condoleezza Rice about the PDB during the 9/11 Commission hearings—wasting the time of the president's national security adviser in wartime—he nearly had to pull out a bullhorn to prevent Rice from revealing its contents:

BEN-VENISTE: Isn't it a fact, Dr. Rice, that the August 6 PDB warned against possible attacks in this country? And I ask you whether you recall the title of that PDB.

RICE: I believe the title was "Bin Laden Determined to Attack Inside the United States." Now, the . . .

BEN-VENISTE: Thank you.

RICE: No, Mr. Ben-Veniste, you . . .

BEN-VENISTE: I will get into the . . .

RICE: I would like to finish my point here.

BEN-VENISTE: I didn't know there was a point. I asked you what the title was.

RICE: You asked me whether or not it warned of attacks.

BEN-VENISTE: I asked you what the title was.

RICE: You said did it not warn of attacks? It did not warn of attacks inside the United States. It was historical information, based on old reporting. There was no new threat information, and it did not, in fact, warn of any coming attacks inside the United States.[11]

This enraged the Jersey Girls. How dare Rice deny that the 9/11 plot had been laid out plainly in a document that issued such clarion warnings as "Bin Laden associates surveilled our embassies in Nairobi and Dar es Salaam as early as 1993, and some members of the Nairobi cell planning the bombing were arrested and deported in

1997." Obviously, this meant nineteen Muslim men were going to wrest control of four commercial aircraft flying out of Boston's Logan Airport, Washington's Dulles Airport, and New Jersey's Newark Airport on the morning of September 11 and fly the planes into the World Trade Center, the Pentagon, and a field in Pennsylvania. Why wouldn't Rice admit she could have stopped the 9/11 attack and saved Kristen Breitweiser's husband?

Mostly the Witches of East Brunswick wanted George Bush to apologize for not being Bill Clinton. Like Monica Lewinsky before her, Breitweiser found impeached president Clinton "very forthcoming." She also found the flamboyant Bush-basher Richard Clarke "very forthcoming."[12] Miss Va-Va Voom of 1968 seemed to think the 9/11 Commission was her nationally televised personal therapy session and as long as government officials issued fake apologies, she could have "closure." (One shudders to imagine how Clinton ministers to four widows.) The rest of the nation was more interested in knowing why the FBI was prevented from being given intelligence about 9/11 terrorists here in the United States more than a year before the attack and would have liked to have top government officials back on the job preventing the next terrorist attack rather than participating in a charade intended to exonerate the Clinton administration.

Needless to say, the Democrat ratpack gals endorsed John Kerry for president. Most audaciously, they complained about the Bush campaign using images from the 9/11 attack in campaign ads, calling it "political propaganda"[13] —which was completely different from the "Just Four Moms from New Jersey" cutting campaign commercials for Kerry. And by the way, how do we know their husbands weren't planning to divorce these harpies? Now that their shelf life is dwindling, they'd better hurry up and appear in **Playboy.**

Other weeping widows began issuing rules about what could be done at Ground Zero in New York City. This is among the contributing factors to the fact that it's been five years since the 9/11 attack and Ground Zero is still just a big empty plot of ground in the most dynamic city in the world. Five years after Pearl Harbor, we had won WWII, fielded armies on two continents, and developed the atom bomb. Construction workers cleaned up the entire World Trade Center site—1.8 million tons of rubble, 16 acres wide, seven stories high, and 70 feet below ground—months ahead of schedule. But since then, the site has remained unchanged, while family members squabble about what may be built on the "sacred" ground. **You have to shut down the No. 1 train because it reminds me of my husband!** If FDR had had to put up with this, no planes would ever have been allowed to fly over Hawaii again. Surely, there can be a proper memorial without leaving the footprints empty. The British burned the Capitol and the White House in the War of 1812. If we'd been smart, those are the places we would have left empty.

A lot of widows support Bush—a lot support Pat Buchanan. But they were not trying to convert their personal tragedy into a weapon to dictate national policy or redesign lower Manhattan. None of the weeping widows issuing demands, I note, were firemen's wives. And how about we hear from some wives of proud fighting Marines? While these professional 9/11 victims turned themselves into the arbiters of what anyone could say about 9/11, some poor woman in Astoria, Queens, was being told her husband died in a car accident. She won't be paid millions of dollars, feted in **Vanity Fair,** or granted federal commissions to investigate why her husband died.

It's especially odd having the angry 9/11 widows fawned over by the same political party that objects to crime victims' delivering victim impact statements. From now on, when someone's loved one is killed by a criminal and given a reduced sentence by a liberal judge, can that judge be hauled before a committee of the family?

■ ■ ■

ANOTHER Democrat who used a tragedy that befell a mate to end an argument was the biggest drama queen of them all: Joseph C. Wilson IV. Wilson is the ne'er-do-well, unemployed WASP who claimed to be a Bush insider accusing the president of lying about prewar intelligence on Iraq. Wilson's prior work experience consisted of drifting through some low-level positions at U.S. embassies over the years until reaching the pinnacle of his career: Ambassador to Gabon. Wilson insists on being called "Ambassador."

Wilson thrust himself on the nation in July 2003. He wrote an op-ed for the **New York Times** claiming Bush had lied in his State of the Union address when he said the famous "16 words": "The British government has learned that Saddam Hussein recently sought significant quantities of uranium from Africa."

The British believed it then and believe it now. A bipartisan Senate Committee that conducted a painstaking investigation believes it. Why, even the French believe it! After Coalition forces conquered Iraq in seventeen days flat with amazingly few casualties, forcing liberals to carp about something other than the execution of the war, they became hysterical about the case for war. Consequently, the British government convened the Butler Commission to evaluate their government's prewar intelligence. Among the commission's conclusions, released in 2004, was this: "It is accepted by all parties that Iraqi officials visited Niger in 1999" and that "the British government had intelligence from several different sources indicating that this visit was for the purpose of acquiring uranium."

But that's not how Wilson saw it. In 2002, he had been sent on an unpaid government make-work job to Niger to "investigate" whether Saddam Hussein had tried to buy uranium ore from Niger. Wilson's method of investigating consisted of sitting around cafés, asking African potentates questions like **Did you commit a horrible crime, which, if so, would ruin your country's relationship with the United States? I have no independent means of corroborating this, so be honest!** It seems not to have occurred to Wilson that his method of investigation might not be watertight. But on the basis of the answers he got, Wilson concluded that Saddam had not sought uranium ore from Niger.

The Senate Intelligence Committee later

learned that Wilson's trip had unwittingly bolstered the case that Saddam had sought uranium from Niger. (Joe Wilson seems to go through life doing things unwittingly.) Almost as an afterthought, Wilson had informed CIA employees that the former prime minister of Niger told him an Iraqi delegation had proposed "expanding commercial relations" with Niger. Since Niger's only major export is uranium, anyone who discusses "expanding commercial relations" with Niger is talking about buying uranium.

But Wilson was floored when he heard Bush's State of the Union address. Listening to Bush's speech, Wilson interpreted "Africa" to mean "Niger" and "British intelligence" to mean "Joseph Wilson," and realized in horror that Bush must have been referring to Wilson's very own report!

Or at least that's what he realized soon after he started working for the Kerry campaign in May 2003. This was a fact the media seemed studiously uninterested in pursuing: Wilson's inadvertent admission that he had begun advising the Kerry campaign one month before he started making his outlandish claims against the Bush administration. In October 2003, the Associated Press reported that Wilson said he had been "advising Kerry on foreign policy for about five months."[14] That means he started working for

Kerry in May 2003—a month before he wrote his **New York Times** op-ed titled "What I Didn't Find in Africa."

Out of love for his country and an insatiable desire to have someone notice his worthless existence, Wilson wrote a column for the **Times** that called Bush a liar. His story was nutty enough to be believed by the entire **New York Times** editorial board.

Though Wilson's defenders later indignantly denied it, he had clearly implied in his op-ed that he had been sent to Niger at the behest of Vice President Dick Cheney and had reported back to him—which was certainly news to Cheney.

Among Wilson's other references to the high-level nature of his trip in his **j'accuse** column in the **Times,** he said:

- "I was informed by officials at the Central Intelligence Agency that Vice President Dick Cheney's office had questions about a particular intelligence report."
- "[A]gency officials asked if I would travel to Niger to check out the story so they could provide a response to the vice president's office." (Curiously, one "agency official" also asked him to take out the trash and be home early for junior's T-ball game that night.)

- "Based on my experience with the administration in the months leading up to the war, I have little choice but to conclude that some of the intelligence related to Iraq's nuclear weapons program was twisted to exaggerate the Iraqi threat."[15] (He neglected to mention that his "experience" with the Bush administration was limited to what he read in the **Washington Post** from his living room couch.)

True, Wilson never unequivocally stated that Cheney sent him to Niger or that he reported back to Cheney. But he sure as hell didn't say his wife had recommended him for the trip. With Wilson's encouragement, soon the entire press corps was reporting that Cheney had sent him to Niger and that Wilson's nonexistent "files" were sitting on Cheney's desk.

In short order, the White House was being forced to deny that the vice president had sent Wilson to Niger. CNN's White House correspondent Dana Bash querulously remarked that the White House "at this time" was "continuing to deny" that Cheney had "ordered" Wilson to make the trip: "Now, with regard to ambassador Wilson's charge that it was actually the vice president's office that ordered him to go and that they did know about his conclusion . . . administration officials are, at this time, flatly denying that. One official is telling CNN, quote, that they were, quote, 'unaware of the mission and unaware of the results or conclusion of his mission.' So this is something that the White House is continuing to deny."[16]

ABC News reported, in a program objectively titled "Bush Administration Deceives America: President Used Known Falsehood to Lead Americans to War," that "Ambassador Joe Wilson says, at the request of Vice President Cheney's office, the CIA sent him to Niger in February 2002."[17]

Wilson not only failed to correct the media's mammoth misunderstanding about the genesis of his trip to Niger, but began claiming that the vice president was aware of his conclusions. On **Meet the Press,** Wilson said, "The office of the vice president, I am absolutely convinced, received a very specific response to the question it asked and that response was based upon my trip out there."[18] Unless he was referring to the vice president of the Screen Actors Guild, this was preposterous. But Wilson assured the **Washington Post**—based on his insider knowledge, no doubt—"When you task a serious organization like the CIA to answer a question, it doesn't go into a black hole."[19] It might go into a black hole, however, if you were sent by your wife.

The **Washington Post** reported that the Bush administration and British government had "ignored [Wilson's] findings" that "helped debunk claims that Iraq had tried to obtain uranium" from Niger.[20] (This was about the same time the Bush administration "ignored" my report that I was running low on dishwasher detergent.)

The **Union Leader** (Manchester, N.H.) reported that Wilson went to Niger "at the request of Vice President Richard Cheney's office" and that Wilson said "he had files with the State Department, CIA and the vice president's office" saying there were no uranium sales to Iraq.[21] Wilson had filed no written report, but suddenly his "files" were sitting on the vice president's desk.

The **Daily Telegraph** (London) went the whole nine yards, calling Wilson a "CIA man" and "a senior CIA envoy sent to investigate the claim" about Saddam seeking uranium. Wilson was finally "[b]reaking his silence" after being sent to Niger "on CIA orders"—that is, by his wife. According to the **Telegraph,** "Mr Wilson said he believed that his conclusions would have been automatically shared with British officials."[22] So now Wilson's nonexistent report was not only on Cheney's desk but had been wired to Tony Blair!

Los Angeles Times columnist Robert Scheer called Wilson "the mysterious envoy" sent to Niger "under pressure from Cheney" and claimed "Wilson reported back the facts to Cheney."[23] And the Democrats' leading geopolitical strategist, Bianca Jagger, said, "Ambassador Joseph Wilson" said "his report got to the State Department, to the White House, to the national security and that he believes that all of them should have that information, and that Vice President Cheney should have had that information."[24]

So don't tell me it wasn't relevant that Wilson had been recommended for the unpaid trip to Niger by his wife.

Soon journalist Robert Novak revealed in his July 14, 2003, syndicated column that Wilson did not go to Niger on a high-level CIA mission for Vice President Cheney, as Wilson had implied.[25] Wilson spoke with no expertise, he was not a "CIA man," he was not sent by Dick Cheney, no one in the White House was ever told of Wilson's make-work "report." He had been sent by his wife, Valerie Plame, a chair-warmer at the CIA who apparently wanted to get him out of the house. Wilson had never even filed any written report, but gave an "oral report" to a few CIA bureaucrats who came to his house—just before Wilson zoomed back to his Austin Powers fantasy camp.

In response to Novak's column, Wilson accused Karl Rove of outing his wife as an undercover "spy" to get her killed and retaliate against him. In the words of the **Washington Post,** Wilson believed his wife had been mentioned "to intimidate other government insiders from talking to journalists." Except Wilson wasn't an insider and his wife wasn't an undercover spy.

Liberals were allowed to boast that Wilson was sent "by the CIA" and "reported back" to Cheney. But—in the traditional liberal definition of **criminal**—Republicans were committing heinous crimes if they responded by pointing out that Wilson's trip was a boondoggle arranged by his wife. The man the Democrats wanted to be commander in chief, Senator John Kerry, said, "it's an 'act of treason' to reveal the identity of intelligence sources." (Not as treasonous as calling your comrades in arms war criminals during the Vietnam War, but still, a pretty serious offense.)

A sampling of headlines from various newspapers indicates the tenor of the coverage:

SO NOW WE SELL OUT OUR OWN?
Santa Fe New Mexican, August 3, 2003

BLOWING CIA AGENT'S COVER
WEAKENS NATIONAL SECURITY

Atlanta Journal-Constitution,
September 30, 2003

BUSH ADMINISTRATION MUST BRING ROGUE
OFFICIALS TO JUSTICE; CIA AGENT OUTED FOR
PARTISAN POLITICAL REASONS
News Tribune (Tacoma, Washington),
October 1, 2003

EDITORIAL: BETRAYAL OF TRUST
Denver Post, October 2, 2003

CIA LEAK LOOSE-LIPPED LEAK
The Sunday Oregonian, October 5, 2003

DIRTY AND DEADLY
Charleston Gazette (West Virginia),
October 26, 2003

DEFIANT NOVAK SHOULD BE INDICTED,
TRIED FOR TREASON
Palm Beach Post (Florida), October 27, 2003

(Noticeably, none of the newspapers screaming about "treason" or "traitors" were papers like
the **Washington Post.** For the really insane stuff
you have to go to bush-league newspapers where
reporters have all the venom of the big-city newspapers, combined with retard-level IQs.)

The real story about Joseph C. Wilson IV was
not "Bush lied, kids died." It was that Wilson and

his wife foisted their mutual fantasies on the nation, instigating massive investigations, the only provable conclusion of which is that Joe Wilson is a nut and a liar.

"CIA man" Wilson's diplomatic career was a joke. Back when he had a job, Wilson was the guy who made sure the toilets at American embassies flushed and the commissary was stocked, in such desirable locations as Niger, Togo, South Africa, Burundi, and Iraq. His big break came when Saddam waited for the U.S. ambassador to leave Iraq on vacation before invading Kuwait—leaving only "deputy chief of the U.S. Mission" Wilson behind. The fact that Wilson had no training in Middle East affairs and did not speak Arabic was no impediment to his post in Iraq because, as the **New York Times** put it at the time, "he has risen within the Foreign Service as an administrative officer, someone usually more concerned that the embassy heating and plumbing work than with what is going on in the host country."[26]

As President Bush (41) prepared for war, he repeatedly dissed Saddam by telling him to talk to Wilson, which, in diplomatic circles, is considered one step above "talk to the hand." Wilson's major assignment during that period was to set up a meeting between Saddam and an actual official from the Bush administration, James Baker. People who do that sort of thing are usually called "secretaries," not "Mr. Ambassador." One of Wilson's friends boasted of Wilson's qualifications to the Associated Press: "He's certainly capable . . . to make any message." Which is so unfair: Joe also made really good coffee.

Secretary of State James Baker sent Wilson a pro forma letter conveying Bush's message that Wilson's work was "truly inspiring" and telling him to "keep fighting the good fight." (Also: "We hope we can count on your vote in the next election!") Wilson instantly began brandishing the letter to reporters. He even shared his fantasy-obituary with reporters, saying it would read: "Joseph C. Wilson IV, who was the last American diplomat to meet with Iraqi President Saddam Hussein, died . . ." Concededly, this was better than "Joseph C. Wilson IV, mostly unemployed his entire life, briefly had a paying job unstopping toilets at American embassies in Togo and Burundi . . ." A 1990 **New York Times** article on the message-boy left behind in Iraq quoted Wilson reminiscing about the last time he had "'faced down' his own mortality" and making dramatic pronouncements about having "signed his will and paid up his [life insurance] coverage." The article noted, "Already framed in Mr. Wilson's office is the Nov. 28 cable sent to him by Secretary of State James A. Baker 3d . . ."**27**

Wilson was never the ambassador to Iraq, but

after he accused the Bush administration of lying in 2003, some reporters decided to give him a promotion. Thus, **Publishers Weekly** reporter John F. Baker referred to Wilson as "the former U.S. ambassador to Iraq."[28] (Of course, John F. Baker refers to himself as "the Queen of Sheba.") Wilson's lucky break of happening to be the guy left behind when Saddam invaded Kuwait was called "a career-maker" by his colleagues. Wilson apparently thought so too, telling reporters his "dream assignment would be France." Alas, Wilson's next posting was to Gabon, which even by my estimate is a country more worthless than France. Then, at age forty-eight, he was—to put it diplomatically—let go, having made only the first of four grades in the foreign service.[29]

So one can well imagine that after reading Wilson's delusional op-ed, top officials at the White House and CIA were scratching their heads wondering who this imbecile was. The answer is: He's nobody. Bush was certainly not relying on anything Wilson said when he referred to the conclusions of "British intelligence" about Saddam seeking enriched uranium from Africa.

I think that's the gist of what Karl Rove was trying to convey to **Time** magazine correspondent Matt Cooper when he told him, according to Cooper's notes, "big warning!" Don't "get too far out on Wilson." Cooper processed this information through the mainstream media filter and produced an article accusing the White House of slandering Wilson: "Has the Bush administration declared war on a former ambassador who conducted a fact-finding mission to probe possible Iraqi interest in African uranium? Perhaps." As long as Wilson was calling Bush a liar, the mainstream media treated his every idiocy as if it were the word of Moses.

Wilson repeatedly denied that his wife was involved in his trip to Niger. In his humbly titled autobiography, **The Politics of Truth: Inside the Lies That Led to War and Betrayed My Wife's CIA Identity: A Diplomat's Memoir,** Wilson stated point-blank: "Valerie had nothing to do with the matter. . . . She definitely had not proposed that I make the trip."[30] And again, he said, "The assertion that Valerie had played any substantive role in the decision to ask me to go to Niger was false on the face of it. . . . Valerie could not—and would not if she could—have had anything to do with the CIA decision to ask me to travel to [Niger]."[31] (How does a publisher react to some pompous jerk who wants to call his book **The Politics of Truth? Okay, seriously, what are you really going to call it?**)

And then the Senate Intelligence Committee

heard testimony from a CIA official who told the committee that it was Wilson's wife who had "offered up" Wilson for the Niger trip. The committee also obtained the memo from Valerie Plame recommending her husband for the assignment. In the memo, Plame notes that her husband "has good relations with both the PM [prime minister] and the former Minister of Mines (not to mention lots of French contacts), both of whom could possibly shed light on this sort of activity." (At the end of the memo she added, "Oh, and as long as you're going out you might as well bring back a quart of milk.") Joe Wilson's response to the production of his wife's memo was, "I don't see it as a recommendation to send me." So Wilson is a liar, an illiterate, or someone who needs new eyeglasses.

With the vast diplomatic experience Wilson had fantasized for himself, he simply could not understand why anyone would imagine he was sent to Niger on the recommendation of his wife. In a state of utter incomprehension, Wilson demanded to know, "And what really did the inclusion of my wife's name add to the story?" Well, let's see now: uh, other than being the entire story, nothing.

That explains Wilson—but what about the objective, fair-minded mainstream media? Did they think this clown was sent to Niger because of his skills and experience? Apparently so. In September 2003, crack newsman Doyle McManus, the Washington bureau chief of the **Los Angeles Times,** said Wilson's wife had been "unmasked" by the Bush administration "for reasons we still don't understand."[32] In fairness, there seems to be a lot Doyle McManus doesn't understand.

There are two interpretations of Karl Rove's tip to the media. Either: (1) He was trying to warn reporters that Wilson was a delusional nutcase, or (2) The White House was punishing Wilson for telling the truth by exposing his wife as a "covert" agent.

Well, now the results are in. Among the reasons we know Rove wasn't exposing Valerie Plame as a covert agent is the fact that Plame wasn't a covert agent. Or rather, she was the type of covert, deep-cover, top-secret spy who poses for two-page color photo spreads in **Vanity Fair** magazine under her real name—you know, that kind of covert. When special prosecutor Patrick Fitzgerald, who was investigating the "leak" of Plame's name, announced his indictment of a lone assistant to Cheney for perjury, he never even mentioned the law about releasing the names of covert agents. To the contrary, Fitzgerald went out of his way to avoid calling Plame "covert," instead saying her employment status was "classified"—which would only be relevant to the 1917 Espionage Act. "Jane Bond" was, in actuality, "Jane Paper Pusher Whose Husband Is a Stay-at-Home Dad Currently, Uh, Between Jobs." The closest Plame has been to "undercover" in recent years was at last year's CIA Christmas party, when she was somebody's secret Santa. It was not a crime to reveal her name, much less tell the press that Wilson's little junket to Niger was a "Take Our Daughters to Work Day" gone bad. The country could have been spared a lot of trouble if the media had not studiously pretended not to grasp Rove's point.

Incidentally, if Wilson ever believed his own Walter Mitty fantasy about his wife being a covert spy—so secret that his entire family could be killed if her identity were revealed—maybe he should have thought twice before writing an op-ed for the **New York Times** calling the president a liar based on information acquired solely because his wife works at the CIA.

Wilson lied about what he "didn't find in Africa." He lied about whether his wife recommended him for the trip. And he lied about his wife being a covert agent. (Other than that, everything Wilson said was perfectly accurate.)

Indeed, Wilson told so many lies, there are some everyone has forgotten. When Wilson first started accusing the Bush administration of lying, he claimed he based his conclusion that Saddam had not tried to buy uranium from Niger on "sales records" that were clearly forged. Even if we skip over the absurd logic that because documents are forged, what they purport to show has been proved false—an old spy trick—it would later turn out Wilson had never seen the forged documents.

But before Wilson wrote his "What I Didn't Find in Africa" column, he was retailing the "forged documents" story to gullible reporters, in news stories now known to be citing Wilson.

On May 6, 2003, the **New York Times**'s Nicholas D. Kristof wrote this in his unintentionally ironically titled column "Missing in Action: Truth":

I'm told by a person involved in the Niger caper that more than a year ago the vice president's office asked for an investigation of the uranium deal, so a former U.S. ambassador to Africa was dispatched to Niger. In February 2002, according to someone present at the meetings, that envoy reported to the C.I.A. and State Department that the information was unequivocally wrong and that the documents had been forged.

[T]he envoy's debunking of the forgery was passed around the administration and seemed to be accepted—except that President Bush and the State Department kept citing it anyway.[33]

On June 12, 2003, Walter Pincus wrote this in the **Washington Post:**

[T]he CIA in early February 2002 dispatched a retired U.S. ambassador to the country to investigate the claims [that Iraqi officials had been seeking to buy uranium in Niger], according to the senior U.S. officials and the former government official.

After returning to the United States, the envoy reported to the CIA that the uranium-purchase story was false, the sources said. Among the envoy's conclusions was that the documents may have been forged because the "dates were wrong and the names were wrong," the former U.S. government official said.[34]

And on June 29, 2003, Andrew Buncombe and Raymond Whitaker reported in the **Independent:**

A high-ranking American official who investigated claims for the CIA that Iraq was seeking uranium to restart its nuclear programme accused Britain and the US yesterday of deliberately ignoring his findings to make the case for war against Saddam Hussein.

The retired US ambassador said it was all but impossible that British intelligence had not received his report—drawn up by the CIA—which revealed that documents, purporting to show a deal between Iraq and the West African state of Niger, were forgeries.[35]

After massive investigations in this country and in Britain into the uranium claim, the Senate Intelligence Committee concluded in 2004 that Wilson had never even seen the forged sales records. The forged documents—which everyone knew were forged, by the way—did not even arrive at the CIA until eight months after Wilson's Niger trip.[36] Apparently, Wilson not only traveled to Niger, but through time! As the **Washington Post** later admitted, "the report also said Wilson provided misleading information to the **Washington Post** last June" when he said his conclusions about Niger were "based on documents that had clearly been forged." In response to questions from committee staff, asking Wilson how he could have known about the forged documents when he had never seen them, Wilson said he may have "misspoken" to reporters. That's what we call "The Politics of Truth."

This is the sort of nonsense that gets spread by a press corps that will believe absolutely any accusation against a Republican administration and will treat any lunatic accusing Republicans of lying as an uncontested truth-teller. The real scandal was how liberals embraced Wilson. "Ambassador" Wilson was about one step above Bill Burkett in terms of reliable sources. Burkett, you'll recall, was CBS's source for accusing President Bush of shirking his National Guard duties based on blatantly forged documents. Burkett admitted to having nervous breakdowns and having been hospitalized for depression, and, according to **USA Today,** an interview with Burkett ended when he "suffered a violent seizure and collapsed in his chair." But any stumbling drunk who attacked Bush was instantly hailed by the media as the next Joan of Arc, no matter how blinding the warning signs.

Liberals' first sign with Wilson should have been his telling the **Washington Post** that he and his wife were discussing "who would play [her] in the movie." Wilson also reverted to fantasizing out loud about the first line in his obituary. This time, his favorites were "Joseph C. Wilson IV, the Bush I administration political appointee who did the most damage to the Bush II administration . . ." and "Joseph C. Wilson IV, the husband of the spy the White House outed . . ."[37]

But after Wilson accused the Bush administration of lying, the **New York Times** nearly put him on their editorial board. He was instantly embraced by Democratic senators like Jon Corzine of New Jersey, awarded a **Nation** magazine "Award for Truth-Telling," and given a lucrative book contract. He was fawned over by **Vanity Fair** magazine, where his wife wore dark glasses and a scarf as if to hide her "secret identity." Meanwhile, the only person who was undercover in the Plame household was Joe Wilson—under cover of his wife's skirt, that is.

He may have been a liar and a fraud, but Wilson could attack the Bush administration with impunity. Liberals took the position that Wilson was free to puff up his worthless credentials by implying he had been sent to Niger on an important mission directly by the vice president and the director of the CIA. But the White House couldn't respond to his delusional accusations by saying his wife sent him.

■   ■   ■

ABOUT the time Wilson was becoming an embarrassment even by the standards of the Democrats—which is a high bar—the Democratic Party's new spokesman became Cindy Sheehan, loon. To expiate the pain of losing her firstborn son, who died bravely fighting in Iraq, Sheehan decided to cheer herself up by engaging in Stalinist agitprop outside President Bush's Crawford, Texas, ranch. It's the strangest method of grieving I've seen outside of Paul Wellstone's memorial. Someone needs to teach these liberals how to mourn. It must be very difficult for people to comprehend the death of a loved one based on abstract ideas like "Islamic fanaticism," "retaliation," and "freedom." Because liberalism is a primitive religion, it tells people like Cindy Sheehan that her loss was the result of some intentionally evil force, like witches, evil spirits, or George W. Bush.

Call me old-fashioned, but a grief-stricken war mother shouldn't have her own full-time PR flack. After your third profile on **Entertainment Tonight,** you're no longer a grieving mom; you're a C-list celebrity trolling for a book deal or a reality show. At that point you're no longer mourning, you're "branding."

Sheehan was joined in her cause by Elizabeth Edwards, wife of former Democratic presidential candidate John Edwards. Edwards sent out a public letter asking people to "Support Cindy Sheehan's Right to Be Heard," which the media almost missed because they were all in Crawford interviewing Cindy Sheehan. Joining the school of thought that says "having a loved one killed violently makes you an expert advocate for liberal policies," Mrs. Edwards noted that she, too, had a son who died. What is this, some kind of weird club or something?

We're sorry about Ms. Sheehan's son, but the entire nation was attacked on 9/11. This isn't a "teachable moment," it's a war. The Left's campaign to turn war into a matter of individuals' personal grief cheapens what we're fighting against. America has been under relentless attack from Islamic terrorists for twenty years, culminating in a devastating attack on U.S. soil on 9/11. It's not going to stop unless we fight back, annihilate Muslim fanatics, destroy their bases, eliminate their sponsors, and end all their hope. A lot more American mothers will be grieving if our military policy is: No one gets hurt!

By the time Sheehan joined the "Surrender Now, Great Satan" bandwagon, there had already been two free elections in Iraq. The Iraqis were busily at work on a constitution. Iraqi women were freely protesting on the street against Sharia law, and crafty Iraqi politicians were preparing to woo the "Burka Mom vote."

Fortunately, the Constitution vests authority to make foreign policy with the president of the United States, not with this week's special guest on the Oxygen television network. But liberals think that as long as they can produce a grieving mother, the commander in chief should step aside and let Cindy Sheehan dictate the nation's foreign policy. As **New York Times** columnist Maureen Dowd said, it's "inhumane" for Bush not "to understand that the moral authority of parents who bury children killed in Iraq is absolute."

I'm not sure what "moral authority" is supposed to mean in that sentence, but if it has anything to do with Cindy Sheehan dictating America's foreign policy, then no, it is not "absolute." It's not even conditional, provisional, fleeting, theoretical, or ephemeral. The only sort of authority Cindy Sheehan has is the uncanny ability to demonstrate, by example, what body types should avoid wearing shorts in public. Dowd's "absolute" moral authority column demonstrates, once again, what can happen when liberals start tossing around terms they don't understand, like **absolute** and **moral.** As someone once said of Norman Mailer, I do not know for a fact that Maureen Dowd was drunk when she wrote that, but for her sake I certainly hope she was. The logical shortcomings of such a statement are staggering. What if the person arguing with you is a mother who also lost a son in Iraq and she's pro-war? Do we decide the winner with a coin toss? Or do we look for a woman out there who lost two children in Iraq and see what she thinks about the war? Ladies, I know logic isn't your strong suit, but come on!

Liberals demanded that we listen to Sheehan with rapt attention—and silence—but she had nothing new to say about the war. At least nothing we hadn't heard from Michael Moore since approximately 11 A.M., September 11, 2001. It's a neocon war; we're fighting for Israel; it's a war for oil; Bush lied, kids died; there is no connection between Saddam Hussein and al Qaeda. Turn on MSNBC's **Hardball** and you can hear it right now. Cindy Sheehan was like a touring company of Air America Radio: same old script and it's not even the original cast. The only thing Cindy added was frequent references to her son, Casey. As she wrote in an August 31, 2005, column on her Truthout.org webpage, "So it is official, Casey had his blood shed in Iraq for OIL. He died so we could pay over 3.00/gallon for gas." It's hard to construct an argument that the war was about stealing the Iraqis' oil when gas was at $3 a gallon. I guess Bush is both evil and yet too inept to steal their oil. It's a very subtle plan for the long horizon.

In any event, back in October 2002, these same anti-war arguments didn't persuade Hillary Clinton or John Edwards to vote against the war. In fact, they didn't persuade any of the liberal senators who want to be president to vote against the war. Democrats in Congress kept voting to give President Bush carte blanche, but then would turn around and deliver angry indignant speeches opposing the war whenever there was no congressional stenographer around to memorialize their positions.

The liberal shock troops didn't even persuade Democratic primary voters, who unceremoniously dumped anti-war candidate (and one-man RNC fundraising machine) Howard Dean in favor of John Kerry, who voted for the war before he voted against it. They certainly didn't persuade a majority of American voters, who re-upped George Bush's tenure as the nation's commander in chief.

But liberals demanded that we listen to the same old arguments all over again, not because Sheehan had any new insights but because she had the ability to repel dissent by citing her grief. She was the angry Left's human shield.

On the bright side, Sheehan shows us what Democrats would say if they were immunized from counterarguments. Sheehan has called President Bush "that filth-spewer and warmonger." She says Bush is "the biggest terrorist in the world"—and that was just on her Christmas card to the Bush family. She says, "America has been killing people on this continent since it was started" and "the killing has gone on unabated for over 200 years." (Is it my imagination, or is somebody angling for Ward Churchill's soon-to-be-available job at the University of Colorado?) She calls the U.S. government a "morally repugnant system" and says "this country is not worth dying for."

Evidently, however, there are some things worth killing for. Speaking at an anti-war rally held by Veterans for Peace, Sheehan said, "So anyway that filth-spewer and warmonger, George Bush, was speaking after the tragedy of the marines in Ohio, he said a couple things that outraged me. . . . And I know I don't look like I'm outraged, I'm always so calm and everything. That's because if I started hitting something, I wouldn't stop till it was dead. So I can't even start, 'cause I know how dangerous that would be, but George Bush was talking . . ." It's a wonder Bush wouldn't meet with her.

We must listen to Sheehan, but we may not respond to her. As Joe Trippi said to Bill O'Reilly on Fox News, she's "had a loss, a painful loss"—

so no one is allowed to criticize her. (And believe me, if anyone knows about painful losses, it's Howard Dean's former campaign manager.) He said Sheehan is "willing to stand up to the most powerful man in the world"—at least as long as no one is allowed to respond.

O'Reilly pointed out that, contrary to Sheehan's claim that Bush was flippant and rude to her during their meeting in June 2004, immediately after that meeting, she said, "I now know President Bush is sincere about wanting to help the Iraqis. I know he's sorry and feels some pain for our loss. And I know he's a man of faith." Finally, someone with the moral authority to contradict Cindy Sheehan: Cindy Sheehan!

Trippi ruled this observation out of order, informing O'Reilly that Sheehan was the "first citizen in the country ever to be charged with flip-flopping." (She had had a "painful loss.") As the Left's Nazi block watcher that week, Trippi informed O'Reilly that only politicians can be charged with flip-flopping. "We as citizens," he decreed, "are allowed to flip-flop any day we want."

When O'Reilly again raised the subject of Sheehan's about-face on her meeting with Bush, saying, "she either lied then or she's lying now," Trippi said it was talk like that that led to the "hate that's spewing around the Net." So that's the way it is with liberals. They can call Bush a "lying bastard," a "filth-spewer and warmonger," but if anyone points out that the bastard used to be "sincere," and a "man of faith," it's "hate."

The story that was lost in the media lovefest over Cindy Sheehan was that her son was a great American. After serving one tour in Iraq, Casey Sheehan reenlisted. He was not an infantryman and consequently was not required to go into combat, but when members of his unit came under attack by Islamic savages in Sadr City, Casey insisted on joining the battle to rescue his comrades. It was during that rescue mission that Casey was killed. Despite having a screwball for a mother, Casey Sheehan was a great American who fought and died nobly for his friends and for his country.

It is supremely ironic that the brave men who died for their country would almost certainly be appalled at the reaction of Moms Against Anyone Dying. Perhaps this note I received by e-mail should be clipped and posted by all brave Americans in Iraq:

> Know this. If I am taken captive or killed by these Arab savages, I shall never disgrace myself or my nation by groveling in the fashion of many hostages and their families.

There shall be no special entreaties on my behalf. I shall condone no disgusting and disloyal attempt by weepy relatives to "distinguish" me from my nation or its brave president, as in "Actually, our whole family opposed the war." If I am taken, and the animales will not let me talk on camera, tell the world I renounced any disloyal relatives and that my last words were: "God Bless America, God Bless President Bush."

We're winning this war and we are winning it because of brave men like Casey Sheehan who do not decide to throw in the towel every time an American dies. More than a hundred Americans died at Lexington Green and Concord. Should we have quit then? The Civil War dragged on for three long years before the Union started making serious inroads against the Confederacy. You want a quagmire? **That** was a quagmire.

In the Battle of Tarawa, one of the first major engagements of World War II, we lost more than 1,000 men in three days. On this small island, far away from home, our Marines faced savagery of epic proportions and took quite a licking. Iwo Jima was yet to happen (7,000 Americans killed). Okinawa was yet to happen (18,000 Americans killed). FDR hadn't "planned" properly and the

Marines were required to hastily improvise mine sweeping. Should we have walked away from that war, too? Liberals keep talking up World War II, why not this war?

Liberals simultaneously demean our current war heroes and beatify (Democratic) war veterans from wars past. While turning D-Day into a religion, similar sacrifice and bravery in the War on Terrorism appalls them. They disparage real religion as pagan worship of ancestral power, but they have turned military service (by Democrats) into a secular religion, mostly honored in the breach. At the mere mention of one of the seven or eight veterans in the entire liberal community, we are required to fall on our knees, mouths agape. Any other reaction is deemed an attack on their patriotism.

It was cruel and unfair to respond to Democratic senator Max Cleland of Georgia about anything he ever said or any votes he ever cast—because he dropped a grenade on himself in Vietnam. Cleland took full advantage of his status as another Democrat Unanswerable by viciously attacking Republicans who criticized Democrats for their repeated proposals that we surrender in the War on Terrorism.

From a stage on which another Democratic senator, Frank Lautenberg of New Jersey, called

Bush and Cheney "chicken hawks," Cleland said, "Dick Cheney got five [draft] deferments. John Kerry volunteered for Vietnam, as did I. President Bush spent that time guarding the shores of Texas and didn't even show up for his final physical in the Guard and got out eight months early."[38]

After Tom DeLay joked to a Republican audience, "I certainly don't want to see Teddy Kennedy in a Navy flight suit," Cleland fired off a nasty letter—a letter, no less!—to DeLay saying, "This country deserves more patriots like Senator Kennedy, not more chicken hawks like you who never served."

Most Democrats shy away from citing Kennedy's "military service" with such bravado. The "military service" at issue consisted of Kennedy's spending two years in NATO's Paris office after he was expelled from Harvard for paying another student to take his Spanish exam.[39] This was during the Korean War. While Kennedy faced down nasty paper cuts in Paris, other American boys his age were freezing and being shot at by the Chicoms at the Yalu River.

Accusing anyone he disagreed with of being a "chicken hawk" became so natural for Cleland that he even said it about military heroes and former POWs. After six Republicans called on John Kerry to apologize for what he said about American troops in Vietnam on the thirty-third anniversary of Kerry's Senate testimony, Cleland called the Republicans "a bunch of chicken hawks who never went to war, never felt a wound, but are so quick to criticize a man who went to war and got wounded doing it."**40**

The Republicans' military service may not have been as awe-inspiring as a desk job in Paris after being thrown out of Harvard for cheating, but it was still pretty impressive. Five of the six Republicans Cleland attacked were combat veterans, and the one who was not had spent thirty years in the Army Reserves. Among the five was Representative Sam Johnson (R-TX), who flew sixty-two combat missions in Korea and twenty-five over North Vietnam, was shot down in combat over North Vietnam, and was tortured as a POW for six and a half years. Another was Representative Randy Cunningham (R-CA), one of only two American Navy aces that the Vietnam War produced. But apparently none of these men had the dauntless courage to drop a grenade on his own foot.

In November 2005, Democratic representative John Murtha called for—as the **New York Times** put it—the "immediate withdrawal of American troops" in the middle of the war. At that point in the war, the U.S. military had deposed a dictator who had already used weapons of mass destruction and would have used them again. We had found evidence proving that Saddam Hussein was working with al Qaeda and was trying to acquire long-range missiles from North Korea and enriched uranium from Niger. Saddam was on trial and his psychopath sons were dead. The American military had captured or killed scores of foreign terrorists in Baghdad. The Iraqi people had voted in two free democratic elections already and were one month away from a third vote for a National Assembly. The long-suffering Kurds were free and no longer required 24/7 protection by U.S. fighter jets. Libya's Muammar Qaddafi had voluntarily dismantled his weapons of mass destruction, and Syria had withdrawn from Lebanon. Last but certainly not least, the Marsh Arabs' wetlands ecosystem in central Iraq that Saddam drained was being restored, so even the Democrats' war goals in Iraq were being met.

The American military had done all this with just over 2,000 deaths. These deaths are especially painful because they fall on our greatest Americans. Still, we were a lot farther along in the Iraq War than we were after the first 2,000 deaths in any other war. There were about 600,000 deaths in the Civil War, 400,000 deaths in World War II, and 60,000 deaths in

Vietnam—before Walter Cronkite finally threw in the towel and declared victory for North Vietnam. No one wants to think about the deaths of Americans in any war, but that's the operative word: **war.** We're in a war.

John Murtha, or what is known as a "hawk" in today's Democratic Party, looked at what our military had accomplished and said, "Many say that the Army is broken." He complained, "This war is not going as advertised; this is a flawed policy wrapped in an illusion." While our allegedly "broken" military was in harm's way, Murtha then demanded that we withdraw our troops, claiming Americans had turned against the war: "The American public is way ahead of us."

Fed up with being endlessly told "the American people" had turned against the war in Iraq, Republicans asked the Democrats to show what they had in their hand. Republicans introduced a resolution that would do exactly what the Democrats claimed the "American people" were clamoring for: withdraw the troops. By a vote of 403–3, the House of Representatives wasn't willing to bet that "the American people" wanted to pull out of Iraq. (This vote also marked the first time in recent history that the Democrats did not respond to getting their butts kicked by demanding a recount.) The vote was all the more shocking because of what it said about the Democrats' motives in attacking the war—as well as alerting us to three members of Congress we really need to keep an eye on: Cynthia A. McKinney (D-GA), Robert Wexler (D-FL), and José E. Serrano (D-NY). All Democrats—go figure.

It is simply a fact that Democrats like Murtha were encouraging the Iraqi insurgents when they said the war was going badly and it was time to bring the troops home. Whether or not there was any merit to the idea, calling for a troop withdrawal—or "redeployment," as liberals pointlessly distinguished—would delay our victory and cost more American lives.

Democrats fondly remember the Vietnam War because their antiwar hysteria at home helped lose that war for us. Anti-war protests in America were a major source of moral support to the enemy. We know that not only from plain common sense but also from the statements of former North Vietnamese military leaders who evidently didn't get the memo telling them to lie. In an August 3, 1995, interview in the **Wall Street Journal,** Bui Tin, a former colonel in the North Vietnamese army, called the American peace movement "essential" to the North Vietnamese victory.

"Every day," he said, "our leadership would listen to world news over the radio at 9 A.M. to follow the growth of the American anti-war movement." And he named names: "Visits to Hanoi by people like Jane Fonda and former Attorney General Ramsey Clark and ministers gave us confidence that we should hold on in the face of battlefield reverses."

What are we to make of the fact that—as we learned from the 403–3 vote—the Democrats didn't even want to withdraw troops from Iraq? By their own account, there was no merit to their demands. Before the vote, Democrats could at least defend themselves from sedition by pleading stupidity. After the vote, we knew even they didn't believe what they were saying about the war. (Fortunately, thanks to that vote, the Islamofascists knew it, too.) The Democrats enjoy giving aid and comfort to the enemy for no purpose other than giving aid and comfort to the enemy. There is no plausible explanation for the Democrats' behavior other than that they long to see U.S. troops shot, humiliated, and driven from the field of battle. They fill the airwaves with treason, but when called to vote on their own proposals to withdraw troops, they disavow their own public statements. These people are not only traitors, they are gutless traitors.

Or—as President Bush put it—Murtha is a "fine man, a good man" who served with "honor and distinction," who "is a strong supporter of the United States military." Bush said he was sure Murtha's "decision to call for an immediate withdrawal of our troops . . . was done in a careful and thoughtful way." Defense Secretary Donald Rumsfeld also called Murtha "a fine man," saying, "[I]t's perfectly proper to have a debate over these things, and have a public debate." National Security Adviser Steve Hadley called in his praise of Murtha from South Korea, saying Murtha was "a veteran, a veteran Congressman and a great leader in the Congress."

The nation hadn't witnessed this much jingoistic hero worship since General Douglas MacArthur returned from Korea. Can't Republicans disagree with a Democrat veteran without praising him for six days straight? Even after Murtha had time to reflect on his insane proposal to withdraw troops in the middle of the war, his explanation was—according to the **Pittsburgh Post-Gazette**—that "his views began to change as attacks on U.S. troops rose this year and he realized that they 'had become the target.'" It took this military genius two and a half years to realize that the Islamic fascists were shooting at U.S. troops? A veritable Patton, this Murtha. In other words, Murtha would support U.S. troops fighting a war, but only provided the enemy does not make our troops "the target." I assume the logic of this position requires no further refutation than stating it.

It is simply axiomatic that any Democrat who ever brushed against the cloth of a military uniform is automatically a saint. How about our veterans? What about Sam Johnson, Duncan Hunter, Oliver North, Tailgunner Joe McCarthy? What about the Swift Boat Veterans? They were all brave men—braver than Kerry. Don't they deserve the same presumption of magnificence as Democrat veterans? You wouldn't know it the way Democrats are constantly carrying on about their military service, but there are a lot more Republican military veterans than there are Democrat veterans. Despite all their bluster about "chicken hawks," in the very Congress whence Murtha issued his demand to withdraw troops Republican veterans outnumbered Democrat veterans 87–62.[41]

Former representative Randy "Duke" Cunningham never did something as insane as proposing that we withdraw troops in the middle of a war. But a week after Murtha was proposing unconditional surrender in Iraq, Cunningham did admit to taking bribes as a congressman. Cunningham is a Navy ace. He shot down five MiGs, three in one day, including a North Vietnamese pilot with thirteen American kills. And yet Democrats don't get sweaty whenever

Cunningham's name is mentioned. Indeed, no Democrat breathed a word of Cunningham's unquestioned heroism before launching into angry denunciations of him. Representative Nancy Pelosi called Cunningham "the latest example of the culture of corruption." Even in his disgrace, Pelosi is not fit to polish Cunningham's boots. No liberal prefaces attacks on Colonel Oliver North with a recitation of North's magnificent service as a Marine. And unlike Murtha's, North's record is known. As long as liberals are going to be jock sniffers for war veterans, let's at least be equal about it. Why aren't Democrats obligated to praise North's war service before disputing his views?

After Murtha proposed withdrawing troops from Iraq, not one Republican attacked him personally. To the contrary, the only personal attacks leveled in response to Murtha's proposal came from John Murtha—who responded to Vice President Cheney's defense of the war by saying, "I like guys who've never been there that criticize us who've been there. I like that. I like guys who got five deferments and never been there and send people to war and then don't like to hear suggestions about what needs to be done." This must have been Murtha's way of thanking Cheney for referring to him as "my friend John Murtha" and "a good man, a Marine, a patriot."

Democrats brag endlessly about their war records and wave the flag like mad until it comes time to cough up the record. When challenged repeatedly over the years by various Vietnam veterans, Murtha has refused to release medical records on file with the Department of Defense proving he was entitled to his two Purple Hearts. A fellow Democrat, decorated Vietnam veteran, and congressional colleague who ran against Murtha in a primary, Don Bailey, has said on numerous occasions that Murtha admitted to him that he didn't deserve his Purple Hearts because he wasn't injured.[42]

But despite the peculiar murkiness of Murtha's war record, I will stipulate that the records he refuses to release are filled with exploits that would put Audie Murphy to shame. I am willing to impute greater courage to Murtha than exhibited outside the gates of Troy. I shall assume he fought at Valley Forge and in the Peloponnesian War. Whatever is in those elusive DOD files, Benedict Arnold was a hell of a better fighter than John Murtha. Benedict Arnold captured Fort Ticonderoga from the British, repelled a British invasion near Lake Champlain, and most significant, led the charge at the Battle of Saratoga. Yet and still, there is one thing we can't forgive even a great military hero for. Benedict Arnold was a traitor and we revile him, his name enshrined as a synonym for treason.

Perhaps the Democrats should resuscitate George McClellan as the original anti-war combat veteran of their party. McClellan was appointed commander of the Union Army by President Abraham Lincoln. But he was constantly carping about the war—he complained it was being fought against slavery instead of against the Confederate Army. McClellan repeatedly refused to go on the attack, saying Lincoln hadn't planned or provided the Union Army with sufficient armor. Finally, Lincoln fired McClellan in a letter that read, "My dear McClellan: If you don't want to use the Army I should like to borrow it for awhile." In 1864, McClellan ran against Lincoln as an anti-war Democrat. Lincoln faced huge internal opposition within the Union from people who didn't care about slavery and had grown weary of the war. Should people have backed McClellan over Lincoln because of McClellan's demonstrably superior military service? He would have allowed the dissolution of the Union and the continuation of slavery. But who could speak with greater certainty of the horrors of war than General George McClellan?

If those of us who didn't fight are wimps who

don't know the real truth of war, I say, Fine. Let's allow only combat veterans and active military members to vote. Everybody else shut up— including me and the vast majority of liberals. Kerry, Kerrey, Cleland, Inouye, and Murtha— that's it; they've got five votes. Until then, I don't want to hear anything more about "chicken hawks." Let's have an end to it.

The media's persistent use of the word **hawk** to describe Murtha was somewhat misleading. His 2005 demand that we withdraw troops in the middle of a war was not the first time Murtha failed to live up to the description. To be sure, in 1991 Murtha supported the Gulf War, as did most sentient primates to the political right of Gore Vidal. He's been dining out on that vote ever since.

In September 2002, amid loud claims that Murtha was "one of the first of President Bush's chief Democratic supporters" in the Gulf War, Murtha was described as a surprising naysayer on the Iraq War resolution. He said the president was going about it "the wrong way." Boasting of his superior credentials in matters of war and peace because he served, Murtha said, "I have found that the guys who haven't been there are more likely to vote to go to war."[43] In the end, ex-marine John Murtha voted in favor of the war resolution so that, henceforth, each one of his repeated criticisms of the Iraq War would be treated as a shocking about-face from an Iraq War supporter and provide reporters with a new excuse to retell the story of his dauntless valor as a soldier (with precious few details).

In September 2003, Murtha complained that the administration had "severely miscalculated" the war in Iraq and noted that the "latest polls show that we've lost the American public."[44] On May 6, 2004, he said, there weren't enough troops "to prevail in this war."[45] In his defense, at that point there had only been one successful free democratic election in Iraq—their first in some fifty years—as opposed to the three we've got under our belts now.

In September 2004—right about the time John Kerry mysteriously took up goose hunting—an increasingly unhinged Kerry began claiming Bush had a secret plan to reinstitute the draft as soon as the election was over. We're still waiting for our draft notices, Senator. Of course, Kerry also predicted during the campaign that he would release his complete military medical records, and that hasn't happened either.

Only one member of Congress backed Kerry's claims of an impending draft: John Murtha—based on secret inside information. Murtha said "he had learned through conversations with Pentagon officials that beginning in November, 'the

Bush administration plans to call up large numbers of the military Guard and Reserves, to include plans that they previously had put off to call up the Individual Ready Reserve.'"[46] What happened to those plans? Did no one in the media ever ask? And why were Democrats constantly excoriating Bush for not having a "plan," while simultaneously accusing him of having plans he didn't have?

But a year after complaining Bush had not deployed enough troops—and, indeed, that there were secret plans to reinstitute a draft—Murtha thought there were too many troops in Iraq. Murtha didn't like the "not enough troops" porridge, so then he tried the "too many troops" porridge, but he never found the "just enough troops" porridge.

So it wasn't that big a surprise when, in November 2005, demurely standing in front of seven American flags and a bust of John F. Kennedy, Murtha called for withdrawing all troops. But once again, the media treated Murtha's carping about the war as especially damaging to Bush inasmuch as it was coming from a "leading Democratic hawk on the Iraq war turned dove," as the New York **Daily News** put it.[47] The **Washington Post** breathlessly reported Murtha's call to withdraw troops under the headline "An Unlikely Lonesome Dove." The article noted that Murtha's "brand of hawkish-ness has never been qualified by the word 'chicken.' "[48]

How many times do we have to hear about the bolt of lightning with this guy? I did not know the road to Damascus was this long, with so many opportunities for conversion.

The Democrats and their pals in the media considered the vote in November 2005 on Murtha's proposal to withdraw troops from Iraq a Republican dirty trick. I see that my handy Democrat-to-Republican phrase book translates "dirty trick" into "up-or-down vote." Democrats think they should have a right to naysay the war effort and embolden the enemy without anyone calling them on it.

Deploying their usual fallacy of composition, liberals say that because they have a constitu-tional right to say stupid things, the stupid things they say must have merit. The Nazis had a consti-tutional right to march in Skokie, Illinois; that doesn't mean we should kill the Jews. Yes, Demo-crats are constitutionally entitled to be stupid. They are, after all, Democrats. But they're wrong and everyone knows it—including them, appar-ently, by a vote of 403–3. They say their "right" to carp pointlessly about Iraq is patriotic because that's what the "troops are fighting for"—

implicitly admitting, I might add, that our cause in Iraq is just. Yes, and I have a right to call Democrats blowhards, moral cowards, and traitors. (But in the interests of brevity I'll spare you the twenty minutes of praising them first.)

No one is disputing whether anyone has a right to say anything. What we're saying is—as indicated above—they are liars, cowards, and traitors. If the same person who told President Bush to nominate Harriet Miers to the Supreme Court were advising him on foreign policy and we invaded the Cayman Islands instead of Iraq, I, too, would be criticizing the war. But I wouldn't pretend that by calling for an immediate troop withdrawal, I wasn't encouraging the Cayman resistance force to hold on and fight harder. Clearly I'd be offering aid and comfort to the poolside waitresses, cabana boys, and scuba instructors we were fighting. But if there were a vote to withdraw troops from the Cayman Islands, I wouldn't pout and say that's not fair and then vote against it. It is simply a fact that naysaying the war and claiming that things are going so badly that troops must be withdrawn will encourage the enemy and demoralize our troops. Why can't the Democrats just admit that?

When our troops came under a bloody attack

in Somalia in 1993, President Clinton ordered a humiliating retreat—on the advice of John Murtha. Calling on Clinton to pull the troops out, Murtha said, "Our welcome has been worn out"—which I think is the essence of battlefield valor: the ability to know when staying another minute would just be tacky. And sure enough, perhaps out of force of habit, Clinton pulled out before finishing. Our troops emerged from a typically incompetent Clintonian mission with unvarnished heroism. They didn't run, Clinton ordered their retreat—a retreat that was later specifically cited by Osama bin Laden as proving to al Qaeda fighters that America was a "paper tiger." After a few blows, bin Laden said, America would run in defeat, "dragging their corpses and their shameful defeat."

In the current war, Democrats make the same proposal over and over again and then attack disagreement by portraying it as an attack on their "patriotism"—and it is a violation of law to question a liberal's patriotism.

Democrats screamed like stuck pigs when White House press secretary Scott McClellan meekly remarked that by proposing to withdraw troops in the middle of a war Murtha had adopted "the policy positions of Michael Moore." The **Chicago Tribune** said the "debate got ugly" when McClellan "lumped Murtha with filmmaker Michael Moore."[49] A **Boston Globe** columnist said the White House was "impugning the reputations and patriotism" of opponents by comparing them to Moore.[50] The **New York Times** called the comparison to Moore a "blistering statement"[51] and "an unusually critical statement."[52] Liberals could conceive of no greater calumny than associating a Democrat with Michael Moore.

To be sure, Moore's propaganda film **Fahrenheit 9/11** was pretty seditious. Moore compared the terrorists in Iraq killing American troops to the Minutemen of the American Revolution saying, "They are not the enemy" and "their numbers will grow—and they will win. Get it, Mr. Bush?"

But since when was Michael Moore persona non grata with liberals? A year earlier, **Times** columnist Paul Krugman had hailed **Fahrenheit 9/11** for telling "essential truths about leaders who exploited a national tragedy for political gain." The only time Democrats tried to dissociate themselves from Moore—other than when they found themselves positioned between him and a buffet table—was when McClellan compared him to John Murtha. Until that moment, virtually every prominent Democrat was rushing to associate himself more closely with Moore.

The Democrats' most beloved president ever, Bill Clinton, gave **Fahrenheit 9/11** a ringing endorsement in an interview with **Rolling Stone** magazine, saying, "I think every American ought to see it. . . . As far as I know, there are no factual errors in it" (and to be fair, it was more factual than Clinton's 1997 grand jury testimony) "but it may connect the dots a little too close—about the Saudis and the Bushes, and the terror and all. I'd like to see it again before making a judgment about whether I think it's totally fair."[53] Clinton might have been a little touchy on the subject of the Saudis, having accepted millions of dollars in donations from the Saudi royal family and Saudi businessmen for his presidential library,[54] to say nothing of their shared viewpoints on the status of women.

When Moore endorsed Democrat Wesley Clark for president, Clark proudly posted the endorsement on his website[55] and invited Moore to speak at his fundraisers. And, of course, Moore sat with Jimmy Carter at the Democratic National Convention, which drew more than a few stares, mostly from people wondering when the luxury box would collapse.

Tom Daschle and Terry McAuliffe attended the Washington, D.C., premiere of **Fahrenheit 9/11,** when Daschle was still Senate minority leader and McAuliffe was chairman of the DNC. David Boies, former election-stealing lawyer for sore loser Al Gore, was cohost of the event.

Moore's movie was being promoted by a veritable Who's Who of Democrat flacks, including Howard Wolfson, Hillary's former press secretary; Michael Feldman, former adviser to Al Gore's 2000 presidential race; and Mark Fabiani and Chris Lehane, former spokesmen for both Bill Clinton and Al Gore. Attending the advance screening of the movie in Manhattan were former UN ambassador and Democrat Richard Holbrooke; former Clinton adviser, Democrat Vernon Jordan; former Democratic presidential candidate Al Sharpton; Democrat Al Franken; and devoted Clinton supporter, Democrat Martha Stewart—representing convicted felons, a key segment of the Democratic vote. It was like a Diddy birthday party in the Hamptons, but with less gunplay.

If the Democrats don't want Republicans associating their good names with Michael Moore, perhaps they should stop associating with Michael Moore.

Or does revealing the Democrats' association with Michael Moore violate some criminal law I'm unaware of? Perhaps liberals will claim Moore is a "covert" agent with the CIA—

assuming a big, sweaty behemoth like Michael Moore could actually be concealed—and McClellan has outed him. Or does the fact that Murtha fought in Vietnam prohibit comment on anything he says? Does he have "absolute moral authority," too?

How about simply repeating what Democrats say? Can we do that? At the end of 2005, the Republican National Committee ran a Web ad showing various Democrats sharing their insights about the war in Iraq, with a white flag waving between each video clip:

> HOWARD DEAN, DEMOCRATIC NATIONAL COMMITTEE CHAIRMAN: The idea that we're going to win the war is an idea that, unfortunately, is just plain wrong.
> **[white flag waving]**
> SEN. BARBARA BOXER (D-CA): There's no specific time frame, but I would say the withdrawal has to start now, right after the elections, December 15th.
> **[white flag waving]**
> SEN. JOHN KERRY (D-MA): There is no reason, Bob, that young American soldiers need to be going into the homes of Iraqis in the dead of night, terrorizing kids and children, you know, women . . .

At the end of the commercial, the camera panned back to show a soldier watching the clips and ends with the message "Our soldiers are watching and our enemies are too."

What are they going to accuse us of now: taking their comments in context?

Guess who the Democrats sent out to attack the RNC ad? We're almost at the end of the chapter, so you shouldn't have to read ahead. Was it "NATO Paris office" Kennedy? Was it "Bad Back" Dean? (Dean avoided Vietnam by producing a note from his doctor and a fake limp at the army recruiting office—before repairing to Aspen for months of skiing.) No! None of these. It was one of the Democrats' surprise military war heroes. Having already used up the war service of Cleland, Kerry, and Murtha, this time it was . . . Senator Daniel Inouye, World War II Medal of Honor winner!

Inouye denounced the RNC ad, saying, "As a veteran of World War II, I know what it's like to fight a war and put your life on the line every day. I also know what it takes to win a war, and I know that politics and an attack machine like the president's plays no part in it." Remember: The alleged "attack machine" did nothing but show clips of Democrats talking about the war—and two of the Democrats weren't veterans or widows, so even under the "Cleland rule" we're allowed to criticize them!

The machismo of liberals about "real war" reached hysterical proportions in a Nicholas Kristof **New York Times** column decrying Bill O'Reilly's Fox News stories about liberals' war on Christmas by lecturing O'Reilly on "real war":

"Look, I put up a 'Christmas tree,' rather than a 'holiday tree,' and I'm sure Mr. O'Reilly is right that political correctness leads to absurd contortions this time of year. But when you've seen what real war does, you don't lightly use the word to describe disagreements about Christmas greetings. And does it really make sense to offer 58 segments on political correctness and zero on genocide?"[56] Kristof knows "real war" not because he's fought, mind you, but because he's covered wars as a scribbler. So no more chatter about liberals' war on Christmas, Fox News! Perhaps Kristof should raise the importance of "real war" with his colleague Frank Rich, who had a column on the gay cowboy movie **Brokeback Mountain,** just above Kristof's column that day. Is "real war" more important than a review of a movie about gay cowboys? Rich's column was one of four articles in the **Times** that day on **Brokeback Mountain,**[57] the tenth in the **Times** that week, and Rich's tenth gay-themed column for the year—out of forty-seven columns in all.

Liberals shape the debate with loud chanting, monopolize your brain through the TV, and then pull cheap parlor tricks to prevent any opposing arguments from being heard. **Her husband died! Her son died! His kid almost died, partly as a result of candidate Al's own negligence! His wife works at the CIA! He's a war hero! He covered a war in Darfur for the** New York Times! **Stop the hate!** They yell in unison, frightening people with their ferocity, and then announce that disagreement will not be permitted.

What crackpot argument can't be immunized by the Left's invocation of infallibility based on personal experience? **Today, a Democrat called for the institution of Communism in America, confiscation of all private property, forcible agricultural collectivization, imprisonment of intellectuals, and seizure of all handguns—moments before her entire family was wiped out in a tornado. Responses?** Perhaps the Democrats could find an orphaned child whose parents were brutally hacksawed to death to put forth their tax plan. If these Democrat human shields have a point worth making, how about allowing it to be made by someone we're allowed to respond to?

6 THE LIBERAL PRIESTHOOD: SPARE THE ROD, SPOIL THE TEACHER

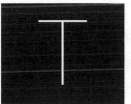

he only group in society that must be spoken of in reverential terms at all times, no matter what, is public school teachers. Attack the Boy Scouts, boycott Mel Gibson, put Christ in a jar of urine—but don't dare say anything bad about teachers. Unless you want it noted on your permanent record . . . We are simultaneously supposed to gasp in awe at teachers' raw dedication and be forced to listen to their incessant caterwauling about how they don't make enough money. Well, which is it? Are they dedicated to teaching or are they in it for the money? After all the carping about how little teachers are paid, if someone enters the teaching profession for the big bucks, aren't they too stupid to be teaching our kids?

Public school teachers are the new priesthood while traditional religion is ridiculed and maligned. As portrayed in the national pulpit of Hollywood, leaders of God-based religions are invariably lying scum. Not since Alfred Hitchcock's **I Confess** (1953) has Hollywood conceived of a priest or minister who was not a Nazi sympathizer, sexual predator, or some other breed of moral viper. Priests and ministers are smarmy, humorless hypocrites in movies like **The People Vs. Larry Flynt** (but the pornographer comes off favorably!), **Judgment** (child-molesting priest), and **The Runner Stumbles** (Dick Van Dyke as a hypocritical priest who impregnates a nun). In **Sister Act,** Whoopi Goldberg is a Reno lounge singer on the lam who shakes up the stodgy convent with her fun, upbeat attitude. The late, briefly aired, and little-missed TV show **The Book of Daniel** was about a drug-addicted Episcopal priest, Daniel, who had an alcoholic wife, a drug-dealing daughter, one gay son, and another son who was having sex with the bishop's daughter. Daniel's lesbian secretary was having sex with his sister-in-law. In other words, it was a typical Hollywood family drama.

By contrast, the moment a teacher walks onto the screen, you know who the hero is going to be. Teachers are Robin Williams in **Dead Poets Society,** Michelle Pfeiffer in **Dangerous Minds,** Jon Voight in **Conrack,** Richard Dreyfuss in **Mr. Holland's Opus,** Kevin Kline in **The Emperor's Club,** Morgan Freeman in **Lean on Me,** and Julia Roberts in **Mona Lisa Smile.** Among the Teacher-as-Saint movies are: **Goodbye, Mr. Chips** (three versions); **The Blackboard Jungle; Stand and Deliver;** and on and on and on. There are only two possible plots in movies about teachers: either inspirational teachers bring their passion and dedication to inner-city schools or inspirational teachers bring their passion and dedication to bored suburban kids.

In real life, these taxpayer-supported parasites are inculcating students in the precepts of the Socialist Party of America—as understood by retarded people. In early 2006, Sean Allen, a student at Overland High School in Colorado, taped his tenth-grade "world geography" teacher Jay Bennish ranting incoherently about Bush for twenty minutes during class. After a brief detour during which Bennish condemned the capitalist system, he proceeded briskly to his main point . . . George W. Bush is like Hitler!

Anyone who uses this adolescent cliché should not be in the tenth grade, much less teaching it. But Bennish thought he was Socrates, telling his students, "What I am trying to get you to do is think more in depth." How about this: Al Gore is like Hitler! Nancy Pelosi is like Hitler! Kanye West is like Hitler! Jay Bennish is like Hitler! And that guy on the Subway sandwich shop TV commercials who lost all the weight—I'm thinking: Hitler! (Are you cogitating deep thoughts?)

Although surely smarter than Bennish, not all American teenagers are bright enough to withstand the constant propaganda from authority figures who are grading them. Part of Bennish's Socratic dialogue that day included this exchange:

BENNISH: Who is probably the single most violent nation on planet Earth?! [sic]

UNIDENTIFIED STUDENT APPLE-POLISHER: We are!

BENNISH: The United States of America!

After Bennish was placed on a short, paid administrative leave, about 150 students—who can't place Spain on a map—"walked out" of the school to protest his suspension.

The new clergy not only teach children clever repartee such as **Bush is like Hitler!,** but they use their positions as taxpayer-supported wards of the state to demote the old religion, treating prayer, Bibles, and Christmas songs like hate crimes. At the Corl Street Elementary School in State College, Pennsylvania, children were led in a chant of "celebrate Kwanzaa" while Christmas carols were stripped of all religious content. At Pattison Elementary School in Katy, Texas, Christmas songs were banned, but students were threatened with grade reductions for refusing to sing songs celebrating other religious faiths. A school district in California prohibits teachers from mentioning Christmas or wearing Christmas jewelry. A New Jersey teacher was forced by an ACLU suit to abandon plans to take children to see the Broadway version of **A Christmas Carol.** In Panama City, Florida, the school principal changed the name of a Bible study group from "Fellowship of Christian Students" to "Fellowship of Concerned Students" and for good measure prohibited the club from advertising. A school administrator in Dallas, Texas, was reprimanded for using her e-mail to forward copies of President Bush's National Day of Prayer Proclamation, though the school district had no problem with employees using e-mail to send jokes, chain e-mails, and secular messages of encouragement.[1]

The worst scandal to hit the real churches in twenty years is the priest child-molestation scandal—which, by the way, pales in comparision to the teacher child-molestation problem. If only the depraved priests had had teachers' unions defending them, they'd still be running amok. All we'd ever hear about is how priests are hardworking, underpaid, and laboring under ghastly parishioner-priest ratios. The hero in every third Hollywood film would be a priest, and letters to the editor pages would be bristling with indignant letters complaining about how poorly priests are paid. Bumper stickers would suddenly appear, saying, "Someday, we'll have enough money for the Lord's House and the Air Force will hold bake sales to pay for its bombers." Most important, every school-age child in America would be required to attend Catholic Church for six hours a day—all subsidized by the taxpayer.

I'm sure there are a lot of wonderful, caring public school teachers out there. But there are also a lot of wonderful, caring Catholic priests. That doesn't stop people from noticing when there's a rash of bad ones. We'd all die without energy companies, but no liberal lips quiver when Enron comes under attack. Why are "educators" in government schools the only people on Earth who must universally be spoken of in hushed tones of religious worship? As it happens, public schools rival Enron when it comes to financial scandals and have more sex scandals per year than Catholic priests—thirty times more. But don't mention it or you'll be accused of hating teachers.

At least the public schools perform such a great service! According to David Salisbury, director of the Center for Educational Freedom at the CATO Institute, "Throughout the twentieth century, the scores of preschool age children on IQ and kindergarten readiness tests have climbed steadily upward. . . . It's not until they move up through grade school and on to high school that their performance declines."[2]

The international comparisons are breathtaking. American students excel on international tests in fourth grade, the earliest grade for which international comparisons are available. In fourth grade—after the public schools have had only a few years to do their damage—American students far outperform other countries in reading, math, and science. Fourth-graders score in the 92nd percentile in science, the 70th percentile in reading, and the 58th percentile in math. They beat 26 of 35 countries in reading literacy, including Germany, France, and Italy. The main educational difference between American children and Western European children at that age is that most American children have not been subjected to preschool, whereas almost all European children have.

But as American children spend more time in

school, their scores decline. By the eighth grade, Americans are merely average in international tests. By the twelfth grade—having received all the benefits of an American education—they are near the bottom. Math scores plummet from the 58th percentile in fourth grade to the 14th percentile in twelfth grade.

Most stunningly, in fourth grade Americans are in the 92nd percentile in science literacy— bested only by students in South Korea and Japan. Eight years later, American twelfth-graders' science scores have fallen to the 29th percentile. (For those of you who learned math in the U.S. public schools, going from 92nd to the 29th means it went down.) The only countries American twelfth-graders beat in science were Lithuania, Cyprus, and South Africa. If the U.S. Olympic gymnastics team could beat only Lithuania, Cyprus, and South Africa, there would be congressional investigations.[3]

Question: Is student achievement inversely proportional to time spent in U.S. public schools, or is there a correlation between poor student achievement and time spent in U.S. public schools?

Discuss.

So that's how schools are doing at their primary mission. But liberals scream bloody murder and accuse you of attacking teachers whenever anyone mentions any problems with the public schools, no matter how meekly (unless "problems" means only "not paying teachers enough").

Through their girly guilt-mongering, Democrats have turned public school teachers (or as I call them, "disinformational facilitators") into religious icons. It's a good gig, especially if you don't even have to teach. At private schools, 80 percent of the personnel are teachers. By contrast, at public schools only about 50 percent of the personnel are actual teachers—most of the rest are cogs in the endless layers of machinery of the "education" bureaucracy.[4] This would be like having 26 full-time coaches for a 26-man baseball team.

It's very important for the Democrats to control the public schools. John Dewey, the founder of public education in America, said, "You can't make Socialists out of individualists—children who know how to think for themselves spoil the harmony of the collective society which is coming, where everyone is interdependent." You also can't make socialists out of people who can read, which is probably why Democrats think the public schools have nearly achieved Aristotelian perfection. For Lenin it was "Give me your four-year-olds, and in a generation I will build a Socialist state." For Hitler it was "Let me control the textbooks and I will control the state." For the Democrats it's "Let us control the schools and in a generation no one will able to read."

Unfazed by international comparisons showing that American children fall behind with each additional year of school, Democrats want to get our students started falling behind even sooner. In his acceptance speech at the Democratic National Convention, John Kerry proposed "investing" in Head Start, Early Start, Smart Start, Jump Start, Kick Start—and got a standing ovation. He mentioned the military and you could hear crickets in the convention hall. Al Gore's 2000 Democratic platform included federal preschool for every child in America. Sandra Feldman of the American Federation of Teachers says America "can't afford not to" adopt a preschool program like the French—whom our fourth-graders crush in international comparisons, by the way. Remember how factories in the old Soviet Union stayed open year after year even though half the products they turned out were defective? U.S. public schools have become like that, which is why Democrats feel so much at home in the education business.

Democrats like to say, "Sure, Republicans are all for fetuses, but once the child is born, do they care?" Their yardstick for caring is: Where do you stand on creating jobs for public school teachers? The rule used to be that you could be anti-abortion provided you supported creating more welfare bureaucrats. **Los Angeles Times** columnist Robert Scheer began a 1995 column with "Love the fetus, damn the child," and then went on a jeremiad against "pro-life"—his quotes—senators Bob Dole and Phil Gramm for putting together a welfare reform bill that "will make abortion a compelling choice for poor women." Scheer referred to this monstrosity as "Dole's bill." Once "Dole's bill" turned out to be a smashing success, it was renamed "Clinton's welfare reform bill" or, for short, "President Clinton's crowning achievement."

So now the new rule is, in order to be the "right kind" of pro-lifer, you don't have to support massive increases in spending on welfare programs; you have to support massive increases in spending on public school teachers. When he was running for president in 2004, Al Sharpton said, Republicans "love the fetus and they cut the funds from the baby. I don't understand this jaded love for children where you cut daycare, cut childcare, cut anything—Head Start—but yet you want to protect the fetus coming into the world." For liberals, a human life begins at the precise moment the person starts filling out his first application for a government job.

Howard Dean says Democrats should not turn their backs on "pro-life people"—but only if they are "the right kind of pro-life person," by which he means supportive of every possible teachers' union giveaway. Whenever the Democrats talk about increasing spending on "the children," what they mean is sending more dollars to useless government bureaucrats, even if they never encounter a child on the job. Until no one in America earns more than a kindergarten teacher, the nation does not value human life.

The only work Senator Chris Dodd has ever done in twenty-five years in the Senate is to try to nationalize kindergarten and prekindergarten child care. It's somehow cruel and unfair not to federalize all education workers in America. And there are a lot of them—teachers, substitute teachers, assistant teachers, substitute assistant teachers, teachers' safety instructors, teachers' pension managers, teachers' health care providers, teachers of teachers—and we haven't even gotten to the principals, assistant principals, and superintendents. Democrats won't rest until we have achieved a national average class size of 1 teacher for every .03 students.

Dodd's 2001 bill on "childcare" is typical. With a title that sounds suspiciously as though a teacher named it—"Focus on Committed and Underpaid Staff for Children's Sake Act"— Dodd's bill spent about two sentences talking about children and the next 90 pages detailing copious benefits packages for public school teachers. In a sentiment born of pure class hatred, teachers are enraged that they often earn less than members of the sweaty working class who probably don't even hold master's degrees in "education theory." Consequently, the Democrats are constantly introducing bills to legislatively proclaim that all teachers are worth more than plumbers, truck drivers, and other professions whose members do not vote for Democrats. Dodd's bill couldn't even make it through the "findings" section without long diatribes about the indignity of bus drivers earning more than teachers.

After two very brief references to "the children" at the beginning, the bill gets right to the heart of the matter: increasing the salaries of "child care providers."

Finding number (3) cites "a growing body of research" showing the value of "well-compensated child care providers."

Finding number (4) bitterly quotes Department of Labor statistics showing that in 1999, "the average wage for a child care provider was $7.42 per hour," and the "median wage of a family child care provider in 1999 was $264 weekly, or $13,728 annually." These figures apparently include the salaries of teenage babysitters and after-school care at Grandma's house. One major reason child care providers show up as being paid so little is the large number of liberal Democrat cabinet nominees who pay their nannies off the books. The average teacher's salary that year was $43,300, compared with $40,100 for other full-time workers—who, I note, don't get summers off or leave work at 3:00 P.M.

Finding number (5) expresses the class hatred of teachers toward the working class, complaining that "child care providers earn less than bus drivers ($26,460), barbers ($20,970), and janitors ($18,220)." Inexplicably, Derek Jeter's income from the previous year was not mentioned here. How about this: When the bus drivers' failure rate of getting kids to school gets up to around 50 percent, which is the teachers' failure rate of teaching kids, then we can talk about equal pay for teachers and bus drivers.

Finding number (6) complains about "woefully inadequate" health care benefits for child care professionals.

Finding number (7) returns to the important matter of paying "childcare workers" more.

Finding number (8) complains, "Teachers leaving the profession are replaced by staff with less education and formal training in early child development."

Finding number (9) complains again about teachers' "low wages and limited benefits." (This can't be mentioned often enough!)

Finding number (10) says that everyone suffers "the consequences of inadequate compensation" for child care providers, principally the providers, of course, but also—way down on the list—even the children.

The eleventh and final finding praises state programs that increase the "compensation of child care providers" and notes that the states could get better child care providers "by offering financial incentives, including scholarships and compensation increases, that range from $350 to $6,500 annually."

The cost of the bill that promised to make our fourth-graders as dumb as the French within five years was $5 billion. Every part of Dodd's Teachers' Union Wish-List bill was calculated to produce stupid children chock-full of behavioral problems.

The main reason good teachers aren't paid more is bills like Dodd's. Educating children is no longer the primary purpose of the public schools. Today their purpose is to employ 2 million people. Back in 1985, Albert Shanker, president of the American Federation of Teachers, said, "When school children start paying union dues, that's when I'll start representing the interests of school children."[5] The public may be confused on this issue, but the teachers' unions— and the Democrats—are not. If you gave all the money in the United States to the public schools, they would not improve; they would simply cost more. The teachers' unions are tenaciously committed to expanding their workforce, and paying every teacher the same salary, whether that teacher is world-class and deserves $200,000 a year or is utterly incompetent and deserves to be fired—possibly imprisoned.

Putting children in government schools at younger and younger ages does not help the children; it merely expands teachers' unions' membership rolls. As any normal human could tell you—and studies now confirm!—it's better for a child under five years old to be at home with his mother than in child care, no matter how "stimulating" the environment. The National Institute of Child Health and Human Development studied more than 1,300 children in ten different states for seven years and concluded that the more time a child spends in nonparental child care, the more behavioral problems the child will have. Yes, perhaps given a choice between being left alone in a crack house as opposed to Chris Dodd's pre-K child care, the child care would win. But in most cases, that's not the choice. The Democrats' solution is to raise taxes to pay for preschool child care, which will require more mothers to work outside the home to pay the taxes, which will require them to put their children in government child care. Except welfare mothers. Those are the only women in America who Democrats think should not work.

The throwing-money-at-it approach to educating children has been tried so often that teachers are now among the highest-paid workers in America, with thousands of teachers—about 20,000—already earning more than $100,000 a year.

Using data from the U.S. Department of Labor on household median earnings, Ohio University economics professor Richard Vedder found, "Weekly pay for teachers in 2001 was about the same (within 10 percent) as for accountants, biological and life scientists, registered nurses, and editors and reporters, while teachers earned significantly more than social workers and artists." Of the seven professions Vedder compared, the only ones with higher weekly pay than teachers were lawyers and judges, which, as Vedder said, "one would expect, given that the educational training to become a lawyer is longer and more demanding."[6]

Of course, only teachers get long summer vacations, "professional development" days, snow days, and every conceivable federal holiday. It appears that the only people who get better compensation than teachers for nine months' work are professional baseball players. So in order to compare apples and apples, Vedder compared hourly wages as calculated by the National Compensation Survey of the Bureau of Labor Statistics, based on the teachers' self-reports for how many hours they worked weekly.

First of all, relying on self-reports of how many hours someone works is like relying on teenage boys' self-reports about how much sex they're having (90 percent say they have had sex, 60 percent with Pamela Anderson). Nonetheless, comparing hourly wages based on the teachers' self-reports, Vedder says, "Teachers earned more per hour than architects, civil engineers, mechanical engineers, statisticians, biological and life scientists, atmospheric and space scientists, registered nurses, physical therapists, university-level foreign-language teachers, librarians, technical writers, musicians, artists, and editors and reporters." Only lawyers, engineers, and doctors earned more. And a lawyer can't call in a "substitute lawyer" when he needs a "personal day." (Plus it's a lot harder for doctors, lawyers, and engineers to have sex with their clients.)

Judging solely by the amount of time teachers spend writing letters to the editor complaining about how poorly paid they are, teachers **seem** to have a lot of free time.

A Nexis search of all news documents during the years 2000 to 2005 that included the words "letters to the editor," "teachers," "underpaid," and "overworked" produced 168 documents. The same formulation for other professions produced these results:

doctors . . . . 60 documents
lawyers . . . . 30 documents
secretaries . . . . 30 documents
reporters . . . . 29 documents
firefighters . . . . 23 documents
marines . . . . 15 documents
priests . . . . 6 documents
carpenters . . . . 2 documents
waiters . . . . 1 document

Of course, we can't be sure that these were all letters to the editor complaining about the low pay of teachers, marines, firefighters, and so on; they might have all been letters complaining that teachers are "overworked" and "underpaid" **compared** to marines, firefighters, and others.

In 2002, Bob Chase, the president of the National Education Association (NEA), complained that teachers don't make as much as engineers ($74,920) or lawyers ($82,712). But I'm thinking, Why stop at engineers and lawyers? Why shouldn't kindergarten teachers earn as much as Tom Hanks and Julia Roberts? A better benchmark comparison for public school teachers might be private school teachers. Teachers in the private sector earn about 60 percent less than public school teachers.[7] And their students actually learn to read.

Comparing hourly earnings still does not quite compare apples and apples or even apples and oranges—more like apples to grapes—because of the massive benefits packages public school teachers receive. Teachers have far more generous pensions than other professional workers, allowing them to retire earlier. In 1995, while the average retirement age for teachers was fifty-nine, for professional workers whose only government pension is Social Security it was almost sixty-four years old.[8] Despite this, the NEA complains about teachers' pensions being offset against their Social Security benefits. So in addition to having taxpayers foot the bill for government pensions more generous than Social Security benefits, they also want the teachers to get their full Social Security benefits.

Pop Quiz: If a private sector retiree has to get by on Social Security and a retired public school teacher is entitled to two pensions, which one is hosing the American taxpayer more? Please show your work.

Then there is health insurance. Many public school medical insurance plans still do not require that teachers contribute any payment whatsoever toward the premium—unheard of in the private sector—and woe to the politician who proposes increasing teachers' co-pay from $5 to $10. Finally, no matter what happens to the rest of the economy, teachers don't have good years and bad years. Public school teachers have absolute job security, which is also worth something.

According to Vedder's analysis of the federal data, teachers receive a package of benefits worth more than 26 percent of their salaries, compared with benefits packages worth 17 percent of a salary in the private sector. "All told," Vedder says, "teachers' average hourly compensation plus benefits exceeds the average for all professional workers by roughly 10 to 15 percent."

Congratulations to the teachers' unions! But do we have to keep hearing about how underpaid, overworked, and underappreciated teachers are? It's like the "Islam is a religion of peace" mantra—and similarly based in reality. One begins to wonder if schools of education teach anything besides how mistreated teachers are. Everyone simply asserts, as one columnist did in the **Los Angeles Times,** "Teachers are underpaid."[9] The author went on to say that teachers "give it their best and try to make it work." That must not be easy, considering they have to labor with the knowledge that someone, somewhere earns more per hour than they do. Only an electorate educated in a school system like ours would fall for the argument that teachers aren't paid enough. Hey—maybe these teachers aren't so dumb after all.

A lot of people in America have difficult jobs. There are men sleeping in their boots in Afghanistan right now so the rest of us can sleep peacefully at night. There are store owners who haven't taken a vacation for twenty years. There are entrepreneurs working weekends and risking everything for an idea that will make the world better or safer—or on the other hand might fail and land them in bankruptcy court. (And they don't get summers off.)

The very fact that teachers have three months off in the summer and can hold other jobs is indignantly cited as further proof that teachers are underpaid. Shelley Potter, president of the San Antonio Alliance of Teachers and Support Personnel, told the **San Antonio Express-News,** "For most teachers, it's a matter of necessity to work that extra job to make ends meet."[10] Teachers seem not to realize that everyone else works in the summer, too.

In fact, almost 80 percent of teachers do not take second jobs in the summer. That's according to a lachrymose op-ed in the **New York Times** bemoaning the idea that teachers should spend any of their three-month summer vacation working. "One day," the writers say, teachers are "shaping minds, a moral force in the lives of the young people they teach and know, and in some ways the architects of the future of the nation"— such as by telling students, "Bush is like Hitler"— "The next day they're serving cocktails and selling plasma TV's at the mall."[11] The indignity!

If we're choosing the most underpaid profession, my pick is doctors. They spend a minimum of seven years in school, with somewhat more rigorous schedules than those of education majors. When they finally graduate from medical school, they will leave with $100,000 to $200,000 of student loan debt. Their reward for all this hard work and deferred gratification is a residency, where they will work up to 120 hours a week, often 36 hours consecutively, for the princely starting salary of $29,000 to $37,000. Finally the big payoff comes—but there are still the student loans to pay off and malpractice insurance premiums of $50,000 to $300,000 per year. Some doctors will clean their own office toilets when they start off just to make ends meet.[12] According to Department of Labor statistics, the mean average salary for doctors ranges from $106,000 a year for podiatrists to $190,000 a year for surgeons. Which isn't bad—why, it's nearly as much as a school principal makes in New York City!

Compare the years of training for a doctor with the educational achievements of teachers. As summarized by Frederick Hess of the American Enterprise Institute—who has a Harvard master's degree in education himself—"Undergraduate education majors typically have lower SAT and ACT scores than other students, and those teachers who have the lowest scores are the most likely to remain in the profession. The lower the quality of the undergraduate institution a person attends, the more likely he or she is to wind up in the teaching profession."[13] In a 1999 interview, Hoover Institution fellow Thomas Sowell was asked what change in America would give him the greatest satisfaction if he could snap his fingers and make it happen. He answered, "Do away with schools of education and departments of education. Close them down." The "Mickey Mouse courses that you have to take to enter the field," he said, were driving away many of the best people from teaching. Sowell also remarked that "the most childish letters I receive in response to my newspaper column come from teachers. . . . They seem to think that they can simply make up their facts, and that they can psychoanalyze me. They like to tell me, for instance, 'You must have had a bad experience of teachers.' "[14]

In 2001, only 60 percent of education students taking the basic teachers' licensing exam in Virginia were able to pass. The test asked questions like these:

Martin Luther King Jr.(*insert the correct choice*) _____
for the poor of all races:

> **a. spoke out passionately**
> **b. spoke out passionate**
> **c. did spoke out passionately**
> **d. has spoke out passionately**
> **e. had spoken out passionate**

Anyone who could not answer that question should not be allowed to serve food in a public school much less teach at one, but nearly half the aspiring teachers got it wrong. Acting quickly to remedy this crisis, the Virginia state board of education lowered the requirements, making it easier to pass while getting the above question wrong.[15]

The same thing happened in Massachusetts in 1998. Fifty-nine percent of candidates for teaching positions failed a basic-skills test geared to eighth-graders. One-third of the test takers couldn't even pass the basic-skills section. In response, the state education commissioner, Frank W. Haydu III, suggested that the passing grade be lowered from 77 percent to 66 percent. When informed that one-third of applicants flunked the test, he said, "Okay, but that's still less than half, right?" (Only the last sentence is a joke.)

Defenders of the illiterate Massachusetts teachers at FairTest.org—presumably illiterate Massachusetts teachers themselves—denounced the exam, claiming there were "major substantive and administrative problems with the test." According to FairTest, the first "fundamental" defect with the test was that some teachers didn't grasp that their scores would count and thus were denied—I quote—"due process legal right to adequate time to prepare for a high-stakes exam." Also, according to FairTest, the company that created the test "has a history of making and selling defective products." (FairTest enclosed an addendum explaining to their members what the terms **history** and **test** meant.) Thus, for example, FairTest says a "study" found that "the exam was 'fundamentally flawed' because of the lack of any demonstrable relationship between test scores and initial teacher competency."[16] Genuine teacher competency is measured by how capable a teacher is at taking away a fourth-grader's Bible and passing out condoms.

In 2005, a Bronx public school teacher paid a homeless man with a history of mental illness to take the state teacher certification test in his place after the teacher had repeatedly failed the test. The test results drew suspicions because the homeless man did so well on the test. (That's not a joke.)

Obviously, the solution is to keep paying teachers more. At least that's the conclusion the courts keep coming to—which is probably why the Constitution did not give judges the power to tax. In the mid-1980s, a federal judge in Kansas City implemented liberals' dream program to improve the public schools. The judge imposed a $2 billion tax hike on the citizens of Kansas City in order to build opulent public school campuses replete with Olympic-size pools with an underwater viewing room, 25-acre wildlife sanctuaries, a model United Nations with simultaneous translation facilities—and of course, higher teachers' salaries. After twenty years of the perfect experiment in liberal education theory, there was less racial integration in the schools—the purported purpose of the plan—and black test scores hadn't improved one jot. Somewhat amazingly, at one high school, the reading scores of black males were completely unchanged from freshman to senior year.

Between 1982 and 2001, spending on New York City public schools increased by more than 300 percent, clocking in at $11,474 per pupil annually. Only Washington, D.C., that hotbed of educational achievement, spends more per student. By contrast, the average tuition for private elementary schools is less than $4,000 and around $6,000 for private secondary schools.

And yet the New York State courts officially found in 2003 that graduates of New York City's public schools are not competent to sit on a jury. The courts found that the schools were not providing children with such skills as "basic literacy, calculating and verbal skills necessary to enable children to eventually function productively as civil participants capable of voting and serving on a jury." In response, the courts ordered that yet more money be spent on the same failing public schools.

It's all academic to judges who send their kids to private schools anyway. They have no contact with all the things they extol, like public education and the marvel that is the New York City subway system. Rich liberals take the subway once a year and are stunned at how big it is. Liberals are quite confident that people in Queens will be happy with their decisions.

When not complaining about their low salaries, teachers say it's not the money, it's respect they want. A New Jersey public school principal complained to the **New York Times** that he has to leave the country to be "reminded of the high regard with which the rest of the world views his occupation." According to the principal, back in America, "You'll be at a party and someone will ask what you do. You'll say you're a teacher and they'll say, 'That's nice,' and move on."[17] They're probably ashamed of how little they make compared with school principals.

It's tough to make the case that teachers are not valued in American society—in addition to being paid more per hour than architects, civil engineers, mechanical engineers, space scientists, registered nurses, musicians, artists, and editors and reporters. According to a Harris poll taken in 2005, teachers were ranked as the third most "prestigious" profession, tied with firemen and just behind scientists and doctors. This placed teachers ahead of military officers, nurses, police officers, and priests.[18]

You would think there would be a little more humility in a profession where the main competition comes from nuns. Even nuns, who have taken a vow of poverty, aren't lavished with praise the way public school teachers are.

When Jason Kamras received his National Teacher of the Year Award from President Bush in 2005, he hailed the other members of his profession for working "tirelessly every day doing wonderful and challenging work." And he added, they "do so almost always without recognition." Without recognition? Kamras was in the Rose

Garden of the White House being recognized by the president of the United States of America. I'm guessing they don't teach irony at schools of education.

But you know who does work tirelessly every day doing wonderful work and almost always without recognition? Electrolysists. Plumbers. Cooks. Cable guys. Farmers. Maids. Deliverymen. In fact, just about everybody who's not a celebrity works tirelessly every day doing wonderful work and almost always without recognition. The president does not give out a Fireman of the Year Award, Policeman of the Year Award, Plumber of the Year Award, Heart Surgeon of the Year Award, Physical Therapist of the Year Award. Apart from Hollywood actors, teachers are the most incessantly praised profession in America. Run a Google search of "Teacher of the Year" and you'll get almost 40 million hits—more even than "Mother of the Year"!

The National Football League has a Teacher of the Year Award for teachers nominated by players, and awards the winner a trip to a bowl game and $5,000. Wal-mart runs an annual Teacher of the Year contest, awarding fifty schools a $10,000 grant and the national winner's school another $25,000. The Veterans of Foreign Wars has a Teacher of the Year Award, giving teachers at three different grade levels $1,000 for themselves and another $1,000 to the schools. Toyota has a Toyota Family Literacy Teacher of the Year Award that awards $5,000 to the winner. The National Fire Protection Association has a Teacher of the Year Award. The World Affairs Council of Washington, D.C., has a Teacher of the Year Award. The California Masons have a Teacher of the Year Award. The Kirksville Chapter of Sigma Xi in Missouri has a Teacher of the Year Award. This is in addition to all the state Teacher of the Year Awards generally announced at a big ceremony with the governor. No wonder kids can't read or write—their teachers are always jetting off to some fancy event to pick up their Teacher of the Year Awards.

In California, teachers get discounted mortgages and car loans, and tuition reimbursement.[19] The Department of Housing and Urban Development has a program that allows teachers to buy homes in revitalized areas at a 50 percent discount off the sale price. In other areas, discounts and special deals are offered to teachers by bookstores, office supply stores, computer stores, and cell phone companies.

Oddly enough, public school teachers aren't offered discounts on condoms, even ones sold for use just on school grounds. They should take that up at the next NEA conference. It's all about respect, people. One teacher who managed to find time to write a letter to the editor—despite the long, long hours teachers work—to complain that her salary was "very sad indeed," proposed yet more goodies that could be given to public school teachers, such as day care "for teachers only."[20] Just don't say teachers already have plenty of benefits or the Democrats will accuse you of hating teachers. You must weep with admiration at the mere mention of "teachers." Soon one of every five people in America will be part of the "education" industry and the rest of us will work to support their salaries and benefits.

In 2004, New York City investigators secretly filmed five assistant principals whiling away their days at Lord & Taylor, Macy's, Kmart, and Duane Reade. About the same time the courts were concluding that New York public schools could not even produce a competent O.J. juror, the five "educators" were caught on tape arriving late, leaving early, and spending the time in between shopping. They could afford it: New York City taxpayers were paying them between $65,000 and $106,000 per year to do nothing. The five assistant principals had been reassigned to administrative duties after some reshuffling in the public schools eliminated their jobs. They refused to perform any of the tasks assigned to them on the grounds that the tasks were not within the job description for "assistant principal."[21] Apparently, buying ballet tickets and shopping at Lord & Taylor were within the job description.

In January 2005, New York public school teacher Frances Levine was arrested for attempted murder in connection with a brutal attack on the principal of her school. According to police, Levine's boyfriend attacked the principal, Wanda Rivera-Switalski, outside her Queens home early one morning, riding up on a motorcycle and slashing her with a box cutter so many times she needed more than a hundred stitches. Before the attack, Levine was overheard haranguing her boyfriend, saying, "When are you going to do it? She already has fired three of my friends. Quit procrastinating." You know a school is hurting when the teachers can't even get murder assignments completed on time. Levine's salary at the time of the attack was $57,804.[22]

In April of that year, a Brooklyn teacher earning $69,359 per year was arrested on the Lower East Side of Manhattan for possessing illegal "gravity knives," which can be opened by the force of gravity alone. When the police ran his name, they discovered he had also been arrested in 1993 for disorderly conduct and in 2001 for possession of marijuana, resisting arrest, and obstruction of governmental administration.[23] In other words, he had a criminal record so extensive he might actually have had trouble landing a job with the New Orleans police department. After his earlier arrest, the teacher had simply been reassigned.

In July, the superintendent of the Yonkers school district was indicted for perjury and evidence tampering for trying to cover up his appointment of a twenty-four-year-old friend of his daughter's to a $90,000-a-year job with the school.[24] He later pleaded guilty.

Also in July, Matthew Kaye, a high school social studies teacher in Queens, faced disciplinary action for calling in sick eleven days in December and February when, in fact, he was pursuing his real job in professional wrestling. I'd long suspected that professional wrestling was fake. Who knew that teaching was, too? The school discovered this deception by the simple expedient of reading Kaye's wrestling website. Randi Weingarten, the president of the city teachers' union, defended Kaye, saying it was the fault of low teacher salaries: "Teachers frequently have second jobs or second careers because you just can't make it on a teacher's salary these days."[25] By his own account, the thirty-one-year-old Kaye was making $42,000 a year, more than double the median income in the state for a one-person family. When he realized he might lose his lucrative teaching job, he said, "I'd work overtime without pay. I told them I'd do anything I could to keep my job."[26]

In addition to grand theft, disorderly conduct, weapons charges, and attempted murder, there were also 180 claims of sexual abuse by New York City public school teachers in 2005—all before May. One involved a male public school teacher in Queens having sex with two female students, sixteen and eighteen years old. A male public school teacher on Staten Island was charged with flashing teenage girls over a period of several months. Two female teachers at the High School for Health Professions and Human Services in Manhattan were caught having sex with male students; one of the two was pregnant with a student's child. Another female public school teacher at a Brooklyn public school—who was twenty-seven years old and earning $45,583 a year—was caught passionately kissing a fifteen-year-old student alone in her classroom.[27] Some of these "stay in school!" campaigns have simply got to be rethought.

Analyzing the data from a survey by the American Association of University Women Educational Foundation, statistics professor Charol Shakeshaft estimates that between 1991 and 2000, roughly 290,000 students were subjected to physical sexual abuse by teachers or other school personnel.[28] In her report for the U.S.

Department of Education, Shakeshaft says that about one in every ten American children has been sexually abused in some way at school.[29]

Compare that with Catholic priests. A study by the U.S. Conference of Catholic Bishops said that 10,667 allegations of sexual abuse of children had been made between 1950 and 2002. Multiply that by four to account—generously—for unreported cases and it comes to 821 children abused by priests per year. Priests: 820 abused children per year; educators: 32,000 abused children per year. For those of you who went to public schools, 32,000 is greater than 820.

It's not just New York City—the school district that spends the second most money per pupil—where the educators are committing major felonies. In the school district that spends the most per pupil, Washington, D.C., members of the Washington Teachers' Union stole nearly $5 million from union coffers. According to the **Washington Post,** the education bureaucrats used the money to purchase "Escada handbags, Ferragamo shoes, St. John knits, Baccarat vases, Rosendorf-Evans furs, Herend plates and a 288-piece set of Tiffany silverware" (or as the teachers' union referred to these items, "school supplies"). Some of the union money was used for a $2,000 donation to Hillary Clinton's Senate campaign and a $9,000 donation to the Democratic National Committee, which was later returned. The president of the union hired the union handyman to be her personal chauffeur, for which she paid him a salary of $125,000.[30] Perhaps Randi Weingarten could start citing this case to complain that even chauffeurs earn more than teachers!

This isn't just a problem of urban schools. Fun teacher felonies pop up in comfortable suburban school districts, too. In June 2004, an assistant superintendent on Long Island was charged with grand larceny for stealing over $1 million from school funds, which she spent on mortgages for four homes, a Lexus, several motorized water scooters, and a massive credit card bill. The "educator," Pamela C. Gluckin, pleaded not guilty (but returned a quarter of a million dollars). One gets the distinct impression that Ms. Gluckin never needed to moonlight as a cocktail waitress.[31]

One month later, a superintendent on Long Island was also accused of stealing over a million dollars from school funds to buy furniture, Caribbean vacations, and a $372,000 home in Nevada he shared with a male exotic dancer. The residents of the town were shocked, because, as the **New York Times** put it, the superintendent was "a progressive leader who spoke of social justice, made condoms available in the high school," which, to my way of thinking, made him a prime suspect for this type of behavior. Between bouts of helping out his male dancer friend, he started a service program dedicated to the idea that "the privileged class should give something back"—most of all to him, apparently.[32] After all, he had two master's degrees and a doctorate in education from Columbia. It's not like he was a bus driver or something.

They are the hardest-working, most underpaid workers in America.

Most public schools are—at best—nothing but expensive babysitting arrangements, helpfully keeping hoodlums off the streets during daylight hours. At worst, they are criminal training labs, where teachers sexually abuse the children between drinking binges and acts of grand larceny.

With public schools like this, students are going to learn, if they are going to learn, because of their parents, not because of any inspiration they get from schools. Dwight Eisenhower, Abraham Lincoln, John Marshall—all these men were taught to read at home by their parents. Felix Frankfurter went to public school on the Lower East Side in Manhattan. Undeterred by the large class size and trifling teacher salaries in his tenement neighborhood, he went on to graduate first in his class from Harvard Law School. So don't tell me smaller class size is the key to educational achievement.

The "class size" shibboleth appeals to yuppies' desire to have the best of everything. The tiniest ratio of students to teachers is a status symbol that is supposed to indicate their commitment to education. Tell it to teachers in Japan, Brazil, and Korea, who routinely teach classes numbering fifty students or more and whose students beat ours on international comparisons. Reducing class size doesn't improve educational achievement; it reduces the workload for each teacher.

How about extending the ratio measure of excellence to other professions, like mailmen and butchers? **We must lower the ratio of mailmen to letters. The optimum number of letters for a single mail carrier to deliver is 500 letters a day. Our mail is too important!** Or: **The butcher/steak ratio is a shame to our nation. We have the highest ratio in the world of butchers to cuts of beef. France has three times as many butchers per cut of meat.**

But if you say that, you will be accused of attacking teachers. People talk about public school teachers with breathless zeal, as if they'll be shot by the Nazi SS if they are not enthusiastic enough. I defy anyone to tell me under a lie detector test that they would not have gone to exactly the same college and gotten exactly the same SAT scores if their entire high school student body had matriculated at the worst public school in New York City. At Harvard, 90 percent of the students come from families above the median income in America ($42,000 a year). Nearly 80 percent come from families in the top 20 percent ($80,000).[33] As this indicates, kids from good families could be taught by lunatics in an insane asylum and they would still do well on their SATs. The professional classes can teach their own, except they can't because they're out working to pay taxes to support high teacher salaries. And students with bad parents are manifestly not being helped by the public schools. They could—if the schools could fire the bad teachers and reward the good teachers. But the teachers' unions won't allow that. The education establishment's answer to its own incompetence is to demand more money so it can keep doing more of the same. The Democrats' answer is to say teachers are the most hardworking, underappreciated, self-sacrificing people in the universe.

It's well past time for liberalism to be declared a religion and banned from public schools. No other religion has the right to propagandize to children for twelve years, six hours a day. In 2001, the **New York Times** hysterically denounced the Supreme Court decision in **Good News Club v. Milford Central School** for allowing religious groups equal standing with other after-school groups. The **Times** complained that "children that young are unlikely to discern that the religious message of authority figures who come to the school each day to teach does not carry the school's endorsement." The school's own "authority figures" are usually teaching the youngsters how to put condoms on zucchini, training them in the catechism of recycling, or telling them Bush is like Hitler. Sending a mixed message about government "authority figures" might interfere with the state's ability to turn small children into Good Germans inculcated in the liberal religion. Allowing Christians to be one of many after-school groups induces hysteria not only because liberals hate real religion. It's also because the public school is their temple. Children must be taught to love Big Brother, welcoming him to take over our schools, our bank accounts, our property, even our toilet bowls. There's nothing the matter with teachers that a little less unionization and more competition couldn't cure. But if liberals insist on making teachers the new priests, at least let's make them take vows of poverty, chastity, and obedience like all the other priests.

7 THE LEFT'S WAR ON SCIENCE: BURNING BOOKS TO ADVANCE "SCIENCE"

istening to liberals invoke the sanctity of "science" to promote their crackpot ideas creates the same uneasy feeling as listening to Bill Clinton cite Scripture. Who are they kidding? Liberals hate science. Science might produce facts impervious to their crying and hysterics. Even at college re-education camps, it's striking that the chemical engineering and economics departments are jam-packed with Republicans, while liberals are all taking French.

As with their sudden new interest in the military, liberals invoke "science" only as a cudgel to end debate. Actual science excites them only if it involves some sort of Nazi experimentation with human embryos.

When Richard J. Herrnstein and Charles Murray's book **The Bell Curve: Intelligence and Class Structure in American Life** landed on the shelves in 1994, liberals responded with their usual open-mindedness to scientific facts. The 850-page book represented eight years of collaboration between Herrnstein, a Harvard psychology professor, and Murray, a political scientist. **The Bell Curve** synthesized mountains of data culled mostly from the National Longitudinal Study of Youth (NLSY), a federal study testing the intelligence of more than 10,000 Americans beginning in 1980, with regular follow-ups for many years thereafter. Contrary to the party line denying that such a thing as IQ existed, the book methodically demonstrated that IQ exists, it is easily measured, it is heritable, and it is extremely important.

The book—all but one chapter—dealt exclusively with the influence of IQ on white people's lives. After years of censorship on the subject of IQ, the entire book was a stunning revelation. Once the taboo was shattered and the unspeakable was spoken, IQ turned out to be an extraordinary commodity. Among many other things, IQ is a better predictor than socioeconomic status of poverty, unemployment, criminality, divorce, single motherhood, workplace injuries, and high school dropout rates. The ability to speak different languages is not correlated with IQ, but near-sightedness is. Spouses tend to have closer IQs than siblings. Although other factors influence IQ, such as a good home environment and nutrition, **The Bell Curve** authors estimated that IQ was about 40 to 80 percent genetic.

In a rare editorial about a book, the **New York Times** said **The Bell Curve** was "a flame-throwing" book with "a grisly thesis."[1] The **Times** was suspicious of the "aura of scientific certitude" to **The Bell Curve,** calling the scientific findings "ugly" and vowing that they would soon be challenged by other experts in the field. Not yet—but soon! The **Times** denounced Murray as "a political ideologue who uses social science data to support his policy preferences," and then launched into an irrelevant tirade on the "long and sordid history" of "bigots" who used "'scientific' evidence that blacks, or American Indians, or Jews, to name three targets, were of inferior stock."[2]

Having spent decades rigorously enforcing the taboo against any mention of IQ in any context, ever—with a narrow exception for remarks about

the IQs of Republican presidential candidates—
the **Times** complained that **The Bell Curve** "be-
labor[s] the well-known fact that the average IQ
of blacks is 15 points below that of whites." I'm
going out on a limb to say that fact was not well
known to readers of the **Times.** Indeed, the indignant denunciations of the book were never
clear on whether the problem was that **The Bell
Curve** was wrong or that it was old news.

An article in **BusinessWeek** said that to call
the "opinions" in **The Bell Curve** "scientific
truth" was "downright dangerous." In fact, the
book was nothing but "a house of cards con-
structed to push a political agenda."[3] **Newsweek**
branded Murray "an intellectual snake charmer"
who wrote a book that took a "deeply angry"
view. The magazine added that Murray "vehe-
mently denies he is racist."[4] Columnist Ellen
Goodman said she suspected Murray and Herrnstein had raised the issue of genes and environment influencing racial differences in IQ solely
"in order to break the 'taboo' against fanning
racist sentiments."[5] **Newsday** columnist Robert
Reno calmly said of the book, "The slop Murray
has served up is not only unappetizing, but
warmed over. Proving the inferiority of races
has for 100 years been the mischief of self-
promoting scholars as credentialed as Murray
and as squalid as the louts who churned out the

'science' behind Dr. Goebbels' loathsome ravings."**6** Only liberals could interpret a statement that people have varying IQs as a call to start killing people.

After the furor over the book died down, it came out that psychometricians had known the truth all along. They had been lying to the public about IQ. In light of the calm and measured response to Murray and Herrnstein's book, one could see why.

A few years later, the American Psychological Association formed a Task Force on Intelligence in response to the publication of **The Bell Curve** and issued a report basically admitting the truth of all the book's major conclusions.**7** Among these were:

- "Differences in genetic endowment contribute substantially to individual differences in [psychometric] intelligence . . ."; and
- "The differential between the mean intelligence test scores of Blacks and Whites (about one standard deviation, although it may be diminishing) does not result from any obvious biases in test construction and administration, nor does it simply reflect differences in socio-economic status."

So much for the **New York Times**'s claim that as soon as "unlike-minded scholars have time to react, they will subject its findings to withering criticism."8

Liberals were afraid of a book that told the truth about IQ because they are godless secularists who do not believe humans are in God's image. Christians have no fear of hearing facts about genetic differences in IQ because we don't think humans are special because they are smart. There may be some advantages to being intelligent, but a lot of liberals appear to have high IQs, so, really, what's the point? After Hitler carried the secularists' philosophy to its bloody conclusion, liberals became terrified of making any comment that seems to acknowledge that there are any differences among groups of people—especially racial groups. It's difficult to have a simple conversation, much less engage in free-ranging, open scientific inquiry, when liberals are constantly rushing in with their rule book about what can and cannot be said.

Among the most absurd results of liberals' unbridgeable commitment to nondiscrimination was their insistence on suppressing the truth about AIDS and scaring Americans into believing that heterosexuals were as much at risk for acquiring AIDS as gays and intravenous drug users.

Once again, the science had to be lied about so no one's feelings got hurt. But in contrast to liberal preachiness about IQ, there would be no moralizing when it came to sex. Anal sex, oral sex, fisting, dental dams, "birthing games"—all that would be foisted on unsuspecting children in order to protect kindergartners from the scourge of AIDS. As one heroine of the sex education movement told an approving **New York Times** reporter, "My job is not to teach one right value system. Parents and churches teach moral values. My job is to say, 'These are the facts,' and to help the students, as adults, decide what is right for them."**9**

At least when Herrnstein and Murray talked about IQ, they got the facts right. Liberal sex educators claimed to be slaves to the facts—not to subjective moral values like promoting abstinence—but they spent most of the eighties orchestrating a massive campaign of lies about AIDS, as copiously documented by science writer Michael Fumento.

The high-water mark of liberal lies about AIDS came in 1985, when **Life** magazine's cover proclaimed, "NOW, NO ONE IS SAFE FROM AIDS."

Newsweek's Jonathan Alter praised the responsibility of the press in writing about AIDS, saying the **Life** cover "may have crossed the line, but not by much."[10] It's been twenty years, and we're still waiting for that heterosexual outbreak.

A 1985 issue of **People** magazine began an article on AIDS warning that the disease "poses a growing threat to heterosexuals." (And the folks at **People** wonder why they're no longer considered a legitimate science journal.) Associated Press "science writer" Malcolm Ritter approvingly quoted an AIDS activist saying "there's nothing inherent in homosexuality or drug use that leads to AIDS."[11] Evidently, Ritter is a "science writer" much the way Cindy Sheehan is a "geopolitical expert."

The **Chicago Tribune** "science writer" quoted the head of California's AIDS research task force saying it was "highly likely that the disease will spread into the heterosexual population." **Tribune** columnist Bob Greene followed up with a piece titled "The AIDS Epidemic: Not for Gays Only," in which he ominously concluded, "If you never gave AIDS a second thought before, it's time to start thinking."[12] This was a few years before Bob Greene was dismissed from his **Tribune** job for having sex with a teenage reader. Let's just hope it was safe sex.[13]

"Dear Abby" informed her readers, "AIDS is not exclusively a homosexual disease. An increasing number of cases are being found among heterosexual (straight) men and women. All sexually active men and women, gay or straight, should be concerned."[14] Yes—especially when they share dirty needles with street junkies!

A few years would go by and the great heterosexual outbreak still wouldn't materialize, but it seemed to be constantly just around the corner. In 1987, Oprah Winfrey said, "Research studies now project that one in five—listen to me, hard to believe—one in five heterosexuals could be dead from AIDS at the end of the next three years. That's by 1990. One in five. It is no longer just a gay disease. Believe me."[15]

In 1987, **U.S. News & World Report** said, "The disease of them is suddenly the disease of us . . . finding fertile growth among heterosexuals."

In 1988, ABC's **20/20** cited a study of AIDS cases on college campuses, claiming these were all heterosexual infections. It struck no one at ABC as odd that 28 of the 30 infections on college campuses had occurred in men.

Then, two years later, CNN reported on the rerelease of that same 1988 study, and concluded, "A new report from CDC indicates that AIDS is on the rise on college campuses." As Michael Fumento remarked, "Only with AIDS can an old study be declared an alarming increase over itself."

In 1992, PBS broadcast a program that claimed a single condom can save "hundreds of lives."[16] It would have to be "a hell of a condom," Fumento said. (Maybe if you used it to plug up a leaky life raft . . .) The program was sponsored in part by a condom manufacturer, so liberals were willing to suspend their opposition to greedy profit-making corporations in this one instance.[17]

After a decade-long epidemic with more than a million infections, in November 1992 the Centers for Disease Control listed only 2,391 cases of AIDS transmission by white heterosexuals—and that included hemophiliacs and blood transfusion patients.

The most recent figures from the CDC—now called the "Centers for Disease Control **and Prevention**" in a stupid bureaucratic redundancy—show that through the end of 2004, almost 70 percent of AIDS victims in America acquired the virus through homosexual sex or intravenous drug use. Only 13 percent of cases are even alleged to be through heterosexual conduct. As Fumento has pointed out, determinations of the method of transmission are based almost entirely on self-reports and no one who got the virus from heterosexual sex lies and says he got it from homosexual sex or intravenous drug use, but the reverse is not true.

Intriguingly, black and Hispanic men—groups that have been slow to embrace Queer Theory—were five times more likely than white men to claim to have gotten AIDS from heterosexual contact. When the CDC performed a follow-up investigation on AIDS reports from two Florida counties, more than half of the cases of men who claimed to have contracted AIDS from heterosexual sex had to be reclassified as homosexual transmissions. This took little effort in some cases. The CDC simply looked at the men's medical records and moved men with rectal STDs from the "heterosexual transmission" category to the "homosexual transmission" category. Men with symptoms that are frequently, but not exclusively, associated with homosexual sex, such as a loose sphincter muscle, remained in the "heterosexual transmission" category.[18]

While liberals loudly proclaimed that absolutely anyone could get AIDS, and that AIDS doesn't discriminate, they simultaneously insisted that no one should worry about sharing towels or utensils with AIDS sufferers. That message might have been a little clearer if someone had simply said, **Just don't have anal sex with them!** Liberals also may have been sending mixed messages by saying in one breath that "AIDS is not a gay disease" and that Ronald Reagan was a homophobe for not allotting more federal funding to find a cure.

At least we could count on the government not to politicize science. That is, unless the surgeon general was more interested in being called brave by the mainstream media than in giving Americans the truth. In June 1987, U.S. Surgeon General C. Everett Koop released a "Report on AIDS" that said, "Although the initial discovery was in the homosexual community, AIDS is not a disease only of homosexuals. AIDS is found in heterosexual people as well. AIDS is not a black or white disease. AIDS is not just a male disease. AIDS is found in women; it is found in children."

The pamphlet droned on and on about the danger of heterosexual AIDS, warning that "[h]eterosexual persons are increasingly at risk" and "[h]eterosexual transmission is expected to account for an increasing proportion of those who become infected with the AIDS virus in the future." Although "[a]bout 70 percent of AIDS victims throughout the country are male homosexuals and bisexuals," Koop said, "this percentage probably will decline as heterosexual transmission increases."[19] Twenty years later and the percentage hasn't budged.

Koop was a major advocate of teaching school-children to use condoms, because, he said,

"There is now no doubt that we need sex education in schools and that it must include information on heterosexual and homosexual relationships."[20] AIDS does not discriminate!

Koop took his campaign on the road, describing heterosexual sex as the sort of "very high risk behavior" that could lead to AIDS. He mentioned homosexual sex third in his list of "high risk behavior" that could transmit AIDS.[21] In 1987, the CDC predicted that AIDS would be the number-one killer on campus by 1991.[22]

It was as if the government had issued a scientific report stating, "Sharks will eat people, but so will rainbow trout!"—so as not to stigmatize sharks.

While gays were being decimated by the AIDS virus, Koop was more interested in not "stigmatizing" them than in saving their lives. See, where I come from being dead also carries a certain type of stigma. Instead of distributing condoms in gay bars and at Madonna concerts where they might have done some good, Koop insisted on distributing condoms in kindergarten classes, in order to emphasize the point that AIDS does not discriminate, which it does.

C. Everett had clearly flown the Koop. Yet with each more insane statement, Koop was hailed in the media for speaking truth to power. It almost got to the point where Dr. Koop's distinctive look—the gay Amish Navy guy in the Village People—seemed more sane than the things he was saying about AIDS. Soon he was advocating teaching kindergartners about anal sex and AIDS.[23] This stance made Koop more popular than John Hinckley with liberals.

In 1987, **New York Times** reporter Maureen Dowd—before she was elevated to the cartoon pages—wrote a heroic portrait of the man. Dr. Koop, she said, "fiercely wants to strip AIDS of its stigma," and for that reason, he talks "about making an animated educational video that would feature two condoms 'with little eyes on them' chatting, and about the need for 'gentle, nonmystifying' sex education for students, starting in kindergarten."[24] I would pay quite a bit of money to hear someone describe anal sex—oh heck, make it any kind of sodomy—to a five-year-old in a gentle, nonmystifying way.

For wanting to teach kindergartners about condoms and anal sex, liberals swooned over Koop. Representative Henry Waxman called Koop "a man of heroic proportions." Koop himself boasted of all the praise he was getting from some of the most heinous people in America: "Obviously, it's gratifying to have people like Senator Edward Kennedy and Henry Waxman saying I have integrity."[25] Koop's sodomy lessons, Clinton's non-euclidean sex romps, Jocelyn Elders's masturbation musings—all you have to do to become a liberal icon in this country is discuss non-coital sex in graphic detail with small children.

Conservatives were not so enthralled with Koop's plan to introduce talking condoms "with little eyes" to kindergartners in response to the AIDS epidemic—an epidemic notable for **not** being spread by show-and-tell, peanut butter sandwiches, and nap time. Naturally, therefore, Koop's conservative critics were accused of being against "science." Koop wrote a letter to the **Washington Post** complaining that "[p]arents are uncomfortable with the science of reproduction,"[26] which would raise questions about how they became parents in the first place. Is Dr. Koop comfortable with the notion of the oxymoron? Inasmuch as the kind of sex Dr. Koop seemed bent on teaching kindergartners does not result in reproduction, he may have been the one who needed a lesson. The **New York Times** echoed Koop, saying conservatives were "enraged" by Koop's "emphasis on science rather than values."[27] Whenever liberals say values must take a back seat to "science," you know you're not getting values or science. In fact, I get a little nervous whenever liberals use the word **backseat.**

For liberals, not making moral judgments is the very essence of science. On that theory, Howard Stern should be curing cancer and inventing cold fusion any day now. To great acclaim, Koop went around saying things like "I'm not here to make moral judgments. I'm here to save people if I can."[28] But of course Koop was making moral judgments. As he courageously told Dowd, "I hate injustice of any kind" (and let the chips fall where they may!). Warming to his subject, Koop continued, more bravely, "and I don't like to see people excoriated in the midst of illness because there's some other part of their life style that people don't like."[29] Koop made the personal decision to withhold true information from gays rather than let them feel stigmatized.

That is what's known as "a moral judgment." Still Koop blathered on and on about his heroism in excluding "morals"—meaning moral codes that have been around for thousands of years in contradistinction to morals about not stigmatizing people because of their "lifestyle," which were invented in 1970. So a lot of gay guys were going to die needlessly, but dead or alive, they'd all feel good about their "lifestyle" choices. Because liberals shared Koop's moral values, they praised him for lying about science and denounced his detractors as anti-science.

A year later, Koop admitted under oath in congressional hearings that only about 4 percent of adult AIDS transmissions worldwide could be traced to heterosexual contact, and that in the

United States only 2.3 percent of AIDS cases came from heterosexual contact, and "most of that is in sexual partners of IV drug abusers."[30] In other words, the entire, years-long AIDS Threatens Straight People Too PR campaign was a total lie from start to finish.

At the end of the year, the U.S. Department of Health and Human Services and the Centers for Disease Control were back at it, unveiling a major AIDS awareness ad campaign in which—according to one perplexed reporter asking questions at the press conference—"All the ads pertain[ed] to heterosexual behavior."[31]

Koop's campaign had its intended effect. (And not just because his freakish appearance discouraged heterosexual relations in general.) First and most important, the **Washington Post** hailed him as "that rarest of Washington officials—a rugged individualist who follows his own agenda, not a predictable ideologue who espouses the party line."[32] This tripe about rugged individualism was, of course, immediately parroted by every other major media outlet.

Second: Everyone was terrified of contracting AIDS. AIDS hotlines were ringing off the hook, mostly with calls from heterosexuals.[33] In San Diego, Mothers Against AIDS—working tirelessly to counter the lies being put out by Mothers for AIDS—organized a demonstration around Mother's Day to encourage women and their families to take AIDS tests in order to "destigmatize" AIDS tests, according to Teddie Pincus, one of the organizers.[34] Yes, there's nothing like a traditional Mother's Day complete with hysterical housewives lecturing one another on the dangers of anal sex.

Let's be clear on what happened here: HHS, the CDC, and the surgeon general's office, with the full cooperation of the media, deliberately put millions of lives needlessly at risk by disseminating misinformation on AIDS rather than risk stigmatizing a single gay person, however slightly. And when parents objected to their schoolchildren being taught about anal sex, Koop said they were uncomfortable with "science."

■　　■　　■

IF SCIENCE must be suppressed to ensure that gays don't feel singled out, there is no limit to the book burning that must be undertaken to avoid upsetting the ladies. At a January 2005 conference on women in the sciences, then–Harvard president Larry Summers commented that men and women might have different innate abilities in math and science, which led to fainting spells by women in attendance and raised questions about a whole different set of innate differences.

In a perfect world, the women's histrionics would have triggered a discussion on women and irony.

Summers began his rather tepid remarks by saying he intended to be "controversial" and "to provoke you." He even laid it on thick about "passive discrimination" against women, which—according to him—no one can deny. But then Summers said, "[I]n the special case of science and engineering, there are issues of intrinsic aptitude, and particularly of the variability of aptitude."

That was the phrase that kicked off the trial of Galileo. The effect was roughly that of telling a room full of gay men that Judy Garland couldn't sing worth a damn. It turns out that innate intelligence differences between the sexes is a topic that may not be discussed on university campuses for fear of giving distaff professors the vapors. Summers ran "continuing discrimination" around the block again, concluding that he "would like nothing better than to be proved wrong." But it was too late. There weren't enough fainting couches in the room to deal with the response from nauseated female professors forced to contemplate the possibility of innate differences in ability between men and women.

Some of the women paired off and went to the ladies' room to discuss possible responses. Others went on eating binges. Most chose to just sit there sobbing. A quick show of hands revealed that every woman in attendance needed a hug.

The Best in Show award went to MIT biology professor Nancy Hopkins, who told the **Washington Post,** "I felt I was going to be sick." She continued, "My heart was pounding and my breath was shallow."[35] (Some might describe Hopkins's response to Summers's remarks as "womanish.") Hopkins told the **Boston Globe** she had to flee the room because otherwise she "would've either blacked out or thrown up,"[36] proving that you can become a full professor of biology at MIT without realizing that women and men are innately different. Can anyone imagine evangelicals behaving this way if someone mentioned evolution? Would they flee a room crying if Dr. Koop showed them talking condoms? Only the feminists can behave like children with so little reflection.

A few days later, Professor Hopkins explained her emotional reaction to Summers's remarks on NBC's **Today** show, saying she was shocked by what he said because "there is research now that shows very clearly that there is unconscious bias in how we make judgments, and this unconscious bias can really influence our decisions in ways we are not aware of."[37] (She also did a cooking segment with Katie Couric on that same show. I guess some gender stereotypes die harder than others.) So in the case of evaluating women's mathematical abilities, liberals' idea of "science" consists of invisible forces that we "are not aware of," but if anyone denies them, liberal women will run from the room, threatening to throw up.

In strict accordance with the scientific method, a Wiccan ritual expelling Summers's remarks had to be performed—rounds of protests, letter writing, marches, apologies, concluding with a "no-confidence" vote on Summers from the Harvard faculty. Written summaries of Summers's noxious remarks were burned in every room like bundles of sage to cleanse the air of negative vibes.

If Summers's milquetoast remarks caused fainting and nausea in the ladies, they should hear what I think about women's genetic endowments! They'd have me burned at the stake—if Cambridge weren't a "smoke-free zone."

These delicate hothouse flowers have a completely neurotic response to something someone else says—and then act like it's Summers's fault. Only a woman could shift the blame this way. If I hit you with a sledgehammer, that is my fault. But if I propose a scientific idea and you vomit, I think that's really more your fault. Perhaps to improve girls' scores on the SATs, a section on blame shifting should be added to the math section.

■ ■ ■

WHAT liberals mean by **science** is never what a normal person would understand the term to convey—facts, subject to independent verification, capable of being disproved, and not alterable by crying jags. They mean banning alar and DDT, or teaching kindergartners about anal sex, or Connie Chung interviewing women who believe their breast implants made them sick. Or they mean former senator John Edwards pretending that unborn children were speaking through him in order to coax large monetary awards from juries.

Using junk science, trial lawyer Edwards engaged in paranormal conversations with the dead to convince jurors that obstetricians—rich obstetricians with big insurance plans—caused cerebral palsy in babies by not performing cesarean sections soon enough. As part of his scientific case, Edwards literally claimed to channel the unborn child in front of juries. "She speaks to you through me and I have to tell you right now—I didn't plan to talk about this—right now I feel her. I feel her presence. She's inside me, and she's talking to you." Edwards—or as he's known in the courtroom, the Fetus Whisperer—continued, "She said at 3, 'I'm fine.' She said at 4,

'I'm having a little trouble, but I'm doing OK.' Five, she said, 'I'm having problems.' At 5:30, she said, 'I need out.'"**38** (Oddly enough, the little critter didn't add, "And by the way, I'm pro-life," which I think would have been prudent under the circumstances.)

In the years since Edwards told juries he could "feel" the unborn babies "inside" him, winning fabulous jury awards—and attorney's fees for himself—it has been quietly admitted that there is no connection between cerebral palsy and the method of delivery. As the **New York Times** reported in 2004, "Studies indicate that in most cases, the disorder is caused by fetal brain injury long before labor begins."**39** During the 2004 presidential campaign, in which Edwards was the Democrats' vice presidential candidate, a Johns Hopkins neurology professor wrote to the **Washington Post** to say "we now know" that the science on which Edwards's jury awards were based was false and that most "cerebral palsy is due to developmental abnormalities occurring during pregnancy or due to subtle infection near the time of delivery."**40** This is another way of saying that the Democrats' 2004 VP candidate was a proven huckster whose $50 million personal fortune of ill-gotten gain was amassed by defrauding doctors, jurors, and insurance compa-

nies. And yet the Johns Hopkins professor—
channeling Zippy the Chimp—said he supported the Kerry-Edwards ticket anyway.

As a result of such lawsuits, there are now
more than four times as many cesarean sections
as there were in 1970. But curiously, there has
been no reduction in babies born with cerebral
palsy. All those cesareans have, however, increased the mother's risk of death, hemorrhage,
infection, pulmonary embolism, and Mendel-
son's syndrome, while also driving up the cost of
medical care for every man, woman, and child in
America. Not only that, but those "little guys"
John Edwards claimed to represent are having a
lot more trouble finding doctors to deliver their
babies. Insurance companies are getting out of
the medical malpractice business and doctors are
getting out of the obstetrics business rather than
pay malpractice insurance in excess of $100,000
a year.[41] All that for a paranormal lounge act just
slightly more believable than Johnny Carson's
mentalist character Carnac the Magnificent.

Then there was the liberal "science" that bankrupted the company Dow Corning. This time,
liberals relied on the research not of serious scientific experts like trial lawyers, but of CBS News
anchorwoman and noted biochemistry authority
Connie Chung. In 1990, Chung hosted a sensa-
tionalistic report on the danger of breast im-

plants, warning that, for some women, "It may be too late."

Pursuing the rigorous fact-checking methods that have made CBS News what it is today, Chung's report consisted of interviews with three women who were "convinced" their breast implants had caused health problems. Apart from fatigue, which they each had, their symptoms were completely different. One woman had "flu-like symptoms—swollen glands, fevers, chills, sweats, sore throats." Based on her indications, my theory is this woman had the flu. I'm not a medical doctor, but then again neither is Connie Chung. Another woman suffered constant pain. The third had mouth ulcers, hair loss, skin rashes, and fevers. As Chung summarized the evidence, "There are no statistics on how many women have become ill because of their implants"[42]—making it one of countless imaginary illnesses for which there are also no statistics. There are no statistics on how many women have become ill from watching Connie Chung. The fact that I frequently experience nausea while watching Connie Chung on TV is "anecdotal," not "statistical," evidence.

It was the perfect David and Goliath story for the media: Erin Brockovich and Halliburton all rolled into one. CBS was so pleased with the program, it ran it again in November 1991, with

Chung smugly remarking that her implant special program had "unleashed a torrent of protests
and investigations around the country"—mostly
by disgruntled topless dancers and their despon-
dent customers. Even so, everybody has a right to
be heard.

The next year, in 1992, FDA Commissioner
David Kessler banned silicone breast implants—
not because the FDA had found anything wrong
with silicone in the body but because women
were hysterical. Kessler was too busy taping up
"No Smoking" signs all over Washington to
bother reviewing the medical literature, so he appointed a panel to review implant safety, and the
panel advised keeping them on the market. He
told them to think it over some more. They did,
and again advised keeping them on the market.
But Kessler was a pediatrician, and if a baby doctor doesn't know about something used exclusively by adult women, who does? Dr. Connie
Chung said breast implants were dangerous, so
there had to be a moratorium.

After Kessler's moratorium, the trickle of lawsuits against implant manufacturers became a del-
uge. Within three years, Dow Corning was in
bankruptcy proceedings. By then, more than
twenty epidemiological studies had been performed on silicone breast implants, all of which
showed no connection between implants and dis-

ease. But juries continued to give plaintiffs massive awards, eventually totaling more than $7 billion—more than one-third of which went to the trial lawyers. Like the implants themselves, the settlements were so large that one began to wonder just how large they could get before they started to look ridiculous.

Finally, federal judges became concerned the courts were becoming accessories to a scam. They convened a panel of scientists to examine the science behind the breast implant litigation. In December 1998, after two years of reviewing all the literature on silicone implants, testimony from the parties' experts, and the advice of their own experts, the panel concluded there was no connection between breast implants and disease.[43]

Where does Dow Corning go to get its money back? Why are trial lawyers allowed to say, "Too late!" Car manufacturers can't say, "Sorry! The defective product we were wrong about is already out there. Can't take it back now." In the case of breast implants, liberal "science" consisted of sensational news reports on CBS's **Face to Face with Connie Chung.**

Alar was a perfectly safe substance that had been used on apples since 1968 to both ripen and preserve them. It made fresh fruit more affordable and available by allowing fruit pickers to make one sweep through the apple grove to pick the apples and then distribute them with less risk of spoilage. Because of a lunatic scare ginned up by a phalanx of Hollywood actresses like Meryl Streep, the EPA banned alar, and poor people went back to eating Twinkies instead of healthy fresh fruit. The tests that persuaded the EPA bureaucrats and Hollywood actresses that alar might cause cancer in humans involved feeding so much alar to rats—tens of thousands times more than what a human would eat—that most of the rats died of poisoning, not tumors. Meanwhile, the World Health Organization advised against a ban on alar, and Europeans continued to eat alar-preserved fruit in their nice warm houses powered by nuclear energy.

Shortly after the tragedy of Hurricane Katrina—to date this, it was around the time liberals were accusing blacks in New Orleans of engaging in cannibalism—Robert Kennedy Jr. wrote a column claiming "global warming" caused the hurricane. The only human malady RFK Jr. hasn't blamed on global warming is Mary Jo Kopechne's death. Even "global warming" devotees at the UN's Intergovernmental Panel on Climate Change have said there is variation in hurricanes from decade to decade, "with no significant trends over the twentieth century evident." RFK's theory might have gotten more traction but for the sudden groundswell of support for the theory that George Bush caused the hurricane.

A sparrow does not a spring make, but in the Druid religion of environmentalism, every warm summer's breeze prompts apocalyptic demands for a ban on aerosol spray and plastic bags. In 1998, President Clinton denounced Republicans for opposing his environmental policies, such as the 1997 Kyoto Protocol to reduce emissions of carbon dioxide. This, after the Senate rejected the Kyoto agreement by the slender margin of 95–0. In fact, all the world's major industrial powers initially rejected the treaty, including Japan. That's right: even Kyoto rejected Kyoto. But soon, some countries began to realize that they could sign Kyoto while being exempt from having to reduce their greenhouse gas emissions, such as China and India, two of the world's biggest polluters. Others signed it and then proceeded to increase their greenhouse emissions, like Canada. By 2005, Canada was producing 24 percent more carbon monoxide than it had in 1990, whereas the United States was producing only 13 percent more.

But Clinton urged immediate action on global warming. As proof that urgent action was needed, he cited Florida's inordinately warm weather in a single month: "June was the hottest month they had ever had—hotter than any July or August they had ever had." Yes, and then November–December 2000 were the two coldest months in U.S. history.[44] It's a big country; it's always the "coldest" or "hottest" someplace.

Adding to the world's supply of hot air, Laurie David, "Environmental Activist" and—more relevantly—wife of **Seinfeld** creator Larry David, said at the end of 2005, "We just came through a September which was the hottest month since records were taken."[45] Except in Aberdeen, South Dakota. Aberdeen's hottest days were in July 1936, when the temperature hit 115 degrees on two days.[46] Ottawa still hasn't matched the record of 1955, its hottest summer ever. January 1977 was Ohio's coldest month ever.[47] In Omaha, the coldest month was February 1936, and its second-coldest month was December 1983.[48] January 1998 was Denver's fifth-driest on record.[49] And in January 2004, Boston had its coldest month in seventy years. In fact, maybe what we're seeing now is the beginning of the new ice age that some of these same scientists were predicting back in the 1970s. The law of large numbers means that someplace will always be having its hottest, coldest, wettest, or driest month.

Environmentalists claim this statistical inevitability proves global warming. As Steven Guilbeault of Greenpeace explained, "Global warming can mean colder, it can mean drier, it can mean wetter." No set of facts can disprove the environmentalists' secular religion. In 2004, former vice president Al Gore gave a speech on global warming in New York City on the coldest day of the year. Warm trends prove global warming. Cold trends also prove global warming. This is the philosophy of a madman.

In 1995, the Intergovernmental Panel on Climate Change produced a computer model purportedly proving "a discernible human influence on global climate." So according to the UN, there was not enough evidence to determine if Saddam Hussein was a threat, but the evidence is in on global warming. The key to the UN's global warming study was man's use of aerosol spray. You have to know the French were involved in a study concluding that Arrid Extra Dry is destroying the Earth. In the big picture, which would be a bigger threat to the global ecosystem: encroaching oceans flooding the world's coastal cities, or the rest of the world adopting French deodorant habits?

According to global warming hysterics, global warming would begin at the poles and melt the ice caps, and then the oceans would rise. On the basis of such fatuous theories, in August 1998 the host of NPR's **Science Friday,** Ira Flatow, told his listeners to look out their windows and imagine the ocean in their own backyards. Explaining that receding glaciers in Antarctica would dramatically lift sea levels, he warned that their grandchildren could be "hanging fishing poles out of New York skyscrapers," thus qualifying as the teller of the world's all-time greatest "fish story." On the plus side, maybe I could get a decent price for my place in Manhattan if I could list it as "steps from the beach."

Since then, evidence disproving "global warming" has been pouring in. In January 2002, the journal **Science** published the findings of scientists who had been measuring the vast West Antarctic Ice Sheet. Far from melting, it turned out the Ice Sheet was growing thicker. The researchers were Ian R. Joughin, an engineer at NASA's Jet Propulsion Laboratory in Pasadena, and Slawek Tulaczyk, a professor of earth sciences at the University of California, Santa Cruz. Taking the contrary view were distinguished research scientists Alicia Silverstone and Woody Harrelson.

About the same time, the journal **Nature** published the findings of scientist Peter Doran and his colleagues at the University of Illinois. Rather than using the UN's "computer models," the researchers took actual temperature readings. It turned out temperatures in the Antarctic have been getting slightly colder—not warmer—for the last thirty years. The chief scientist for the Environmental Defense Fund, Michael Oppenheimer, responded to the new findings by urging caution and warning that "there is simply not enough data to make a broad statement about all of Antarctica." That's interesting. Global warming devotees don't shy away from making broad statements about the temperature of the entire Planet Earth. We also didn't have to wait for more data when lunatics curtailed the use of nuclear energy in this country. The movie **The China Syndrome** was hard scientific evidence.

We didn't wait for more data when DDT (dichlorodiphenyltrichloroethane) was banned on the basis of Rachel Carson's book **Silent Spring.**

DDT was a miracle invention: tiny amounts of the chemical kill disease-carrying insects with no harm to humans, protecting them from malaria, dengue, and typhus. American soldiers in World War II were bathed in DDT. Jews rescued from Nazi death camps were doused in it. During the debate on DDT prompted by Rachel Carson's book, J. Gordon Edwards, mountain climber, park ranger, author, and professor of biology at San Jose State University, would eat spoonfuls of DDT at lectures to prove its safety to humans. Edwards lived a long and healthy life, finally dying in 2005 at the age of eighty-four while hiking. But children in America were indoctrinated with the idea that DDT would kill all the birds, and that made them sad. So in 1972, American environmentalists working through the EPA banned one of the greatest inventions in modern history. Millions upon millions of people in Africa had to die on the basis of a book by a woman dying of cancer who was obsessed with the idea that it was caused by modern chemicals.

Continuing its tradition of helping the poor and enslaved, in 1986 the State Department informed African nations that the United States would no longer provide aid to countries using DDT. Last year, 80,000 people in Uganda alone died of malaria, half of them children. So environmentalists are again in a panic that African nations will use DDT to save millions of lives each year. The United States and Europe have threatened to ban Ugandan imports if they use DDT to stop this scourge. Environmentalists would prefer that millions of Africans die so that white liberals may continue gazing upon rare birds. Liberals don't care about the environment. They want humans to die—or at least to smell like they have by abandoning their infernal deodorant use.

Tellingly, liberals' one example of **The Repub-lican War on Science,** as one book title puts it,[50] is the Christian objection to Nazi experimentation on human embryos. As with other "sciences" admired by liberals, their enthusiasm for embryonic stem-cell research is based on lies. Liberals lie about the science on stem-cell research because they warm to the idea of destroying human embryos. If they can desensitize Americans to the idea of harvesting human embryos for imaginary medical cures, liberals believe it will help advance the cause of killing the unborn. As columnist Anna Quindlen said, the "pro-choicers" were always "at a loss" when faced with moral arguments in defense of an unborn baby. But with embryonic stem-cell research, Quindlen said, the "battle of personification will assume a different and more sympathetic visage in the years to come"—taking the form of Michael J. Fox, Christopher Reeve, Ronald Reagan, and other beloved public figures for whom embryonic stem-cell researchers can promise miracle cures they are not close to producing.[51]

Although there has been research on both adult stem cells and embryonic stem cells since the fifties, only adult stem-cell research has produced any cures—and lots of 'em. Adult stem cells have been used for decades to treat dozens of diseases, including Type 1 diabetes, liver disease, and spinal cord injuries. Currently, adult stem cells are used to treat more than eighty different diseases.

Harvard medical researcher Denise Faustman has used adult stem cells to cure diabetes in mice. Other cures from adult stem cells are being tested in hundreds of clinical trials. Adult stem-cell researchers in Switzerland take a few strands of hair from burn victims and use the follicular stem cells on the tips to create entire disks of new skin, a vast improvement on ugly skin grafts. Recently, patients with damaged livers have been helped by injections of bone marrow adult stem cells collected not directly from their marrow (an extremely painful procedure) but simply cultivated from their blood.

By contrast, the embryonic stem-cell researchers have produced nothing. They have treated nothing. They have not even begun one human clinical trial. They've successfully treated a few rodents, but they keep running into two problems: First, the cells tend to be rejected by the immune system. Second, they tend to cause malignancies called teratomas—meaning "monster tumors."

The idea that embryonic stem cells are on the verge of curing anything is absurd. It's possible embryonic stem-cell research could find a cure for Alzheimer's disease someday only in the sense that it is possible that a biologist's toenail clippings could be used to find a cure for Alzheimer's someday. Liberals aren't demanding that taxpayer money be used for research on toenail clippings: that would not advance their governing principle, which is to always kill human life (unless the human life being killed is likely to fly a plane into American skyscrapers, in which case, it is wrong to kill it).

The only advantage embryonic stem cells once had over adult stem cells was their ability to transform into any type of cell. But fast-advancing research on adult stem cells has stripped away even that theoretical advantage. As of 2002, adult stem cells were being converted into all three types of cells the body produces during early embryonic development. And adult stem cells were already curing people!

Embryonic stem-cell researchers were in trouble. It was as if thirty years after the invention of electricity, they were still trying to get someone to fund their research on candles. Results tend to draw more research dollars than pie-in-the-sky claims to maybe, possibly someday find a cure for Alzheimer's disease, diabetes, paralysis, Parkinson's disease, PMS, balding, and hemorrhoidal itch. No one is going to buy a drawing of a potential cure when somebody else is already selling the cure.

Embryonic stem-cell researchers had only one choice: Accuse anyone opposed to taxpayer funding of embryonic stem-cell research of being "anti-science." As Michael Fumento says, it was the very success of adult stem-cell research compared with the abject failure of embryonic stem-cell research that led to the all-out PR campaign: "Savvy venture capitalists have poured their money into ASCs, leaving ESC researchers desperate to feed at the federal (or state) trough."[52]

While adult stem-cell researchers were in their labs quietly discovering cures, embryonic stem-cell researchers were mounting a massive public relations assault that not only promised cures for every known human malady but also viciously attacked adult stem-cell research as useless. This is perhaps not surprising, since—in contrast to researchers on adult stem cells—embryonic stem-cell researchers are virtually never doctors. They're biologists. They don't care about healing people, they just want to be paid to push petri dishes around the lab, cut up a living human embryo, and sell it for parts like a stolen Toyota at a chop shop.

It's always the same thing with liberals. Time

and again doctors are just minding their own business trying to cure people and liberal special interest groups swoop in and take all their money. The most valuable people in society are under constant attack from trial lawyers, biologists, and class-warfare Democrats.

Appropriately, the spokesman for liberal "science" was once again a rich white male Southern lawyer doing a passable impression of Miss Cleo. At an Iowa campaign stop during the 2004 presidential campaign, John Edwards promised, "We will stop juvenile diabetes, Parkinson's, Alzheimer's and other debilitating diseases. . . . When John Kerry is president, people like Christopher Reeve are going to get up out of that wheelchair and walk again."[53] Long predicted, it had finally happened: the Democrats had put Elmer Gantry on their presidential ticket. If one wanted to cure the lame, one could reasonably start with John Edwards.

Extravagant promises of miraculous cures turned out to be an extremely effective argument with people who knew nothing about the science involved, such as actors. In a grim irony, Christopher Reeve died waiting for the miracle cure promised by embryonic stem-cell researchers about the same time a South Korean woman who had been paralyzed for nineteen years began to walk again with the help of a walker—thanks to an injection of umbilical cord stem cells into the injured part of her spine.[54] Long before Reeve died, two paralyzed American women with spinal cord injuries, Laura Dominguez and Susan Fajt, were treated with adult stem cells in Portugal. Both regained feeling and movement. Dominguez regained most upper body movement and began to walk with braces.

At a debate in New York before Reeve died, the head of a biotechnology company actually put his hand over the mouth of Reeve's debating partner to prevent Reeve from hearing about the stunning advances being made with adult stem-cell cures.[55] Plan B was to plug up Reeve's ears with his fingers while humming loudly. They're all about the dignity of the disabled, these liberals. Until Michael Fumento wrote about Hwang Mi-soon, the South Korean woman who began to walk again thanks to adult stem cells, there was no mention of it in any document on Nexis.[56]

At least the embryonic stem-cell researchers have a clear financial incentive to lie about adult stem-cell research. Liberals just want to kill humans. Everyone with a doddering ninety-year-old parent is suddenly gung-ho on experimenting on human embryos—or "blastocysts," as they are affectionately known to the "scientific community." The Worst Generation is so appalled at the idea of having to take care of Mom and Dad, they're lashing out at embryos.

Stem-cell research on embryos is an even worse excuse for the slaughter of life than abortion. No woman is even being spared an inconvenience this time. We don't have to hear the ghastly arguments of mothers against their own children, the travails of girls being sent away to live with their aunt for a few months, or the stories of women carrying the babies of rapists—as if that's happened more than twice in the last half century. This is just harvest and slaughter, harvest and slaughter. There's a famous book about this practice. It's called **Brave New World.**

Nobody ever heard of this incredibly important research on human embryos until ten minutes ago, yet everyone makes believe he's known about the undiscovered bounty in human embryos forever, and talks about it with real moral indignation. This whole debate is a hoax designed to trick Americans into yielding ground on human experimentation.

What great advances are we to expect from experimentation on human embryos—as opposed to adult stem cells, which have already produced cures? Liberals don't know. It's just a theory. But they definitely need to start slaughtering the unborn. Why not have the government give me a lot of money so I can sit around and think. Who knows what I might come up with? I'm clever. It's possible. **Give money to Ann or condemn the world to disease and pestilence!** It is simply asserted that scientists need to experiment on human embryos if they are ever going to find a cure for Alzheimer's disease, cancer, AIDS, Parkinson's disease, and so on. Maybe. If it's true, but no one has demonstrated that it **is** true. Liberals are sobbing and groaning that we don't know if the Strategic Defense Initiative will work. We shot a missile out of the sky. What's their proof? Decades of research are called for in the case of human embryos. We don't know if this will work or not, but just to be on the safe side we'd better start chopping up as many human embryos as we can get our hands on. Whereas global warming is a closed matter in need of no further study.

The last great advance for human experimentation in this country was the federal government's acquiescence to the scientific community's demands for money to experiment on aborted fetuses. Denouncing the "Christian right" for opposing the needs of science, Anthony Lewis of the **New York Times** claimed in February 2000 that the experiments were "crucial to potential cures for Parkinson's disease."[57]

Almost exactly a year later, the **Times** ran a front-page story describing the results of those experiments on Parkinson's patients: Not only was there no positive effect from injecting fetal brain tissue into the recipients, but about 15 percent of the patients had nightmarish side effects. The unfortunate patients "writhe and twist, jerk their heads, fling their arms about." In the words of one scientist, "They chew constantly, their fingers go up and down, their wrists flex and distend." And the worst thing was, the scientists couldn't turn it off.[58]

But the science that is working—adult stem-cell research—gets attacked and lied about in order to elevate the science that has produced nothing. In the August 24, 2004, **New York Times,** science writer Gina Kolata claimed that no one had succeeded in using adult stem cells "to treat diseases."

A short list of the successful treatments achieved by adult stem cells are these:

- Rebuilding livers wracked by otherwise irreversible cirrhosis
- Repairing spinal cord injuries by using stem cells from nasal and sinus regions
- Completely reversing Type 1 diabetes in mice using adult spleen cells

- Putting Crohn's disease into remission with the patient's own blood stem cells
- Putting lupus into remission using stem cells from the patient's bloodstream
- Treating sickle-cell anemia using stem cells from umbilical cord blood
- Repairing the heart muscles in patients with congestive heart failure using adult stem cells from bone marrow
- Repairing heart attack damage with the patient's own blood stem cells
- Restoring bone marrow in cancer patients using stem cells from umbilical cord blood
- Restoring weak heart muscles using immature skeletal muscle cells
- Putting leukemia into remission using umbilical cord blood
- Healing bone fractures with bone marrow cells
- Restoring sight in blind people using an ocular surface stem-cell transplant and a cornea transplant
- Treating urinary incontinence using stem cells from underarm muscle
- Reversing severe combined immunodeficiency (SCID) with genetically modified adult stem cells
- Restoring blood circulation in legs with bone marrow stem cells[59]

Meanwhile, embryonic stem cells have never cured anything in any living creature.

What's so disarming about the Left's pretend interest in "science" is that they have the audacity to shut down debate in the name of "science." Science is the study of the world as it exists, which, to their constant annoyance, is not the world liberals would like it to be. Liberals are personally offended that the AIDS virus seems to discriminate against gays. So they lie about it. They are sad that IQ is not infinitely malleable but has a genetic component. So they lie about it (and denounce people who tell the truth as racists). They are angry that men and women have different innate abilities. So they lie about it (also cry and stamp their feet).

Liberals are hostile to the very notion that things are a certain way and there generally isn't much we can do about it. They want everything to be fluid, flexible, up for grabs. That is one reason they are so fixated on the idea of evolution. Darwin's theory of evolution says that organisms don't have a real essence but have "emerged" from something else and are in the process of becoming something different yet again.

The same people who angrily waved "science" in our faces to claim that embryonic stem-cell research is more valuable than adult stem-cell research, global warming causes hurricanes, cerebral palsy is caused by noncesarean deliveries, breast implants caused autoimmune diseases, DDT caused Rachel Carson's death, AIDS is easily transmitted by heterosexuals, and women and men have the same innate aptitude for math and science are now waving the crucifix of "science" to shut down debate on evolution. Intelligent design, they say, is not "science"—like the hard science behind heterosexual AIDS. Real science requires a belief that we all evolved from a common earthworm. No questions will be allowed.

8 THE CREATION MYTH: ON THE SIXTH DAY, GOD CREATED FRUIT FLIES

iberals' creation myth is Charles Darwin's theory of evolution, which is about one notch above Scientology in scientific rigor. It's a make-believe story, based on a theory that is a tautology, with no proof in the scientist's laboratory or the fossil record—and that's after 150 years of very determined looking. We wouldn't still be talking about it but for the fact that liberals think evolution disproves God.

Even if evolution were true, it wouldn't disprove God. God has performed more spectacular feats than evolution. It's not even a daunting challenge to a belief in God. If you want something that complicates a belief in God, try coming to terms with Michael Moore being one of God's special creatures.

Although God believers don't need evolution to be false, atheists need evolution to be true. William Provine, an evolutionary biologist at Cornell University, calls Darwinism the greatest engine of atheism devised by man. His fellow Darwin disciple, Oxford zoologist Richard Dawkins, famously said, "Darwin made it possible to be an intellectually fulfilled atheist."[1] This is why there is mass panic on the left whenever someone mentions the vast and accumulating evidence against evolution.

The ACLU sued a school district in Cobb County, Georgia, merely for putting stickers in biology textbooks that urged students to study evolution "with an open mind, studied carefully, and critically considered."[2] According to the ACLU, an open mind violates the "separation of church and state," which appears in the Constitution just after the abortion and sodomy clauses. In Lebec, California, parents represented by Americans United for Separation of Church and State sued to prevent the school from even offering an elective philosophy class on intelligent design, creationism, and evolution.[3] In Dover, Pennsylvania, a small group of parents backed by the ACLU and Americans United for Separation of Church and State sued to prevent any discussion of intelligent design in a ninth-grade biology class.[4] The judge ruled in their favor and ordered the school district to pay the plaintiffs' legal fees, which will probably exceed $1 million.

So that's that. After Dover, no school district will dare breathe a word about "intelligent design," unless they want to risk being bankrupted by ACLU lawsuits. The Darwinists have saved the secular sanctity of their temples: the public schools. They didn't win on science, persuasion, or the evidence. They won the way liberals always win: by finding a court to hand them everything they want on a silver platter.

This isn't science, it's treating doubts about evolution as religious heresy. Darwinism, as philosopher and mathematician David Berlinski says, is "the last of the great 19th century mystery religions." The only reason a lot of Christians reject evolution is that we are taught to abjure big fat lies. You can look it up—we have an entire commandment about the importance of not lying.

Just to clean the palate of a century of evolutionists' browbeating everyone into saying evolution is a **FACT** and we'll see you in court if you criticize the official state religion, we begin with a story from the late Colin Patterson, respected paleontologist at the Natural History Museum in London. Like Diogenes searching for one honest man, Patterson was on a quest to find someone who could tell him—as he puts it—"anything you know about evolution, any one thing, any one thing that you think is true." Patterson said, "I tried that question on the geology staff at the Field Museum of Natural History, and the only answer I got was silence. I tried it on the members of the Evolutionary Morphology Seminar in the University of Chicago, a very prestigious body of evolutionists, and all I got there was silence for a long time."[5]

Not surprisingly, the Darwiniacs, as author and columnist Joe Sobran calls them, would apparently prefer to discuss anything but evolution, since they are always pretending evolution means something utterly uncontroversial, like "change over time." Describing "evolution" as "change over time" is like describing abortion as "choice." Aren't we all for "choice"? Don't animals change over time? The boring point that organisms "change over time" is not what the Darwiniacs are teaching schoolchildren, and that's not what the fuss is about.

Darwin's theory of evolution says life on Earth

began with single-celled life forms, which evolved into multicelled life forms, which over countless aeons evolved into higher life forms, including man, all as the result of the chance process of random mutation followed by natural selection, without guidance or assistance from any intelligent entity like God or the Department of Agriculture. Which is to say, evolution is the eminently plausible theory that the human eye, the complete works of Shakespeare, and Ronald Reagan (among other things) all came into existence purely by accident.

To avoid discussing the theory of evolution, Darwiniacs keep slipping irrelevant little facts into the debate like spare parts, leaving the impression that to deny evolution is to deny that the sun rises in the east. So, to be clear, by "evolution," I mean Charles Darwin's theory of evolution.

Evolution is not selective breeding, which produces thoroughbred horses, pedigreed dogs, colored cotton, and so on. Evolution is not the capacity of bacteria to develop antibiotic resistance, but which never evolves into anything but more bacteria. Evolution is not the phenomenon of an existing species changing over the course of many years—for example, of Frenchmen becoming shorter during the Napoleonic era or Asians becoming taller after immigrating to North

America. In fact, evolution is not adaptive characteristics developing within a species at all. Darwin's theory says we get a new species, not a taller version of the same species. Evolutionists call such adaptations "microevolution" only to confuse people. This would be like the Flat Earth Society referring to the Sahara Desert as a "micro-flat Earth," as if they are halfway to proving their theory. Well it's flat, isn't it?

Evolution is not proved by genetic similarities among living things, the heritability of characteristics, or the age of the Earth. (Though the neurotic obsession of Darwiniacs to always claim their opponents must believe in a "young Earth" is so bizarre that if they raise it one more time, I'm demanding a full-fledged investigation into the Earth's age.) Finally, one can believe evolution is not true without also believing that the Earth was created in six days by a man with a long white beard who lives in the clouds and looks eerily like Charlton Heston.

What the theory of evolution posits is an accidental, law-of-the-jungle, survival-of-the-fittest mechanism for creating new species—as indicated in the title of Darwin's book, **The Origin of Species.**

Leave aside the thornier issues, like how the accidental process that gave us opposable thumbs could produce a moral sense and consciousness of mortality. Let's consider just the basic steps of evolution.

The "theory" of evolution is:

1. Random mutation of desirable attributes (highly implausible)
2. Natural selection weeding out the "less fit" animals (pointless tautology)
3. Leading to the creation of new species (no evidence after 150 years of looking)

Step One: Unless You Are a Bacterium, Random Mutation Can't Produce Anything Worth Having

With a few exceptions, the higher organisms are not going to get anything good out of a single mutation. Most of the time, it takes more than one lousy mutation to create anything really useful, like an eye or poisonous fangs or a tail. In order to get to the final product, each one of the hundreds of mutations needed to create a functional wing or ear would itself have to make the mutant animal more fit, otherwise it wouldn't survive, according to Darwin's theory of natural selection. To the contrary, the first mutations toward a nose would just make you look funny and no one would want to reproduce with you.

The vast majority of mutations are deleterious to the organism. But evolution demands a whole parade of them that not only are individually advantageous, improving upon what existed before, but also lead to an all-new structure that is also better than what existed before.

The evolutionist's answer is **Assume that each one of the hundreds of mutations necessary to create the final product is itself "fit" in ways we don't understand but must accept on faith because it's Holy Scripture.** We haven't even gotten to the second step, and evolutionists are already asking us to assume a miracle. That's what they mean by "science, not faith."

In Darwin's day, it was only seemingly simple mechanisms like gills and eyes that had to be explained—and, by the way, natural selection couldn't explain those. Darwin knew nothing of DNA and the vastly complex systems studied by molecular biologists, such as the information processing, storage, and retrieval in DNA. Now we do. If Darwinism sounded fishy (get it?) as a means to create the eye, it's comical as an explanation for the intricacies of the cell. This isn't a minor gap in the theory of evolution: it is the theory of evolution.

Until relatively recently, scientists didn't know what the inside of a cell looked like. The cell was a mysterious "black box," as Lehigh University biochemist Michael Behe puts it. Darwiniacs prefer to ignore modern scientific knowledge so that they can pretend the cell is still a black box and tell us the mutation god created it. In his 1996 book **Darwin's Black Box,** Behe used discoveries in microbiology to refute Darwinism on Darwin's own terms. Darwin had set forth this extremely self-serving standard for himself: "If it could be demonstrated that any complex organ existed which could not possibly have been formed by numerous, successive, slight modifications, my theory would absolutely break down."

This is a fantastic formulation I intend to remember in case I ever need to defend one of my own crackpot theories. On one hand, Darwin makes what appears to be a sweeping concession that his theory might "absolutely break down." But in the same breath, he says that will happen only if an impossible test is met: If it is demonstrated that his theory "could not possibly form" a complex organ. Would the Darwin believers take that standard as a scientific test for God? **If it could be demonstrated that any complex organ existed which could not possibly have been formed by God, my God theory would absolutely break down.** If only traffic court judges would fall for that line of reasoning: "Your honor, can you prove that the photo of me running the red light wasn't staged? Oh, you can't? I move for an immediate dismissal so I can return to my home planet, Zircon."

Nevertheless, Behe disproved evolution—unless evolution is simply a nondisprovable pseudoscience, like astrology. Behe produced various "irreducibly complex" mechanisms, of which there are thousands—complex cellular structures, blood-clotting mechanisms, and the eye, among others. A bacterial motor, called a flagellum, depends on the coordinated interaction of 30–40 complex protein parts. The absence of almost any one of the parts would render the flagellum useless. An animal cell's whiplike oar, called a cilium, is composed of about 200 protein parts. Behe compared these cell parts to a simple mousetrap, with far fewer necessary components than a cilium or flagellum. Though there are only a few parts to a mousetrap, all of them have to be working together at one time for the contraption to serve any function whatsoever. If one of the parts is missing, Behe says, you don't get a mousetrap that catches only half as many mice: you don't get a mousetrap at all. Behe then demonstrated that it is a mathematical impossibility for all 30 parts of the flagellum (or 200 parts of the cilium) to have been brought together by the "numerous, successive, slight modifications" of natural selection. Life at the molecular level, he concluded, "is a loud, clear, piercing cry of **design.**"

Although clearly annoyed with him, many evolutionists were forced to concede Behe's point. Evolutionary biologist Tom Cavalier-Smith, at the University of British Columbia, said, "For none of the cases mentioned by Behe is there yet a comprehensive and detailed explanation of the probable steps in the evolution of the observed complexity." Yale molecular biologist Robert Dorit said, "In a narrow sense, Behe is correct when he argues that we do not yet fully understand the evolution of the flagellar motor or the blood clotting cascade." But still they believed that evolution must be true. They'll figure out how to prove it eventually.

But most of the cult reacted to Behe's argument the way feminists do to the suggestion that men and women might possibly have different aptitudes for math and science—they got nasty, they cried, and they denied that anything had been proved. Darwin fundamentalist Richard Dawkins denounced Behe as "cowardly" for believing in God—before admitting he couldn't answer Behe's argument.[6]

You will begin to notice that the Darwiniacs' answer to everything is to accuse their opponents of believing in God—and a flat Earth for good measure—even when responding to an argument based on biochemistry, physics, or mathematics.

Jerry Coyne, evolutionary biologist at the University of Chicago, said of Behe's cell structures, "There is no doubt that the pathways described by Behe are dauntingly complex, and their evolution will be hard to unravel. . . . [W]e may forever be unable to envisage the first proto-pathways." Or it could take hundreds of billions of years! But by then, maybe we'll have evolved into a species that doesn't exhibit anti-religious hysteria whenever anyone questions the theory of evolution. After having had several years to work on unraveling the complexity, Coyne wrote a 13,000-word jeremiad in the October 2005 **New Republic** magazine denouncing proponents of intelligent design as creationist nuts. But, curiously, Coyne never got around to addressing Behe's argument for intelligent design—the centerpiece of the very subject Coyne claimed to be discussing.[7]

Coyne simply asserted that it was possible for irreducibly complex mechanisms to have arisen by natural selection. "We have realized for decades that natural selection can indeed produce systems that, over time, become integrated to the point where they appear to be irreducibly complex." If it can, there is no evidence that it can.

Evolutionist Robert Pennock said of Behe's evidence, "I have not addressed the biochemical details of his real examples, but as we have noted, the evidence is not yet in on those questions."

The evidence isn't in? According to Behe, many of the biochemical systems he cited "have been well understood for 40 years." Much like George Bush's alleged draft dodging, there are only two possible answers from the Darwiniacs: Either evolution is true or more research is needed.

The "science" writer for the **Wall Street Journal,** Sharon Begley, begins her attack on Behe's argument by, in effect, confirming Larry Summers's point about women lacking aptitude for the hard sciences. Begley says, "Even before Darwin, critics attacked the idea of biological evolution with one or another version of, 'Evolve this!' Whether they invoked a human, an eye, or the cell's flagella that propel bacteria and sperm, the contention that natural processes of mutation and natural selection cannot explain the complexity of living things has been alive and well for 200 years."[8]

First, no one was attacking the "idea of biological evolution" before Darwin because there wasn't a lot to attack. "Evolution" before Darwin was just a teleological claim about the chain of life, having nothing to do with natural selection, which was Darwin's contribution to the subject. Indeed, before Darwin, the accepted explanation for the chain of life was design.

Second, no one knew precisely what the flagellum was until around the late 1960s, when the flagellum was first discovered to be the bacterial cell's tiny little outboard motor. So it would be difficult to make an argument for or against any particular method of the flagellum's creation when no one knew what the flagellum was or what it did.

Third, the fact that the eye has been cited as an argument against natural selection for 200 years is true, but this is hardly an argument in favor of evolution. Despite having 200 years to work on it, evolutionists still don't have an answer.

Darwin himself noted the difficulty of explaining the eye in **The Origin of Species,** admitting he could not do it—which science reporter Begley might have mentioned. Darwin hypothesized that the eye might have begun as a patch of light-sensitive cells upon which natural selection could then work its magic, making gradual improvements—creating an eye socket and slowly increasing focus and perspective and so on—until these special cells became light-sensitive pits and then a full-fledged eye. Apart from the fact that his explanation explained nothing—like all evolutionary myths, it was just a story about how something might have happened—even Darwin didn't have a story for where these amazing "light-sensitive cells" came from. That's the big enchilada.

Darwin catapulted over the whole problem to

be solved by beginning his thought experiment at a point after the major characteristic to be evolved—light-sensitive cells—already existed. For light-sensitive cells to work, the cells would have to have the capacity to initiate an electric signal, a nerve capable of carrying the electric signal to a brain, and a brain capable of processing the signal and using it to emit other electric signals.

No one disputes that organisms can develop small improvements on something that already exists, otherwise there would be no health clubs. The interesting question is not: How did a primitive eye become a complex eye? (And for the record, Darwinism can't explain that either.) The interesting question is: How did the "light-sensitive cells" come to exist in the first place? Darwin's solution is like explaining how humans evolved by saying, "Assume Dennis Kucinich. Now, through slight improvements over a billion years, successive generations would eventually become taller, grow opposable thumbs, and generally become more humanlike until one day—wham!—you have yourself a human being."

Even if they start with light-sensitive cells, Darwin's apostles still can't get to an eye. There have long been bald assertions by Darwiniacs of the existence of a computer simulation of the evolution of the eye. The webpage of the National Science Teachers Association baldly states, "Computer simulations of natural selection are common, such as the computer simulation of the evolution of the eye as described in [Richard] Dawkins."9

In his book **River Out of Eden,** Dawkins blathers on and on about "**computer models** of evolving eyes." But the computer simulation turned out to have as much basis in reality as the idea that domestic violence increases on Super Bowl Sunday. David Berlinski got to the bottom of the famed computer simulation, tracking down the scientists alleged to have performed this wondrous feat, and discovered—as described in a tour de force article in **Commentary** magazine—it didn't exist.10

In **The Politically Incorrect Guide to Science,** Tom Bethell quotes Berlinski's summary of the evidence:

> This notion that there is somewhere a computer model of the evolutionary development of the eye is an urban myth. Such a model does not exist. There is no such model anywhere in any laboratory. No one has the faintest idea how to make one. The whole story was fabricated out of thin air by Richard Dawkins. The senior author of the study on which Dawkins based his claim—

Dan E. Nilsson—has explicitly rejected the idea that his laboratory has ever produced a computer simulation of the eye's development.11

In other words, **River Out of Eden** is the Darwiniacs' version of **The Protocols of the Elders of Zion.**

Back to the **Wall Street Journal**'s "science reporter." After demonstrating that she is an ignoramus, Begley accuses critics of evolution of having small minds for refusing to believe in evolution. She calls the Behe argument a variant on all arguments against evolution (which she's apparently growing a little tired of): "the argument from personal incredulity." This, Begley defines as "I can't see how natural forces could produce this, so it must be the work of God."

Begley's argument is called the "argument from the counterintuitive," which says, "It's counterintuitive, so it must be true" (and I'll sound really smart if I say so). "It's the same compulsion that drives insecure adolescents to make counterintuitive, cryptic, and otherwise odd statements." ("Play the game, don't let the game play you." Huh?) I'd be more impressed by Begley's outré spirit if she took up smoking.

Taking its place among such giants as the theory of relativity and quantum mechanics, evolution is, indeed, counterintuitive. So it's got the counterintuitive part down pat. What it doesn't have, and what the theory of relativity, curved space, and black holes do, is any evidence that it is true.

Begley imagines she has proved Behe wrong by announcing that some of the 200 parts of the animal cell's motor have other functions. This is like explaining that the **Mona Lisa** is an accident of nature by saying paint has many other functions. There's still that crucial step of assembling them all together, at one time, into the **Mona Lisa.** It doesn't matter if 200 mutations happened at once or over a billion years. All 200 mutations would have to (1) occur, (2) be the "most fit," (3) survive long enough to exist at the same time and place, in order to (4) assemble themselves into a working flagellum. The cell is as complicated a structure as the entire city of New York. Natural selection has never been demonstrated to change anything fancier than the shape of a bird's beak.

The evolutionists' response is **Well, it's possible. You can't say it couldn't "possibly" happen—and that was the test Darwin of Nazareth set for himself.** It's also possible that galactic ruler Xenu brought billions of people to Earth 75 million years ago, piled them around volcanoes, and blew them up with hydrogen bombs, sending their souls flying every which way until they landed on the bodies of living humans, where they still invisibly reside today—as Scientology's L. Ron Hubbard claimed. Yes, it's possible.

On April 7, 2006—more than two years after Sharon Begley informed **Wall Street Journal** readers that the irreducible complexity argument had been solved eons ago and she was frankly bored with the subject—the **New York Times** ran a front-page article declaring that researchers had finally produced a "counterargument to doubters of evolution who question how a progression of small changes could produce the intricate mechanisms found in living cells." This was under the headline "Study, in a First, Explains Evolution's Molecular Advance."[12] At least we finally had a clear admission that the irreducible complexity argument had not been answered before this. But look at the allegedly "complex" mechanism that scientists asserted—not proved, asserted—might have arisen by natural selection: a two-part molecular mechanism, the hormone and its receptor. Two parts! Even a mousetrap—Behe's simplest example of a complex mechanism—has three parts. And, of course, they still hadn't shown that the hormone-receptor pair could be produced by natural selection, only that this simple two-part mechanism might be produced by natural selection. That's front-page news for the state religion.

Evolutionists believe—purely as a matter of faith—that individual, unrelated mutations facilitated the production of all 200 necessary parts, completely by chance, and thus created the flagellum. And then they tell us they want to keep "faith" out of the classroom. Okay.

The late Cambridge astrophysicist Sir Fred Hoyle and his collaborator Chandra Wickramasinghe came to a similar conclusion as Behe while trying to explain the origin of life. Contrary to the image of evolution skeptics portrayed in the movie **Inherit the Wind,** Hoyle and Wickramasinghe were not millenarian fundamentalists making moonshine by the river. In 1986, they were jointly awarded the International Dag Hammarskjold Gold Medal for Science. Hoyle has won the Crafoord Prize from the Royal Swedish Academy of Sciences, the Klumpke-Roberts Award of the Astronomical Society of the Pacific (1977), the Royal Medal (1974), the Bruce Medal (1970), and the Gold Medal of the Royal Astronomical Society (1968).

Wickramasinghe holds the highest doctorate (Sc.D.) from the University of Cambridge and an honorary doctorate from the Soka University of Tokyo. He is a fellow of the Royal Society of Arts and a fellow of the Royal Astronomical Society. He is a professor of applied mathematics and astronomy at Cardiff University of Wales and director of the Cardiff Centre for Astrobiology. Wickramasinghe was the first to propose the theory that dust in interstellar space and comets was mostly organic, a theory that has now been proved correct.

Finally, Hoyle and Wickramasinghe were both atheists. Consequently, they had some odd ideas about the origin of life—but they knew enough about science to know Darwin's theory of evolution for the creation of life was preposterous.

Hoyle ran the numbers to determine the mathematical probability of the basic enzymes of life arising by random processes. They concluded that the odds were 1 to 1 followed by 40,000 zeroes, or "so utterly minuscule" as to make Darwin's theory of evolution absurd.[13] Hoyle said a "common sense interpretation of the facts" is that "a superintellect has monkeyed with physics, as well as with chemistry and biology and that there are no blind forces worth speaking about in nature." His calculations from the facts, he said, "seem to me so overwhelming as to put this conclusion almost beyond question."

In order to explain the creation of the universe while carefully excluding God, Hoyle and Wickramasinghe came up with a theory called "panspermia," which holds that life began in space and spread to Earth by a steady influx of microscopic infectious agents delivered to Earth on comets. It's sort of a galactic version of commercial air travel. It's a little nutty but, unlike evolution, "panspermia" has the virtue of not being demonstrably false.

Francis Crick, winner of the Nobel Prize for his codiscovery of DNA, also realized that the spontaneous evolution of life could not be reconciled with the facts. As he said, "The probability of life originating at random is so utterly minuscule as to make it absurd." Consequently, Crick hypothesized that highly intelligent extraterrestrials sent living cells to Earth on an unmanned spaceship, a theory he sets forth in his 1981 book, **Life Itself.** Thus was God narrowly averted!

While evolution fetishists turn themselves into modern-day phrenologists, real scientists are making important scientific discoveries about complex structures that keep making the random mutation part of evolution look increasingly silly.

(And that's not to knock phrenology, which actually made some pretty good predictions. A 1921 article on phrenology, for example, observed, "The small-nose man can not have a judicial mind, whatever his other excellencies may be. And a man whose nose upturns can no more be expected to administer justice than a pug dog can be expected to act as a shepherd.")

The evolutionists attack the idea of design in the universe, claiming it is a theory based on what we don't know. The truth is exactly the reverse. The less you know about the physical world, the more plausible Darwinian evolution seems. Primitive people believed in sun gods, moon gods, and fertility gods. But as soon as humans understood the science of astronomy and reproduction (except C. Everett Koop, who still doesn't understand that one), make-believe gods moving the sun and creating babies became a less persuasive explanation.

Similarly, the more we know about molecules, cells, and DNA, the less plausible Darwin's theory of natural selection becomes. So the evolutionists bring lawsuits to prevent schoolchildren from being told that natural selection can't begin to explain such complex parts as the flagellum. DNA is—as Bill Gates says—"like a computer program, but far, far more advanced than any software we've ever created."[14] Darwiniacs want us to believe that DNA—something vastly more perfect and powerful and complex than Windows XP, a program that represents the culmination of tens of thousands of years of human progress—came to exist by means of nothing more than a series of random accidents starting in a puddle of prehistoric goo.

Step Two: Survival of the Fittest Is a Tautology

The second prong of Darwin's "theory" is generally nothing but a circular statement: Through the process of natural selection, the "fittest" survive. Who are the "fittest"? The ones who survive! Why look—it happens every time! The "survival of the fittest" would be a joke if it weren't part of the belief system of a fanatical cult infesting the Scientific Community.

The beauty of having a scientific theory that's a tautology is that it can't be disproved. Evolution cultists denounce "Creation Science" on the grounds that it's not "science" because it can't be observed or empirically tested in a laboratory. Guess what else can't be observed or empirically tested? Evolution!

But, you say, there must be some characteristics that are inherently desirable without regard to whether or not the organism survived, such as intelligence, strength, or—to take something really obvious—a tendency to avoid eating poison. In one experiment attempting to prove evolution (and those are the only evolution experiments allowed by law), fruit flies were bred to avoid eating poison. One would think that if we could settle on one characteristic that is a priori "fit," it would be: "Avoids eating poison."

Alas, the fruit flies bred to avoid eating poison did not survive. They died out while the original dumb fruit flies with no aversion to eating poison survived to reproduce. Thus, the scientists concluded: Stupid is more fit. As the headline in the **New Scientist** put it, "Cleverness May Carry Survival Costs." Yes, it's been observed for centuries that it's the truly stupid who are the most successful, live the longest, are the happiest, the wealthiest, the most desirable, and so on. Let's face it: It's the stupid who have the inside track in this world.

This is what's known as "A Theory Incapable of Disproof." (Or perhaps, "A Theory Born of Self-Interest.") The fruit fly experiment is now cited as scientific proof of evolution. So whenever you hear about the "overwhelming scientific evidence for evolution," remember that evolutionists have put the fruit fly poison-eating experiment in their "win" column.

Or consider the argument for evolution made in the **New York Times** Science section based on the human appendix. After describing how the appendix is a useless organ that can kill you, the author snidely remarks, "You sometimes hear people who say they reject evolution's claim that our bodies show clear signs of being 'intelligently designed.' I wonder how many of them have had appendicitis."

As I understand the concept behind survival of the **fittest,** the appendix doesn't do much for the theory of evolution either. How does a survival-of-the-fittest regime evolve an organ that kills the host organism? Why hasn't evolution evolved the appendix away? (Another sign that your scientific theory is in trouble: When your argument against an opposing theory also disproves your own.)

For those of you opposed to "faith" being taught in the classroom, reflect on the answer the **Times** gave:

> Imagine a trait that helps an animal survive to adulthood, but that also has side effects that can cause trouble later in life. If, on balance, animals produce more offspring with the trait than without it, natural selection will favor it. [P]erhaps the appendix lifted the odds that our ancestors could resist childhood diseases and live to childbearing years. Even if it also caused deaths by appendicitis, the appendix might have been a net plus.[15]

So there it is: the theory of evolution is proved again. When the appendix's use was a mystery, it proved evolution. When the appendix was thought to help humans resist childhood diseases—well, that proved evolution, too! Throw in enough words like **imagine, perhaps,** and **might have**—and you've got yourself a scientific theory! How about this: **Imagine** a giant raccoon passed gas and **perhaps** the resulting gas **might** have created the vast variety of life we see on Earth. **And if you don't accept the giant raccoon flatuence theory for the origin of life, you must be a fundamentalist Christian nut who believes the Earth is flat.** That's basically how the argument for evolution goes.

You will begin to notice that the evolution cultists' answer to everything is the punchline to the joke about the economist. A physicist, a chemist, and an economist are stranded on a desert island with one can of food but no can opener. The physicist says, "If we drop the can from 30 meters, the velocity plus the force will break the can open." The chemist says, "We could heat the can to 101 degrees Celsius and the boiling reaction will burst the can." The economist says, "Assume a can opener."

That's all you ever get from evolution cultists: **Assume a can opener.** Assume each one of the many, many mutations necessary to create a complicated structure—like a cell or an eye—is itself beneficial and somehow makes the organism more fit. Assume completely random mutations—all individually beneficial—could come together in 200 individual parts to form a perfectly functioning mechanism such as the flagellum. Assume the appendix is a cornucopia of unknown benefits (until it kills you). Assume eating poison is good for you. These people make L. Ron Hubbard look like Aristotle.

They ridicule us for saying, "The Bible is true because it says so right in the Bible"—which I've never said, by the way. Then they expect us to swallow their circular argument in support of Darwinism. To paraphrase Chico Marx, "Who are you going to believe? Me or your brilliantly designed eyes?"

Step Three: Creating a New Species Is Still on Evolution's "To-Do" List

We haven't even gotten to the third prong of Darwin's theory of evolution—the point of the whole contraption—and we've already had to assume miracles and stifle giggles at the key definitional term "fittest." The big payoff of the theory that must be taught as scientific fact to small schoolchildren throughout America is this: If we combine (1) absurd assumptions about random mutation with (2) a tautology ("survival of the fittest"), we get . . . a whole new species!

If you get your news from the American news media, it will come as a surprise to learn that when Darwin first published **The Origin of Species,** in 1859, his most virulent opponents were not fundamentalist Christians but paleontologists. It was a nice yarn Darwin had spun, but there was absolutely nothing in the fossil record to support it. Far from showing gradual change with one species slowly giving way to another, as Darwin hypothesized, the fossil record showed vast numbers of new species suddenly appearing out of nowhere, remaining largely unchanged for millions of years, and then disappearing (almost like there was a big flood or something).

Darwin's response was to say: Start looking! He blamed the absence of fossil support for his theory on the "extreme imperfection of the geological record." With a little elbow grease, he was sure, paleontologists would soon produce the necessary evidence. Well, we've been looking for 150 years now, we've found a lot of fossils, and what the fossil record shows is: New species suddenly appearing out of nowhere, remaining largely unchanged for millions of years, and then suddenly disappearing.

In 1979, David Raup, a geologist at the Field

Museum of Natural History in Chicago, described the problem this way:

> The evidence we find in the geologic record is not nearly as compatible with darwinian [**sic**] natural selection as we would like it to be. Darwin was completely aware of this. He was embarrassed by the fossil record because it didn't look the way he predicted it would and, as a result, he devoted a long section of his **Origin of Species** to an attempt to explain and rationalize the differences. There were several problems, but the principal one was that the geologic record did not then and still does not yield a finely graduated chain of slow and progressive evolution.[16]

Things have only gotten worse in the intervening twenty years. It was one thing for Darwin to rationalize the lack of fossil evidence on the grounds that "only a small portion of the world is known with accuracy." It's another thing entirely for today's biologists to be still clinging to the argument from ignorance. One hundred fifty years have passed with vast awards and accolades dangling before any paleontologist who could locate a fossil proving evolution.

Dr. Raup said:

[W]e are now about 120 years after Darwin and the knowledge of the fossil record has been greatly expanded. We now have a quarter of a million fossil species but the situation hasn't changed much. The record of evolution is still surprisingly jerky and, ironically, we have even fewer examples of evolutionary transitions than we had in Darwin's time. By this I mean that some of the classic cases of darwinian [**sic**] change in the fossil record, such as the evolution of the horse in North America, have had to be discarded or modified as a result of more detailed information—what appeared to be a nice simple progression when relatively few data were available now appears to be much more complex and much less gradualistic.[17]

Darwin's disciples simply assert that evolution led from this species to that by the process of random mutation—with cruel nature striking down the genetic losers—and to hell with the fossil record's showing nothing of the sort. At some point, it's not even pseudoscience anymore, it's just a crazy religious cult. If mutations are utterly random—as Darwinism claims—there ought to be an infinite variety of transitional animals with small mutations that eventually led to a magnificent new attribute like a wing or a lung. Unlike most high school biology teachers lying to your children about evolution, Darwin was at least aware of what the fossil record ought to show if his theory was correct. He said there would be "interminable varieties, connecting together all the extinct and existing forms of life by the finest graduated steps."[18]

But we don't have "interminable varieties." We don't have fossils "connecting" the extinct to the extant. We don't have the "finest graduated steps." What the fossil record shows is sudden bursts of all manner of animals, modest change, and then sudden and total extinction. Dinosaurs appeared, lived for 150 million years, and then disappeared, only to be quickly replaced with mammals. Neither the creation nor the extinction of dinosaurs was accomplished by a gradual process of any sort.

You also never see the mutations that turned out to be clunkers, like the dog that mutated webbed feet or the fish that mutated fur. To the contrary, all the changes always seem to follow a straight line.

But if the mutations were really random, with Mother Nature ruthlessly striking down the genetic losers, then for every mutation that was desirable, there ought to be a staggering number that are undesirable. Otherwise, the mutations aren't random, they are deliberate—and then you get into all the hocus-pocus about an "intelligent de-signer" and will probably start speaking in tongues and going to NASCAR races. But that's not what the fossil record shows. We don't have fossils for the vast quantity of hapless creatures that ought to have died out in a survival-of-the-fittest regime.

The evolution cultists hypothesize—since this is a real science, as opposed to intelligent design, which is just a bunch of crazy conjectures—that the bad mutations didn't stick around long enough to leave fossils. Pay no attention to the man behind the curtain: the clunkier mutations simply never fossilized, and why are you asking so many questions?

Or they revert to Darwin's excuse of 150 years ago about the paucity of the fossil record. If that explains anything, it only explains why we wouldn't find one particular unfit mutation—say, if we went looking only for the dog with webbed feet. It doesn't explain why we don't find **any** bad mutations—a dog that mutated anten-nae, or gills, or a tail on its head. In order to mu-tate the good stuff, like a bird's lung, there would have to be countless mutations that were at least better than what existed before. If each one of the incremental mutations is more "fit" than what preceded it—which it has to be in order to survive—those transitional mutations should have stayed around long enough to appear in the fossil record, before mutating their way to something even better. But in the course of millions and millions of years, all we see are slight variations on the final product.

There is no reason to expect, for example, that the first place our eyes ever appeared was on the front of our faces. Why don't we have ancestors with eyes on the bottom of their feet, on their arms, or on the top of their heads? Eyes might be best positioned in the front of our heads, but eyes on the bottom of our feet are better than no eyes at all, and so should have stuck around at least for a while in the fossil record. But they're not there.

We're not talking about **The Swan** on NBC. This is evolution! This is the completely accidental process that created butterfly wings, bat radar, the human brain, and the millions of species alive today. The theory of evolution requires hundreds, thousands, maybe millions of mutations just to create an eye. (No one has any idea how many mutations would be required to create an eye.) A process that is supposed to have transformed an amoeba into Jerry Garcia by "random mutation" must have produced some spectacular failures. Why can't we find any of the amusing ones?

The late Harvard paleontologist Stephen Jay Gould,[19] one of evolution's most passionate defenders, called the "extreme rarity" of transitional animals the "trade secret of paleontology." He said, "The evolutionary trees that adorn our textbooks have data only at the tips and nodes of the branches; the rest is inference, however reasonable, not the evidence of fossils." (Gould was also the guy who tried to disprove the idea of IQ and lost that debate, too. Poor Gould will go down in history as the Robert E. Lee of science, the last passionate defender of lost causes.) Paleontologist and evolutionary biologist Robert Carroll admits, "Very few intermediates between groups are known from the fossil record."[20]

For over a hundred years, evolutionists proudly pointed to the same sad birdlike animal, Archaeopteryx, as their lone transitional fossil linking dinosaurs and birds. Discovered a few years after Darwin published **The Origin of Species,** Archaeopteryx was instantly hailed as the transitional species that proved Darwin's theory. This unfortunate creature had wings, feathers, teeth, claws, and a long, bony tail. If it flew at all, it didn't fly very well. Alas, it is now agreed that poor Archaeopteryx is no relation of modern birds. It's just a dead end. It transitioned to nothing.

But could Archaeopteryx be our one example of bad mutations eliminated by natural selection? Archaeopteryx can't fill that role either, because it seems to have no predecessors. The fossils that look like Archaeopteryx lived millions of years **after** Archaeopteryx, and the fossils that preceded Archaeopteryx look nothing at all like it. The bizarre bird is just an odd creation that came out of nowhere and went nowhere, much like Air America Radio.

The **Washington Post** defended the state religion by referring to evidence that does not exist—the countless bad mutations—in order to rationalize the apparent designed progression of the fossil record: "This appearance of 'perfect fit' makes it seem as if organisms must have been the product of an intelligent force. But this appearance of perfection is deceiving. It gives no hint of the numberless evolutionary dead ends—lineages that, according to the fossil record, survived for a while but then died out, probably because changes in the environment made their once-perfect designs not so perfect anymore."[21]

That would have been a creditable defense of the Darwiniacs' crackpot religion in 1859. But if there were—as Darwin supposed and the **Washington Post** asserts 150 years later in defiance of the facts—"numberless evolutionary dead ends," we ought to have found a whole bunch of them by now. In fact, we ought to have found more dead ends than evolutionary advances—a lot more.

Niles Eldredge, Gould's collaborator, has devoted himself to reconciling evolutionary theory with the fossil record. But even Eldredge complained of the famous "evolutionary" horse sequence purporting to show diminutive horses "evolving" into modern stallions, saying the sequence is entirely "speculative" and yet is "presented as the literal truth in textbook after textbook." Evolutionary biologist Jerry Coyne at the University of Chicago claims it is "flat wrong" to say that the fossil record does not show "a smooth, unambiguous transitional series linking, let's say, the first small horse to today's horse." Coyne ought to apply for a job at the American Museum of Natural History. Much to its embarrassment, the museum has had to rearrange its famous "horse sequence."

The more advances paleontologists make in uncovering the fossil record, the more absurd the evolution fable becomes. Most nettlesome for evolutionists is the Cambrian period, showing a vast quantity of plants and animals appearing on the scene in the blink of an evolutionary eye more than 500 million years ago. In a period of less than 10 million years, there is a sudden explosion of nearly all the animal phyla we have today. As leading Darwin cultist Richard Dawkins describes the Cambrian fossils, "It is as though they were just planted there, without evolutionary history." Darwin himself referred to the great difficulty of explaining the absence of "vast piles of strata rich in fossils" before the Cambrian explosion.

Origin of Species–thumpers prefer to ignore the Cambrian explosion and prattle instead about the "evolution" of "girl crushes"—as one article did in the **New York Times** Style section. ("Social scientists suspect such emotions are part of women's nature, feelings that evolution may have favored because they helped women bond with one another and work cooperatively"[22]— and you know how cooperative we gals are.) This is where all the deep thinking about evolution is being done these days, in the "social sciences" and the Style section of the **New York Times.**

Or the Darwiniacs lie about the duration of the Cambrian period, as Jerry Coyne does to nerd public policy wonks reading the **New Republic** who don't know any better. Referring to "the so-called 'Cambrian explosion' "—as if even the name is a fraud—Coyne writes, " 'Short period' here means geologically short, in this case 10 million to 30 million years."[23] This is both misleading and false (which isn't easy!). The best estimate for the duration of the Cambrian explosion is not 10 to 30 million years, as evolutionists like Coyne often claim, but 5 to 10 million years. And that is the maximum length. When dealing with rocks half a billion years old, it's impossible to resolve times to less than 5 to 10 million years (just as with a telescope it's impossible to distinguish two faraway objects if they are close together). In other words, the explosion of animal life could have happened in an instant, but from our present perspective we can't narrow it down to anything more precise than a window of about 5 to 10 million years. If intelligent design is a crackpot theory being hawked by religious nuts, why are its opponents the ones always caught telling big whoppers?

These great practitioners of the scientific method, dispassionately pursuing the evidence wherever it may lead, simply pretend the Cambrian explosion didn't happen (the "so-called" Cambrian explosion, as Coyne says), and anyone who mentions it is a creationist nut. The **New York Times** will write honestly about Air America's ratings before high school biology textbooks will tell the truth about the Cambrian explosion.

When forced to pony up an answer, Darwin's disciples say, Assume a can opener. Assume that the creatures that preceded the Cambrian era failed to fossilize (as they said about the intermediate fossils that also aren't there). Assume they were soft-bodied creatures evolving like mad, but leaving no record because of their squishy little microscopic bodies. Yes, that would explain it!

The evolutionists had no evidence to support that assumption, but at least it couldn't be disproved—so it was at least on a par with the Flatulent Raccoon Theory of life's origins.

Alas, in 1984, Chinese paleontologists discovered fossils just preceding the Cambrian era, and it turned out the pre-Cambrian creatures were extraordinarily well preserved.[24] But instead of a glut of evolutionary ancestors, all we have at the outset of the Cambrian explosion are some sad little worms and sponges. The interesting thing about the pre-Cambrian organisms is that they are soft-bodied, microscopic creatures—precisely the sort of animal the evolution cult claimed wouldn't fossilize and therefore deprived them of crucial evidence. But now it turned out fossilization was not merely possible in the pre-Cambrian era, the pre-Cambrian beds were positively ideal for fossilization—better even than in the Cambrian period. And yet the only thing paleontologists found there was a few worms.

The Chinese fossil discovery was, as the **New York Times** put it, "among the most spectacular in this century." Scientists were calling it "genesis material." The discovery showed "that the dramatic transformation of life from primeval single-cell organisms to the complex multicellular precursors of modern fauna was more sudden, swift and widespread than scientists had thought."**25** For 3 billion years, nothing but bacteria and worms and then suddenly nearly all the phyla of animal life appeared within a mere 5 to 10 million years—"as though they were just planted there." Jan Bergstrom, a paleontologist who examined the Chinese fossils, said the Cambrian period was not "evolution," it was "a revolution."**26**

Even the famously difficult-to-evolve eye appeared at the beginning of the Cambrian period. And there were no light-sensitive pits. And yet, in 2005—or two decades after the discovery of the Chinese fossils—the **New Scientist** was still clinging to Darwin's speculation that the first eyes "probably evolved from light-sensitive cells."**27** At least when Darwin invoked light-sensitive pits, it was merely question begging. The assertion of the "light-sensitive pits" hypothesis after the discovery of the Chinese fossils is a religious belief held in defiance of the facts.

Andrew Knoll, Harvard professor of natural history, described the importance of the Chinese fossils, saying, "Most of everything that was going to happen, all the ways of making invertebrate animals, had already happened by the mid-Cambrian. Now, it seems the new life forms were invented within the first few million years of the Cambrian."**28** Unable to keep using the excuse that they had no fossil evidence because their evidence failed to fossilize, the Darwiniacs quietly returned to pretending the Cambrian explosion never happened.

In 2005, Jerry Coyne was still trying to pass off the "hard to fossilize" argument to readers of the **New Republic,** writing, "We still do not understand why many groups originated in even this relatively short time, although it may reflect an artifact: the evolution of easily fossilized hard parts suddenly made organisms capable of being fossilized." Twenty years after the Chinese fossils were discovered, Coyne was still pretending not to have heard of them.

The preposterous conceit that the fossil record has produced a beautiful mosaic of organisms consistent with evolution except for the occasional "gap" is absurd. Evolution is nothing but a gap. It's a conjecture about how species might have arisen that is contradicted by the fossil record and by nearly everything we have learned about molecular biology since Darwin's day.

Things do evolve, in a figurative sense. The fifth draft of a script is usually better than the first draft. People do get taller when there's more protein in their diets. Ellen DeGeneres's third TV show is better than her first two were. Okay, fine. The cult cites evidence that looks like Michelangelo's studies for the Sistine Chapel and then claims it has proved the absence of a designer—

and brings lawsuits to prevent anyone from saying otherwise.

Scientists in Communist China have more freedom of speech to discuss scientific facts bearing on evolution than we do in the United States. Chen Jun-Yuan, of the Nanjing Institute of Geology and Paleontology, who performed the excavations, says that contrary to Darwin's tree of life, which predicts a few primitive organisms gradually branching out into many others, the fossil record shows just the opposite. "The base is wide," Dr. Chen says, "and gradually narrows." Chen concluded, "Darwinism is maybe only telling a part of the story for evolution." (Fortunately, Dr. Chen is not in Dover, Pennsylvania, or Judge John E. Jones III would have prohibited him from saying that.)

Meanwhile, when a high school biology teacher in America tries to tell his students about the Chinese fossils, he is banned from teaching biology. Roger DeHart used to teach biology at Burlington-Edison High School in Washington State, where he supplemented his curriculum with newspaper stories on the Chinese fossils from newspapers like the **Boston Globe** and the **New York Times.** He never mentioned God.[29] The ACLU threatened to sue and the school removed DeHart from his class, replacing him with a recent teachers' college graduate who had majored in physical education. Thus were the students of Burlington-Edison High School saved from having to hear scientific facts that might cause them to question their faith in the official state religion. The liberal clergy prohibit students from hearing about a fossil bed described in the **New York Times** as "among the most spectacular in this century." Then they say it's because they want to keep faith out of the classroom.

The Cambrian period isn't a small gap in the fossil record chock-full of evolutionary evidence. There is no evidence in the fossil record—only "ingenious excuses," as Berkeley law professor Phillip Johnson says.

Remarking on the discovery of the pre-Cambrian fossils in China, primitive-chordate specialist Nicholas Holland of San Diego's Scripps Institution of Oceanography, said, "You just hardly know what order to put the material in now. I mean, you might as well just present the phyla alphabetically. It's come to that."[30] As Gould admits when he says transitional forms "are generally lacking at the species level," even the cult members can't point to fossils showing the transition from one species to another, which I gather is the general point of the theory of evolution, subtly alluded to in the title of Darwin's book, **The Origin of Species.**

The sad state of the fossil record has led to a

schism in the church of evolution. Both sets of Darwin's disciples demand that we assume miracles to reconcile Darwinism with the fossil record, but the two branches disagree—passionately—about whose miracle is more convincing. As already mentioned, the "neo-Darwinists" respond to all problems in the fossil record by asking us to assume all the creatures we would expect to find if evolution was true and really did exist (really!)—but somehow **never fossilized.**

Their hated rivals, the Darwin revisionists, tend to reside at places like Harvard and the American Museum of Natural History and have too much intellectual pride to subscribe to a clunky, obvious miracle like "none of the animals that would support our theory fossilized." Consequently, the revisionists have given up on trying to defend the fossil record as consistent with evolution. Instead, the revisionists concocted a more sophisticated supernatural occurrence. The miracle proposed by Gould and Niles Eldredge, a curator at the American Museum of Natural History, is called "punctuated equilibrium." The gist of "punctuated equilibrium" is: Evolution, but this time—let's make it consistent with the fossil record!

Instead of gradual change occurring by random mutation and natural selection choosing the most "fit" to survive and reproduce—in other words, "Darwin's theory of evolution"—Gould and Eldredge hypothesized that evolution could also happen really fast and then stop happening at all for 150 million years. Basically what happens is this: Your parents are slugs and then suddenly—but totally at random—you evolve into a gecko and your brother evolves into a shark and your sister evolves into a polar bear and the guy down the street evolves into a porpoise and so on—and then everyone relaxes by the pool for 150 million years, virtually unchanged.

The important thing is: This happened completely by chance. In other words, the most prominent apologist for evolution came up with a theory of evolution that's not evolution, it's a nontheological miracle.

9 PROOF FOR HOW THE WALKMAN EVOLVED INTO THE iPOD BY RANDOM MUTATION

arwiniacs do not have a single observable example of one species evolving into another by the Darwinian mechanism of variation and selection. All they have is a story. It is a story that inspires fanatical devotion from the cult simply because their story excludes a creator. They have seized upon something that looks like progress from primitive life forms to more complex life forms and invented a story to explain how the various categories of animals

originated. But animal sequences do not prove that the Darwinian mechanism of natural selection caused the similarities. It is just as likely that the similarities are proof of intelligent design, creationism, or the Giant Raccoon's Flatulence theory. The animal-sequence drawings allegedly demonstrating evolution by showing, for example, a little runt horse gradually becoming a grand stallion, are just that: drawings.

Evolutionists act as if they were the first people on Earth to notice similarities among various species, but this wasn't a new concept. Biologists had always grouped animals by what they looked like. No one disputes that a monkey looks like a human, especially in the case of Al Franken. Evolution fetishists then position the different species in a make-believe "tree of life" and announce that they have proved evolution. The capacity to draw a diagram and come up with a story about how things might have happened is not science. Janet Reno looks like Elton John. That is not proof that Janet Reno gave birth to Elton John.

The seductiveness of Darwinism resides in its confusion of similar structures with the engine of creation. The Darwinian sleight of hand consists of the claim that because a human hand, for example, is similar to a bat's wing, there must be an ancestral relationship. Clearly apes look like us, but that doesn't mean there is a lineal connection between us and the apes. It certainly does not establish the mechanism responsible for the differences.

Despite the cult members' occasional calm assurances that this animal evolved into that, we have no idea whatsoever if one animal descended from another. Fossils do not reveal parent/descendant relationships. It's all guesswork, requiring frequent revision in light of new fossil discoveries. The animal-sequence drawings in biology textbooks are presented as if they are hard fact, and then a few years later, new fossil discoveries require the sequence to be completely disassembled, rearranged, and put back together again. Then the all-new animal-sequence drawing is presented as if it were hard fact, and the existence of an earlier, completely different sequence drawing is flushed down the memory hole.

But every few years, the Darwiniacs find some odd creature that looks a little like another creature, and it is triumphantly announced that evolution has been "proved true." Thus, for example, on April 6, 2006, the **New York Times** gave prime front-page, above-the-fold space to an article headlined "Fossil Called Missing Link from Sea to Land Animals." The article quoted unnamed scientists as saying that this discovery "should undercut the argument that there is no evidence in the fossil record of one kind of creature becoming another kind." So they found an odd-looking fish with weird appendages and pronounced the missing link between fish and land animals. But only if evolution is assumed to be true is there any basis for assuming that the fish is related to fishes without appendages or to land animals—much less for assuming that each step was produced by a brutal battle of survival of the fittest. And there is no reason to assume evolution is true until, among other things, the Darwiniacs can produce a whole glut of transitional animals—i.e., a entirely new fossil record.

The successive appearance of more complex species does seem to show something that looks like progress. But that has nothing to do with the Darwinian mechanism of natural selection. One also sees progress in the Wright brothers' increasingly complex airplanes, a master's paintings, and the advance from the peace pipe to Marlboro Lights—progressions all notable for being the product of "intelligent designers." The appearance of progress hardly establishes mutation and natural selection as the engine of change. To the contrary, the similarities that so mesmerize Darwiniacs look more like the progress of a designed object than the result of a series of lucky accidents. Far from the fantastic competition of a dog-eat-dog struggle to survive, we see a fossil record that reveals a rather clean, well-organized sequence.

This is why Stephen Jay Gould referred to the absence of transitional fossils as the "trade secret" of paleontology. As a consolation prize to evolution's lackeys who still wanted to believe the fossil record wasn't a complete bust, Gould offered this hopeful spin: "Transitional forms are generally lacking at the species level, but they are abundant between larger groups."[1] Transitional forms between larger groups means evolutionists can point to reptiles appearing in the fossil record, followed by mammal-like reptiles, followed by mammals. This, they say, proves the mammals came from the reptiles.

They have no idea if the reptiles are even related to the mammal-like reptiles, much less to the mammals. Again, fossils do not reveal a parent/descendant relationship. The cultists certainly don't know whether any particular mammal descended from any particular reptile. But more important, the apparent progress from simple animals to more sophisticated higher animals—with no transitional species—looks a lot more like planned, deliberate progress than a series of random mutations.

Darwiniacs love to cite, for example, the progress from the reptile's multiboned jaw to the jaw of mammal-like reptiles with fewer bones, leading inexorably to the single-boned mammal jawbone with two bones moving to the ear. The jawbone metamorphosis didn't prove evolution, but here at last was one small part of the fossil record that was not wildly inconsistent with the theory of evolution—in contradistinction to the Cambrian period and the absence of transitional species, for example. That's "proof" when it comes to the state religion: For not disproving evolution, the vertebrate jawbone is said to prove evolution. Michael Moore's essence is consistent with the Flatulent Raccoon Theory for the origin of life. On Darwiniacs' standard of proof for themselves, the Flatulent Raccoon Theory has thus been proved true.

In fact and to the contrary, the much-celebrated migration of the reptile jawbone raises more questions for the theory of evolution than it answers. How did that happen? How, that is, did those bones figure out just where to go? One would think that if they had perfect independence in migrating anywhere, the bones would have landed all over the place, but no, we have no evidence, over the course of the reptile-to-mammal transition, that those wandering bones had any other destination in mind than the one they ultimately found.

When asked for proof, all evolutionists can do

is point to structural differences in broad categories of animals—the "larger groups" mentioned by Gould—as if the very thing they were trying to explain constituted an explanation. Yes, we know a lizard is different from a squirrel. Despite the claims of Darwin's apostles, people knew that **even before Darwin!** The question is: Was it the process of natural selection that turned the lizard into the squirrel?

The evolutionists' proof is their capacity to concoct a story. They say the whale "evolved" when a bear fell into the ocean. The bat "evolved" when squirrels developed flaps that helped them leap longer distances and fall to the ground more slowly. This isn't a joke. Cult member Richard Dawkins writes in **Climbing Mount Improbable:**

> To begin with, an ancestor like an ordinary squirrel, living up trees without any special gliding membrane, leaps across short gaps. [It could leap farther if it had something to slow a fall.] So natural selection favors individuals with slightly pouchy skin around the arm or leg joints, and this becomes the norm. . . . Now any individuals with an even larger skin web can leap a few inches further. So in later generations this extension of skin becomes the norm, and so

on. . . . It is possible that true flying, as seen in bats, birds and pterosaurs, evolved from gliding ancestors like these. Most of these animals can control their direction and speed of their glide so as to land at a predetermined spot. It is easy to imagine true flapping flight evolving from repetition of the muscular movements used to control glide direction, so average time to landing is gradually postponed over evolutionary time.[2]

But unlike a squirrel, the bat has a complicated set of elongated bones to support powered wings and, most famously, a sophisticated form of sonar. How did all that evolve, without making the squirrel less fit? Elongated bones would help a bat fly, but it's hard to see how they would make a squirrel more fit, rather than gangly, unsteady, and slow.

Needless to say, these hypothesized half-squirrel, half-bat animals do not appear anywhere in the fossil record. So however persuasive one finds the squirrel-falling-from-a-tree explanation for the evolution of the bat, there are no fossils to support it. To the contrary, the bat appears in the fossil record millions of years ago, fully formed and largely indistinguishable from today's bats. But Darwiniacs have a squirrel and they have a bat and they have a story. Their idea of a "scientific theory" makes psychic readings look like a hard science.

Moreover, if all species evolved from the same single-celled organism beginning in the same little mud puddle, why hasn't the earthworm made a little more progress? Was it never, ever desirable in any of the worm's many dirt holes to mutate eyes or legs or wings or a brain? How could one clump of cells starting in the same little puddle become a human being while others never makc it past the amoeba stage? Forget getting to humans, which liberals rank as the lowest form of life. Why hasn't the earthworm evolved into a beagle? Just for being cute, a beagle can acquire a six-room coop apartment on Park Avenue, surely an evolutionary advantage.

The cult members are especially dazzled by the similar DNA in all living creatures. The human genome is 98.7 percent identical with the chimpanzee's.[3] On the basis of this intriguing fact, psychology professor Roger Fouts of Central Washington University argues that humans "are simply odd looking apes"[4] in a book titled **Next of Kin: What Chimpanzees Have Taught Me About Who We Are.**

Except the genome argument proves too much. The human genome is 35 percent identical to that of a daffodil. I think even a Darwiniac would admit humans are not 35 percent identical to a daffodil. Again, the cult's smoking gun of evolutionary proof turns out to be an imaginary water pistol.

■   ■   ■

THE "mountains of evidence" for evolution we keep hearing about mostly consist of changes less impressive than those produced every day at the Bliss Spa in New York City. Now and then, nature gives some species a Botox shot, but it generally wears off and the basic model returns. Finches on the Galápagos Islands with deeper beaks begin to outnumber finches with shallower beaks during a drought—and then the population of shallow-beaked finches immediately rebounds after a rainy season. Bacteria develop a resistance to antibiotics and viruses develop resistance to antiviral medication—but nothing new is ever created. A bacterium remains a bacterium, a virus remains a virus, a finch remains a finch. Even the evolution fetishists do not claim that a mutating AIDS virus is on its way up the tree of life, soon to be a kangaroo. If a rapidly mutating bacterium or virus were proof of "evolution," then after 3 billion years of nonstop evolution, the only life forms we would have on Earth would be extremely sturdy bacteria and viruses.

Humans develop a tolerance for alcohol, tobacco, and caffeine, but no one imagines a high tolerance for alcohol will somehow lead to a new organ, like a tail or a pair of wings.

Darwin's Galápagos finches are boldly cited as living proof of the creative power of natural selection. It is triumphantly stated that "now" there are thirteen finch species in the Galápagos Islands, which allegedly evolved from a single finch species. Yes, today there are thirteen species of finches on the Galápagos Islands. Guess how many there were when Darwin first discovered them in 1835? That's right! Thirteen species. Darwin hypothesized that the thirteen species he found might have "evolved" from one species, just as evolutionists hypothesize that the bat might have "evolved" from a clumsy squirrel. The Galápagos finches are evidence of nothing but the evolutionists' ability to make up stories.

If anything, the finches are a major blow to Darwin's theory of evolution. Despite major changes in the environment on the Galápagos Islands, the formation of new species has never been observed there. There were thirteen species in 1835, and after more than 170 years of wild variation in the environment, mutation, and "natural selection," there are still thirteen species. The finches' beaks have moved back and forth in shape and nothing more.

In a 1991 **Scientific American,** Darwinist Peter Grant effused about the famous finches, saying that if droughts came only once a decade, natural selection "would transform one species into another within 200 years." Well, it's been 170 years since Darwin first saw them and we're still waiting. If it rained this year, the Galápagos finch population would look exactly like the finch population Darwin first found there. If it was dry, it would look like the finch population he would have found a few years later.

Human breeders have not been able to produce one biologically novel structure in the laboratory—much less a new animal species— even under artificial conditions. No such demonstration exists; none has ever been provided. The fruit fly has been abused, mutilated, and stressed over the course of thousands and thousands of generations. The poor dumb creature remains what it has always been, a fruit fly in the first instance, dumb in the second. This negative result is perfectly consistent with the long history of breeding experiments, which demonstrate beyond question that species may be changed only within very narrow margins of variability. No practical breeder imagines, for example, that he will ever succeed in creating a chicken with antennae or a pig with a dorsal fin.

Amid this dismal record, there have been a few

exciting developments for the Darwiniacs. There was the discovery of a manlike ape that looked like a transitional fossil between ape and man— the long-sought after "missing link." There were drawings of embryos demonstrating that vertebrates all looked alike in the earliest stages of development. There was the peppered moth that became darker—allegedly to better camouflage itself from predatory birds—when industrial air pollution blackened the trees in England. It wasn't terribly impressive in terms of "evidence," but it filled out a few pages in biology textbooks claiming evolution was a **FACT.**

And then, one by one, each of these pillars of evidence for evolution was exposed as a fraud. (Ironically, each appeared to have been an intelligently designed prank.) It's difficult to imagine that any other "scientific" theory has been beset with as many hoaxes as the theory of evolution— always a good sign of a serious scientific endeavor.

On April Fools' Day, 2005, **Scientific American** magazine ran a mock editorial apologizing for accepting the "so-called theory of evolution." (**Scientific American** also sneered at the "alleged" flights of the Wright brothers in 1906— two years after they had flown their first airplanes.) The magazine sarcastically apologized for its belief in the theory of evolution, saying scientists had "dazzled us with their fancy fossils, their radiocarbon dating, and their tens of thousands of peer-reviewed journal articles. As editors, we had no business being persuaded by mountains of evidence."

The only time "radiocarbon dating" was used in connection with the theory of evolution was the time it was used to expose the Piltdown Man as a hoax being pawned off as proof of evolution. It was one of the greatest scientific frauds of all time, right up there with the Pepsi challenge and that commercial where ordinary laundry detergent gets red wine out of a white blouse. For half a century, Piltdown Man constituted a major piece of evidence for Darwin's theory. After decades of being embarrassed by the fossil record's stubborn refusal to come to Darwin's aid, in 1912 the Piltdown Man miraculously appeared in a gravel pit in Sussex, England. Amateur paleontologist Charles Dawson claimed to have discovered a skull with a humanlike cranium and an apelike jaw in Piltdown quarry. It was a creature that was not quite ape, not quite man, but a transitional species between the two, rather like the actor Pauly Shore. This Pauly Shore–like fossil wouldn't have proved evolution, but it would have given evolutionists a possible link between apes and man on their imaginary "tree of life."

Like a doctor's excuse note written to a seventh-grade teacher signed, "Timmy's mommy," it was almost uncanny how precisely Piltdown Man matched what prevailing scientific theory predicted the "missing link" would look like. The **New York Times** headline for the article on the Piltdown Man proclaimed, "Darwin Theory Is Proved True." (My headline the day Clinton was impeached: "God Theory Is Proved True.")

The Piltdown fossil was "peer-reviewed"—so we know it would pass muster with the editors of **Scientific American,** still flush with success after triumphantly exposing the "Ohio flight hoax." Experts confirmed the age and origin of the bones. Indeed, the Piltdown Man received the approval of Arthur Smith Woodward, the leading geologist at the British Museum (Natural History). **Eoanthropus dawsoni** was born.

Dawson was showered with praise, fame, and awards. If only **Vanity Fair** had been around, Dawson could have been photographed in his Jaguar and hailed for "speaking truth to power." He was made a fellow of the Geological Society and a fellow of the Society of Antiquaries. (He was even offered a position writing editorials for **Scientific American.**)

For more than forty years, the Piltdown Man was taught as scientific fact. Then, in 1953, it was exposed as a complete and utter fraud—in part

through the process that so dazzles the editors of
Scientific American: radiocarbon dating. (Note
to **Scientific American:** Steer clear of any mention of "radiocarbon dating" when disparaging
the critics of evolution as uneducated rubes.)

Yes, the same process that recently helped us
pin down the exact year of Helen Thomas's birth
also determined that the Piltdown Man's skull
was from a thousand-year-old human fossil and
the jaw from a modern orangutan. It wasn't even
a particularly good fake: The jaw had been
stained with potassium bichromate and the teeth
filed down to make them look more human.
(Cher had a similar procedure done recently and
she looks amazing.) Evolution's Piltdown Man
makes Scientology's "e-meter" look like a particle
accelerator at Los Alamos.

There was even a Piltdown bird, an incredible
fossil that was half-dinosaur, half-bird—which,
amazingly, was entirely composed of white meat,
had four drumsticks, and was self-basting. "Archaeoraptor" made the cover of **National Geographic** with the sensational headline "Feathers
for T. rex?" And then "Archaeoraptor" was exposed as a hoax, too.

On the empirical side of evolution there was
the celebrated peppered moth. According to the
peppered moth of legend, when pollution first
began to blacken tree trunks in industrial

England in the mid-nineteenth century, the once-pale moths turned black. It was theorized that light moths against sooty tree trunks were easily spotted by birds and eaten, while the dark moths evaded predators, and survived to reproduce. A new black peppered moth had "evolved"—just as Darwin said it would. Thus began the secular Left's short-lived love affair with air pollution.

It wasn't a particularly dazzling example of evolution. Black, white, or purple, they were still peppered moths. Nothing new was created. The moths didn't become birds or grow opposable thumbs or develop a capacity for introspection. The miracle engine of natural selection had merely produced a minor variation within the species of animals known as "moths." New Yorkers not only transform from pale to dark, but also from fat to skinny, during the annual summer migration to the Hamptons, and no one writes scientific articles about that. This is not the sort of metamorphosis that turns a mosquito into a German shepherd.

Still, it was something, and the Darwiniacs didn't have much. Until the peppered moth, evolution fetishists had not been able to produce a single example of natural selection in real time. Here, at last, a light gray moth had been magically transformed into an altogether different and distinct life form—a slightly darker gray moth. Voilà! Evolutionists were so excited about the peppered moth's changing hue, they couldn't be bothered with testing the theory. It had to be true. The Darwiniacs happily announced that the peppered moth proved evolution and presumably went back to calling critics of evolution anti-science know-nothings.

It wasn't until the early fifties that anyone thought to test the theory. Oxford biologist E. B. Ford sent his assistant out to capture hundreds of the moths and stage an experiment. For two years black moths were bused out of the inner-city areas to the suburbs, while white moths were bused into the inner-city areas. Then both groups were monitored to see how long each survived. (Is it just me, or does this scenario sound oddly familiar?) After two years of observation, Ford triumphantly announced that birds easily spotted light moths on black city trees and dark moths on the light country trees. There it was—evolution was proved.

For the next fifty years, the peppered moth experiment was a major part of the "mountains of evidence" for evolution referred to by **Scientific American.** Evolution fundamentalist Jerry Coyne called the peppered moth the "prize horse" of natural selection. Every schoolchild has seen the photo of the light peppered moth clearly visible on a black tree trunk next to a photo of the dark moth nearly invisible against the same tree trunk.

It was so logical, so intuitive, and so fake. Decades later, researchers who had not been informed by the editors of **Scientific American** or Judge John Jones III that questioning evolution was a hanging offense noticed some problems. American lepidopterist Ted Sargent and others pointed out that peppered moths do not rest on tree trunks, but on the undersides of high branches. Not only that, but the peppered moth sleeps during the day, coming out to fly only at night, when the birds are asleep.

It turned out Ford and his assistant had rigged the game by physically placing light moths on black tree trunks in the bright light of day— someplace the moths would never have been if left to their own devices. It was rather like testing the theory that birds developed wings to avoid sharks by dumping wingless birds into a shark tank and seeing if they survived. As described in the **New York Times,** "The most famous example of evolution in action must now become the most infamous."[5]

But what about those photos? The famous photos of the peppered moths were staged, often by literally gluing dead moths to tree trunks. Their "proof" of evolution was suddenly reduced to a variation on Monty Python's dead-parrot sketch. ("I took the liberty of examining that parrot when I got it home, and I discovered the only reason that it had been sitting on its perch in the first place was that it had been **nailed** there.")

Now let's examine how evolutionists responded—you know, the ones who claim to be slaves to the scientific method. Except for a thimbleful of serious scientists who admitted the jig was up, the cult members wholly ignored the truth about the peppered moth. They demonized Sargent, the lepidopterist who had exposed the fraud, marginalized his work, and attempted to ruin his career. To this day, evolutionists cite the peppered moths as proof that evolution is based on "science." The staged photos still appear in biology textbooks, as detailed in Jonathan Wells's book **Icons of Evolution.**

An article in the **New Scientist** on July 9, 2005, authoritatively stated, "Evolutionary biologists have long known that the process can happen rapidly—Charles Darwin himself pointed out the observable changes wrought by pigeon fanciers and dog breeders. A century later biologists showed that peppered moths in England's industrial heartland had evolved darker colours to camouflage themselves against soot-blackened trees."

Maybe the new name for the **New Scientist**

should be the **1950s Scientist.** And I don't think selective breeding directed by a human being goes in the "hidden hand of nature" column.

Also in 2005—three years after it had been acknowledged in the **New York Times** that the peppered moth example was a fraud—University of Rochester biology professor H. Allen Orr wrote an article in the **New Yorker** treating the peppered moth scandal as an open question: "[D]id the peppered moth evolve dark color as a defense against birds or for other reasons?"[6] ("And what role, if any, did the several empty cans of black spray paint found at the scene play in their evolutionary odyssey?") Orr called the darkening of the peppered moth one of the "minor squabbles among evolutionary biologists" that had been inflated by skeptics of evolution.

Peppered moths sleep during the day; they fly at night; they do not normally alight upon tree trunks. These are observable facts, sort of like the Earth revolving around the sun. It would be as if a college professor had lightly dismissed the "minor squabble" among scientists about "whether it's possible to sail off the edge of the Earth" and denounced critics of the flat Earth theory as "fanatical pro-elliptical orbists." What is so peculiar about the Darwiniacs is that they perpetrate comical frauds in defense of their religion and then angrily accuse their opponents of being driven by religious zeal. They're constantly acting like you're the idiot for refusing to admit the **fact** that we're living on the back of a giant turtle.

At least the evolutionists still had the embryo drawings. Almost every biology book for the past century has included pictures of vertebrate embryos made by German biologist and enthusiastic eugenicist Ernst Haeckel, purportedly demonstrating the amazing similarity of fish, chickens, and humans in the womb. Without the Darwinist priesthood to explain, it's not clear what this proved in the first place. It seems that Haeckel believed the development of the embryo imitated an organism's entire evolution as a species—a theory precisely as scientific as molding an animal out of Play-doh and claiming that you have just demonstrated how God made the animals. Haeckel's other big contribution to science, by the way, was the scientific claim that "woolyhaired Negroes" were "psychologically nearer to the mammals (apes and dogs) than to civilized Europeans . . . [and therefore] we must . . . assign a totally different value to their lives."

If Haeckel's imaginative theory were true, then he could show what humans looked like 500 million years ago by pointing to a fertilized human egg. And he could show what humans looked like, say, 100 million years ago by showing a baby in the second trimester. And he could show what humans looked like 1 million years ago by pointing to James Carville. Finally and most important, if his wackadoodle theory were true, then Haeckel could "prove" all vertebrates evolved from a similar-looking organism 500 million years ago. (I note in passing, evolution would **still** not explain why some of us became humans and others never made it past the gecko stage.) You can see why the scientific community sat up and took notice at this point. The last scientific theory to generate this kind of buzz was alchemy.

Amazingly enough, according to Haeckel's drawings, vertebrate embryos did look alike.

To give you a sense of the mountains and mountains of evidence supporting the theory of evolution, until Haeckel's drawings turned out to be frauds, his crackpot theory constituted one of the main pieces of evidence in support of evolution. Charles Darwin himself said the "facts" in embryology were "second to none in importance"[7] and "by far the strongest single class of facts" supporting his theory.[8]

And then, in the 1990s, British embryologist Michael Richardson was looking at vertebrate embryos through a microscope and noticed that they look nothing at all like Haeckel's drawings. Richardson and his team of researchers examined vertebrate embryos and published actual photos of the embryos in the August 1997 issue of the journal **Anatomy & Embryology.** It turned out that Haeckel had used the same woodcuts for some of the embryos and doctored others to make sure that the embryos looked alike. "It looks like," Richardson said, "it's turning out to be one of the most famous fakes in biology"— which, in a field crowded with other evolutionary "proofs," was quite a claim.

After Richardson published his photos of the embryos, the scientific community demonstrated its fearless commitment to the truth by completely ignoring his exposé. It turned out that Haeckel's drawings had been known to be fakes for a century. Stephen Jay Gould responded in the March 2000 issue of **Natural History** magazine, saying he had known all along. And yet the keepers of the state religion had kept mum.[9]

Fully five years later, the **New York Times** reported that biology textbooks were still running Haeckel's doctored drawings. The **Times** specifically singled out the third edition of **Molecular Biology of the Cell,** "the bedrock text of the field," as one of the culprits. Caught red-handed hawking fake evidence, one of the authors of the "bedrock text" justified the use of the Haeckel fakeries with the sort of pompous non sequitur you always get from the cult members: He said Haeckel's drawings were "overinterpreted." If they were fakes, why were they being interpreted at all? Why were they still in his textbook? If it took evolutionists fifty years to notice the "ask me about my prehuman grandchildren" decal on the back of Piltdown Man's skull, needless to say the Darwiniacs aren't giving up just because Haeckel's drawings were fake.

You're probably asking yourself, Why would the **New York Times** be printing the truth? The only reason the **Times** even mentioned the continued publication of Haeckel's phony drawings was to complain that the fakery was helping intelligent design proponents who were screaming from the rooftops about the long-running hoax. As the **Times** said, "Intelligent design has helped its cause by publicizing some embarrassing mistakes in leading biology textbooks." The article concluded with this stirring declaration of faith: "Biologists say the findings do not shake their confidence in the theory of evolution." No evidence will ever shake their confidence in the theory of evolution.

Then there was the famous Miller-Urey experiment in 1953, which seemed to re-create the beginnings of life in a test tube. In a genuinely groundbreaking experiment, scientists Stanley Miller and Harold Urey reconstructed what was thought to be the Earth's early atmosphere. They sent a spark of electricity through the primordial soup and—wham!—simple amino acids appeared. They had produced the building blocks of life with the laboratory equivalent of a bolt of lightning. It could only be a short step to discovering how life came from nonlife on the early Earth. Next stop, David Hasselhoff in a test tube!

The first problem to arise was that for the next twenty years, scientists couldn't get close to the next step, which was to produce proteins. Simple amino acids aren't even proteins, much less life, so the bridge between nonlife and life remained elusive. The primitive "building blocks" created by Miller have no proven pathway to life. Still, it was something.

But the real fly in the primordial soup arose in the early seventies, when geochemists realized that the Earth's early atmosphere was probably nothing like the gases used in the Miller-Urey experiment. Miller-Urey's experiment used an "atmosphere" modeled on what we knew of Jupiter, composed of methane, ammonia, hydrogen, and water. In the 1970s, geochemists discredited this theory of the Earth's early atmosphere and concluded that it probably contained more carbon dioxide, almost no hydrogen, and possibly some oxygen. Creation of even simple amino acids would have been impossible in such an environment. As Miller himself has said, "Either you have a reducing atmosphere [i.e., with lots of hydrogen atoms] or you're not going to have the organic compounds required for life."[10]

The revolutionary 1953 Miller-Urey experiment has been moot since the seventies. It proved nothing about the origin of life because the atmosphere assumed by the experiment was the opposite of what existed on ancient Earth. There is still no plausible account for the origins of life. You would think that fact might interest people who are always boasting that they are impartial scientists, going wherever the evidence leads them, with no ideological predispositions.

Guess what is still taught in biology textbooks as proof of evolution? That's right! The 1953 Miller-Urey experiment.

The Darwin cult has the audacity to compare the theory of evolution to Einstein's theory of relativity, saying that it is "just a theory," too. Okay, but when Einstein announced his theory of general relativity, he also offered a series of empirical tests that would prove it false. That's what made it a "scientific theory" and not, say, "an astrological profile." If light had not appeared to bend away from the Sun during the 1919 solar eclipse or if his equations could not account for Mercury's orbit around the Sun, Einstein would have abandoned the theory. In the end, of course, his theory accounted for both phenomena and has been repeatedly retested and proved true.

By contrast, Darwin imagined a mechanism that would account for how life in its infinite variety might have arisen and offered a nondisprovable standard to test his theory. You will recall, Darwin's test for his theory was this: "If it could be demonstrated that any complex organ existed which could not possibly have been formed by numerous, successive, slight modifications, my theory would absolutely break down."

The great philosopher of science Karl Popper said any theory that cannot conceivably be refuted is not science. The very fact that it is nondisprovable is an "immunizing stratagem," distinguishing pseudoscience from real science. Either there is no evidence that could possibly disprove Darwin's theory of evolution—or it has been disproved for about half a century. So it's possible that Darwin produced an actual scientific theory, but his disciples have turned it into a pseudoscience by their refusal to admit it can be—and has been—disproved.

The evolutionists' other great contribution to the scientific method is to cite obvious, undisputed facts having nothing to do with evolution and brandish them as if they've just grown John Travolta from an earthworm.

A masterful example is this inane passage from the **New York Times:**

Nowhere has evolution been more powerful than in its prediction that there must be a means to pass on information from one generation to another. Darwin did not know the biological mechanism of inheritance, but the theory of evolution required one. . . . Darwin may have been the classic scientific observer. He observed that individuals in a given species varied considerably, variations now known to be caused by mutations in their genetic code.

The idea that Darwin was the first person ever to notice that traits were hereditary and that there was variation within a species is absolute lunacy. Even B.D., before Darwin, people noticed that their children looked like them—but not **exactly** like them. And they didn't understand the mechanisms of inheritance either! Yet the **Times** claims Darwin was the first to notice that information was passed from one generation to the next and then boasts, "The discovery of DNA, the sequencing of the human genome, the pinpointing of genetic diseases and the discovery that a continuum of life from a single cell to a human brain can be detected in DNA are all a result of evolutionary theory."

Using the same logic, one could also claim that DNA, human genome sequencing, the discovery of genetic diseases, and the growth of the human brain are also a direct result of generations of humans saying, Hey! Look—little Billy has his father's nose! But we don't teach, Hey! Look—little Billy has his father's nose! as a groundbreaking scientific discovery.

The same article reports that Darwin "also realized that constraints of food and habitat sharply limited population growth; not every individual could survive and reproduce." Will Darwin's wondrous feats never end? Darwin's **The Origin of Species** was published in 1859—about ten years after the Irish potato famine killed one million people and drove another million to flee the country (1845–48). I believe other people besides Darwin may have noticed that the absence of food limited population growth. Darwin's innovation was that mutation + death would produce a new species. And yet the Irish are still Irish. The only new species we got out of the Irish potato famine was the blight-resistant Idaho potato, invented by intelligent designer Luther Burbank, American plant breeder.

The only evidence for Darwin's theory of evolution is fake evidence, and every time Darwiniacs are caught hawking fake "proof," they complain that it's merely a "gap" in the theory. The Darwiniacs play a shell game with the evidence, but the evidence is never under any of the shells. The point isn't that schoolchildren should be "taught the controversy"—schoolchildren should be taught the truth. This includes:

- the truth about the entire fossil record, which shows a very non-Darwinian progression, noticeably lacking the vast number of transitional species we ought to see
- the truth about the Cambrian explosion, in which virtually all the animal phyla suddenly appeared, with no Darwinian ancestors
- the truth about the Galápagos finch population changing not one bit since Darwin first observed the finches more than 170 years ago
- the truth about the peppered moth experiment
- the truth about Haeckel's embryos being a fraud perpetrated by a leading German eugenicist
- the truth about the Miller-Urey experiment being based on premises that are no longer accepted

- the truth about the nonexistence of computer simulations of the evolution of the eye

These aren't gaps in a scientific theory—there is no scientific theory. There is only a story about how a bear might have fallen into the ocean and become a whale. As Colin Patterson asked, What is any one true thing about evolution?

In the end, evolutionists' only argument is contempt. The cultists know that if people were allowed to hear the arguments against evolution for just sixty seconds, all would be lost. So they demonize the people making those arguments. **You're just saying that because you believe in God! You probably believe in a flat Earth, too! You sound like a Holocaust revisionist!** That's all you ever get.

The evolutionists' self-advertisements paint a different picture. A **New York Times** review of a book on intelligent design summarized the situation this way: "As Michael Ruse points out, modern science's refusal to cry miracle when faced with explanatory difficulties has yielded 'fantastic dividends.' Letting divine causes fill in wherever naturalistic ones are hard to find is not only bad theology—it leaves you worshiping a 'God of the gaps'—but it is also a science-stopper."[11] Far from chastely refusing to acknowledge miracles, evolutionists are the primary source of them. These aren't chalk-covered scientists toiling away with their test tubes and Bunsen burners. They are religious fanatics for whom evolution must be true and any evidence to the contrary—including, for example, the entire fossil record—is something that must be explained away with a fanciful excuse, like "our evidence didn't fossilize."

Meanwhile, and by stark contrast, intelligent design scientists do not fill the "gaps" with God. They simply say intelligence is a force that exists in the universe and we can see its effects and what it does—in Behe's flagellum, in the Cambrian explosion, in Gould and Eldredge's "punctuated equilibrium."

Evolutionists keep modifying their theory to say, "Assume a miracle," and the intelligent design scientists say, "Hey, does anyone else notice that it's always the same miracle?" It's a miracle of design. Design in the universe may well be explained by something other than God, but we'll never know as long as everyone is required to pretend it's not there. To say intelligent design scientists are merely "filling in the gaps" with God is like saying Sir Isaac Newton "filled in the gaps" with the theory of gravity. He saw stuff dropping to the ground and tried to explain it. If only the Darwiniacs had been around, they could have told Newton, **I don't see anything dropping! It's just an accident! Do you believe in God or something?**

Nor are intelligent design scientists looking at things they can't explain: Quite the opposite. They are looking at things they **can** explain but which Darwin didn't even know about, like the internal mechanism of the cell, and saying, That wasn't created by natural selection—that required high-tech engineering. By contrast, the evolution cult members look at things they can't explain and say, We can't explain it, but the one thing we do know is that there is no intelligence in the universe. It must have been random chance, or it's not "science."

10 THE SCIENTIFIC METHOD OF STONING AND BURNING

he single greatest victory of the Darwiniacs is in the realm of rhetoric, not science. They have persuaded the slumbering masses that anyone who questions the theory of evolution must do so out of religious fervor. No matter what argument you make against evolution, the response is **Well, you know it's possible to believe in evolution and believe in God.** Yes, and it's possible to believe in Spiderman and

believe in God, but that doesn't prove Spiderman is true.

I admire the rhetorical technique and plan to use it during all future disputes.

Your time is up on the StairMaster.
You're just saying that because you believe
   in God.
This is the express checkout lane.
Oh, I get it—you believe in God.

On August 24, 2005, the **New York Times** was required to run this amusing "correction":

A front-page article on Sunday about the Discovery Institute, which promotes the concept known as intelligent design to explain the origins of life, referred incorrectly to the religious affiliation of the institute's fellows. Most are conservative Christians, including Roman Catholics and evangelical Protestants—not fundamentalist Christians.

Liberals can make dazzling distinctions between different types of Muslims. Osama bin Laden, for example, was a "fundamentalist" who would **never** have worked with a "secular" Muslim like Saddam Hussein—although liberals think Osama was willing to suspend his principles long enough to work hand-in-glove with Ronald Reagan. But anyone who questions evolution is ipso facto a "fundamentalist Christian."

The intelligent design movement is exactly the opposite of what the Darwiniacs would have you believe. Far from six-fingered lunatics handling snakes and speaking in tongues, the ID proponents are the real scientists—biochemists, astrophysicists, chemists, and mathematicians. As Behe says, intelligent design has been around since Aristotle and its "rising fortunes have been boosted by discoveries principally in physics and astronomy," such as the life-sustaining "coincidences" of the universe discovered by astronomers like the late Cambridge astrophysicist Sir Fred Hoyle.

Bill Dembski has developed complicated mathematical formulas for detecting design in the universe, as distinct from chance or accident. Dembski has a doctorate in mathematics from the University of Chicago and a master of divinity degree from Princeton Theological Seminary. He has done postdoctoral work in mathematics at MIT, in physics at the University of Chicago, and in computer science at Princeton. He has held National Science Foundation graduate and postdoctoral fellowships. When faculty members at Baylor University erupted in rage at the research center Dembski had started up at the university to test theories of design in the universe, not one professor on the committee investigating Dembski could understand the mathematical arguments he had made.[1] (But just to be safe, they abolished his research center anyway.)

In an article in the **New York Times** on intelligent design, the design proponents quoted in the article keep rattling off serious, scientific arguments—from Behe's examples in molecular biology to Dembski's mathematical formulas and statistical models. The **Times** reporter, who was clearly not trying to make the evolutionists sound retarded, was forced to keep describing the evolutionists' entire retort to these arguments as: **Others disagree.**[2]

That's it. No explanation, no specifics, just "others disagree." The high priests of evolution have not only forgotten how to do science, they've lost the ability to formulate a coherent counterargument. You keep waiting to hear a serious response to arguments by people like Behe, Dembski, and Hoyle, but the evolutionists just scream that evolution is a **FACT** and if you don't believe it, you must be a fundamentalist who believes the Earth is flat.

Which is rather presumptuous, considering the scientific standing of the typical evolutionist. Their grandiose self-conceptions to the contrary, the cult members are rarely scientists at all.

They're almost always biologists—the "science" with the greatest preponderance of women. The distaff MIT "scientist" who fled the room in response to Larry Summers's remarks was, of course, a biologist. While I'm sure there have been groundbreaking discoveries about the internal digestive system of the earthworm, biologists are barely even scientists anymore. They're classifiers, list-makers, like librarians with their Dewey decimal system. Except librarians don't claim the Dewey decimal system holds the Rosetta Stone to the universe. There were once great biologists, but the morally vacuous ones began to promote their own at the universities. It was a sort of intelligently designed devolution. Like Marxists gradually dominating the comp lit department, biologists will only be given tenure today if they forswear any doubts about the evolution pseudo-science. Consequently, "biologist" almost always means "evolutionary biologist," which is something like an "ESP biologist."

Curiously, the **science** writers at the **New York Times**—as opposed to opinion writers like Paul Krugman or Style section reporters writing about "girl crushes"—have generally been extremely circumspect in what they say about evolution. The principal source for idiotic statements about the "overwhelming evidence for the theory of evolution" in the **Times** is letters to the editor.

Writing a letter to the **New York Times** is what people who don't fight think of as fighting: **That's it! I'm writing a letter! Why, I'll take him to court!** One letter writer said evolution was a "fact" equivalent to the "fact" that there was no connection between al Qaeda and Iraq.[3] A woman doctor wrote in to say that DNA evidence "shows our common heritage with the animals with whom we share this planet."[4] (And Elton John gave birth to Janet Reno.) If little Miss Smartypants could prove "common heritage" from similar DNA, she'd be awarded the Nobel Prize.

■   ■   ■

THE only evolutionist who ever tried to answer questions about evolution was Stephen Jay Gould, which meant he had to keep conceding key points—so much so that Phillip Johnson called Gould the "Gorbachev of Darwinism." If you can ever get the cult past the argument that their opponents are "fundamentalists," it's Game Over. I gather this is their strongest argument, since it's the only one you hear.

When the Kansas State Board of Education decided to hold hearings to determine what school-children should be taught about evolution, they sought the views of prominent evolution defenders. They invited evolutionary biologist Kenneth Miller of Brown University. They invited Eugenie Scott, Keeper of the Faith at the National Center for Science Education, a front group dedicated to banning any questioning of evolution. (Liberals love organizations with names that are the opposite of the truth, like all the Communist front groups with "American," "peace," and "democracy" in their titles.) And they invited anyone at all from another organization devoted to banning discussion of evolution, the American Association for the Advancement of Science.

Not one of them was willing to defend evolution in a public forum. The evolution fanatics justified their disappearing act on the grounds that members of the school board did not have open minds. "The people running things," Miller said, "were people whose minds were already made up." This is as opposed to the minds of people who refuse to discuss the issue and keep suing to prevent anyone from challenging their theory.

Miller admitted that the refusal to debate "can be made to look as if you do not want to defend science in public, or you are too afraid to face the intelligent design people in public." But the real reason he refused to debate, he said, was that it was not a genuine debate. Evolution is true and everyone please stop asking questions!

Scott, of the American League for Peace and Democracy, remarked sadly that she had once debated critics of evolution. "I was one of the holdouts, saying yes, appear with these guys, yes, tell them what is wrong with their ideas, go to their conferences, treat them like scholars." Scott is to "science" what the "Reverend" Barry Lynn is to Christianity. (And both are proud recipients of the Playboy Foundation's "First Amendment Award" for blocking the speech of religious people while not infringing on the right of overweight women to dance in public wearing only pasties.) When the evolution skeptics refused to acquiesce to Scott's badgering, she concluded they were being dogmatic. "Our willingness to engage their ideas," Scott said, "was not being reciprocated." Scott had deigned to "treat them like scholars." And yet they refused to capitulate. This is the liberal definition of an ideologue: Someone who won't give in to them.

Nazis can march in Skokie, Democrats can fill the airwaves with treason, and Air America Radio can give Randi Rhodes access to literally hundreds of listeners every day, but the teaching of alternative theories to evolution is prohibited by law. They would prefer it if heretics from the official state religion could be put in prison and burned at the stake like Giordano Bruno.

A good example of the Darwiniacs' "willingness to engage" others' ideas occurred when a small school district in Pennsylvania proposed to read a statement to high school biology students mentioning intelligent design. The statement read as follows:

> The Pennsylvania Academic Standards require students to learn about Darwin's theory of evolution and eventually take a standardized test of which evolution is a part.
>
> Because Darwin's theory is a theory, it continues to be tested as new evidence is discovered. The theory is not a fact. Gaps in the theory exist for which there is no evidence.
>
> A theory is defined as a well-tested explanation that unifies a broad range of observations.
>
> Intelligent design is an explanation of the origin of life that differs from Darwin's view. The reference book "Of Pandas and People" is available for students who might be interested in gaining an understanding of what intelligent design actually involves.
>
> With respect to any theory, students are encouraged to keep an open mind. The school leaves the discussion of the origin of life to individual students and their families.

As a standards-driven district, class instruction focuses upon preparing students to achieve proficiency on standards-based assessments.

That was it. Just an alluring reference to dissent from the official state religion that the students might look up in non–school hours.

From the reaction of the evolutionists, you would think the Dover schools were teaching fisting to twelve-year-olds (when, as any student knows, that's not covered until junior year).[5] Going for his own Playboy First Amendment Award, federal district court judge John E. Jones III ruled that this tepid statement violated the First Amendment of the United States Constitution by establishing a religion. The last person to demonstrate such mastery of the First Amendment was erstwhile Supreme Court nominee Harriet Miers.

Judge Jones—or as he came to be known, "the well-respected, Bush-appointed judge"—had spent the better part of his career on a state liquor board determining such matters as that Zippers gelatin shots may not be sold in Pennsylvania. But now he had a case that would get him noticed. As Jones confided to a **New York Times** reporter, when he saw the Dover evolution case mentioned on the cover of **Rolling Stone** magazine, he excitedly brought a copy home to his wife, telling her, "I'm on the cover of **Rolling Stone**!" At least he didn't pose for **Vanity Fair** in a Jaguar. At least not yet.

The judge who had spent his career handing out T-shirts to Little Leaguers with catchy antidrinking messages like "Stop underage drinking—Make the world a better place" concluded that alternative theories to evolution are unconstitutional. Jones wrote, "[T]he fact that a scientific theory cannot yet render an explanation on every point should not be used as a pretext to thrust an untestable alternative hypothesis grounded in religion into the science classroom." Maybe some crazy scientific theory like quantum mechanics could be questioned, but not a rock-solid scientific theory that says a flying fish flew out of the ocean and became a bird. That's hard science. At least according to No Zipper Shots Jones, who held, "[I]t is unconstitutional to teach I.D. [intelligent design] as an alternative to evolution in a public school science classroom."

The **Times** nearly ran out of fawning adjectives in its praise for Jones. Liberals hadn't been this alarmed by the activities at a high school since hearing about a high school football coach in East Brunswick, New Jersey, who allegedly prayed with his players for a good, clean game. In a single article, Jones was called "a man of integrity and intellect," "moderate, thoughtful and universally well regarded," and a "renaissance man." Needless to say, Jones was a "lifelong Republican appointed to the federal bench in 2002 by President Bush." The **Times** still won't mention that John Ashcroft went to Yale, but it managed to work in that Judge Jones's **father** graduated from Yale. All you need to know about Jones's breadth of intelligence is that he calls Tom Ridge the "singular inspiration of my life."

This is the scientific method when it comes to the state religion: **Rolling Stone** magazine and Jayson Blair's employer browbeat a hack judge into declaring the mere mention of alternatives to evolution "unconstitutional."

The cult loves to boast that there are no "peer-reviewed" articles on intelligent design,[6] but then treats the publication of such an article as a fireable offense. (Peer review is very important, because otherwise you might have South Korean scientists claiming they've used cloning techniques to create embryonic stem cells, as Hwang Woo-Suk did in a peer-reviewed paper published in the journal **Science.** Oops.)

In 2004, Richard Sternberg (Ph.D.s in molecular biology and theoretical biology) published an article by Stephen Meyer (Ph.D. in the history and philosophy of science from Cambridge University) in what the **Washington Post** described as the "hitherto obscure" journal **Proceedings of the Biological Society of Washington.**

Meyer's article was peer-reviewed by three renowned scientists and "complied with all editorial requirements of the proceedings," according to a subsequent investigation by the U.S. Office of Special Counsel. Among Meyer's points was the one about the Cambrian period having no Darwinian antecedents—something your children are not allowed to hear about in high school. Apparently, the six readers of **Proceedings of the Biological Society of Washington** weren't supposed to be told about the Cambrian period either.

It wasn't ever clear whether Sternberg actually believed in the heretical doctrine of ID, but for permitting the publication of a peer-reviewed article about it, he was adjudged a witch and banished from the Smithsonian. The obscure journal disavowed the article, and Sternberg was warned not to come to future meetings. As is always the case with the witch-burners, they went straight to Sternberg's sources of employment, demanding that he be fired.

The U.S. Office of Special Counsel, which investigates retaliation against federal employees, was soon looking into the Smithsonian's treatment of Sternberg. The Smithsonian not only objected to any inquiry into intelligent design, it especially objected to any inquiry into its treatment of Sternberg.

The independent counsel investigating the attacks on Sternberg issued a harsh report on the behavior of the alleged scientists at the Smithsonian and Eugenie Scott's National Center for Science Education. In her usual role as Enforcer of the Faith, Scott had led a campaign of vilification against Sternberg. Leaping to action like angry gay David Brock when he's cranky because he's retaining a lot of water and has just seen a Bill O'Reilly broadcast, the NCSE immediately posted hysterical responses to the Meyer article on its website. Scott's organization helped draft a repudiation of Meyer's article for the journal to print, and then turned around and cited that very repudiation as proof that the article should not have been published.[7]

The NCSE, the government report said, had worked closely with the Smithsonian "in outlining a strategy to have [Sternberg] investigated and discredited."[8] In the flurry of e-mails between the NCSE and the "scientists" at the Smithsonian Institution, Sternberg was accused of being a Young Earth Creationist. He was accused of taking money under the table to publish the article. His religion was investigated. He was accused of having no scientific training at all but only "training as an orthodox priest." None of this was true. But according to the independent counsel, the claim that Sternberg was not a scientist became so persistent that a colleague had to circulate his résumé to dispel the rumor. Remember, he has Ph.D.s in molecular biology and theoretical biology.

The Smithsonian's chief spider torturer, Jonathan Coddington, began making inquiries about Sternberg's religious beliefs and politics—in particular, questioning if he was a fundamentalist or right-winger.[9] Another "scientist" at the Smithsonian wrote in an e-mail, "We are evolutionary biologists and I am sorry to see us made into the laughing stock of the world, even if this kind of rubbish sells well in backwoods USA."[10]

Scott defended the inquiry into Sternberg's religious beliefs, saying, "They don't care if you are religious, but they do care a lot if you are a creationist. Sternberg denies it, but if it walks like a duck and quacks like a duck, it argues for zealotry."[11] I'm no evolutionary biologist, but I think if it walks like a duck and quacks like a duck, that argues for it being a duck.

The report concluded, "[R]etaliation came in many forms . . . misinformation was disseminated through the Smithsonian Institution and to outside sources. The allegations against [Sternberg] were later determined to be false." The Smithsonian was unrepentant. Asked about the report by the **Washington Post,** Smithsonian spokesperson Linda St. Thomas said only, "We do stand by evolution—we are a scientific organization."[12]

Whatever else can be said of academics in cushy, comfortable jobs, they tend not to be big risk takers. If this is what one Cambridge Ph.D. goes through for publishing a peer-reviewed article simply because he dared question evolution, you can be sure we're not getting honest answers from the rest of the scientific community. One tends to hear about prominent academics who doubt evolution in the same hushed tones one hears about Hollywood actors who oppose abortion (Martin Sheen, Jack Nicholson, and Warren Beatty).

You could have ten times the IQ of Eugenie Scott—and most do—but if you gingerly raise scientifically based questions about evolution, you will be denounced as a creationist nut, your life will be turned upside down, and your employers will be hounded. You will probably be fired and certainly have to hire a lawyer. Now let's take a show of hands: Any Darwin skeptics? Good. Evolution has been proved again!

■   ■   ■

THE most fanatical defenders of evolution are not Harvard professors, curators at the American Museum of Natural History, or **Times** science reporters. They are cretinous high school biology teachers and liberal know-nothings trying to relive their fantasy of the Scopes trial. HBO Documentary and Family president Sheila Nevins says she doesn't "shy away from such R-rated topics as 'G-String Divas' and 'Taxicab Confessions,'" but she complained of the imagined persecution she would face if she "made a movie about Darwin." If HBO ran such a documentary, Nevins said, "I'd get a thousand hate e-mails."[13] (Maybe, but only from lonely guys upset about missing "G-String Divas.")

Evidently, it isn't **that** hard to make a fawning movie about Darwin in Hollywood. A partial list of movies and documentaries with Darwin's name in the title on the Internet Movie Database includes:

Darwin's Nightmare (2004)
Genius: Charles Darwin (2003)
Freud and Darwin Sitting in a Tree
   (2000)
Darwin's Evolutionary Stakes (1999)
A&E Biography: Charles Darwin—
   Evolution's Voice (1998) (TV)
Darwin (1997)

Galápagos: Beyond Darwin (1996) (TV)
Darwin (1993) (TV)
Darwin on the Galápagos (1983)
Terre des Bêtes: Darwin (1982) (TV)
The Voyage of Charles Darwin (1978)
The Darwin Adventure (1972)
Darwin Was Right (1924)
Felix Doubles for Darwin (1924)
Darwin (1920)
What Darwin Missed (1916)
A Disciple of Darwin (1912)

Cowardly people who run from the room crying at the idea that men and women could have different abilities in science like to play-act that they are John Scopes speaking truth to power against hate-filled fundamentalist Christians ("truth" being defined as "a discredited scientific theory from the Victorian age"). They are like geeks playing air guitar in front of the mirror pretending to be Keith Richards. Except there really is a Keith Richards. (In fact, some scientists argue that Keith Richards is actually the missing link.) The John Scopes of liberal imaginations never existed.

In the great Hollywood tradition of **All the President's Men, Erin Brockovich, Silkwood, Good Night and Good Luck,** and every single movie made by Oliver Stone, there are two separate and distinct stories: the one that actually happened and the movie version. Despite the raw fear that grips the Hollywood community at the thought of making a movie that reflects favorably on Darwin, there have been four movie versions of **Inherit the Wind,** in 1960, 1965, 1988, and 1999.

In the Book of Hollywood, it is taught that a brave high school biology teacher named John Scopes tried to educate his illiterate, toothless students in backwater Dayton, Tennessee, by teaching them "science." For his trouble, he was nearly lynched by fundamentalist Christians, who stormed his classroom and arrested him on the spot for teaching Darwin's theory of evolution. As told in **Inherit the Wind,** clergymen and businessmen immediately threw Scopes in prison, where he remained throughout the trial, with fundamentalist Christians screaming that they would lynch him and throwing things at his window. Scopes was crucified, died, rose again, and now sits—no, wait, that's a different story.

The real story of the Scopes trial is told in the book **Summer for the Gods** by Edward Larson.[14] The Scopes trial was nothing but a publicity stunt. The idea for a trial on evolution was hatched by the ACLU in New York and seized upon by civic leaders in Dayton, Tennessee, as a way to drum up publicity for their town. Scopes was in on the prank, agreeing to be prosecuted even though he had never taught evolution and was not even a biology teacher. He did not spend one minute in jail, was never at risk of being sent to jail, was friends with the prosecutors, with whom he went swimming during the trial, and was even given a scholarship put together by the expert witnesses in gratitude for his star turn in the Monkey trial. When the trial was over, the school offered to renew his teacher's contract.[15]

Darwin's theory of evolution was a hot topic in the summer of 1925, with lots of public debates on the subject. The theory of natural selection was being used to justify racialist theories, eugenics, and German militarism—which I seem to recall took a turn for the worse shortly thereafter but I'd have to check my notes. The most important witnesses the defense considered calling as "expert witnesses" for the Scopes trial were all champions of forced eugenics.

A few other state legislatures around the country had prohibited the teaching of evolution, but other state laws were merely proscriptive, with no punishment attached. Even in Tennessee, teaching evolution was only a misdemeanor offense, punishable by a nominal fine, much like drowning a girl in Massachusetts if your last name is "Kennedy." The Scopes trial is, as Larson says, "the most widely publicized misdemeanor case in U.S. history."

The day the Tennessee governor signed the ban into law, he said it would never be enforced. And it never would have been—but for the bright idea of a native New Yorker who had recently moved to Dayton. Upon reading in a newspaper that the ACLU was offering to defend any Tennessee teacher who violated the law, George Rappleyea decided a trial on evolution would be a terrific way to get publicity for Dayton as a nice place to live and work (especially for busybody former New Yorkers with axes to grind).

Rappleyea took his idea to the town elders assembled in the local drugstore, telling them that a trial on evolution would put Dayton on the map and boasting of his connections with the New York ACLU. Civic leaders warmed to the idea as a splendid way to promote the town— raising the possibility that they were serving more than milkshakes at the drugstore. Even the school superintendent—who had supported the law— liked the idea of a cooked-up trial as a way to get Dayton national recognition. The ACLU signed on, agreeing to pay the costs of both the defense attorneys and the prosecutors.

All they needed was a teacher to teach evolution—or at least to cop to teaching evolution—and a prosecutor to take the case. One of the town prosecutors was friends with John Scopes, a twenty-four-year-old teacher who sometimes taught biology when the regular biology teacher was out.

There was the small problem of Scopes not recalling whether he had ever taught evolution—and indeed, not even being the school's biology teacher. The pharmacist pulled a popular biology book off his shelf, **Hunter's Civic Biology,** and asked Scopes if he had ever used it to prepare for class when he substituted for the regular biology teacher. (Among the scientific facts taught in **Hunter's Civic Biology** is that Caucasians, "represented by the civilized white inhabitants of Europe and America," are "the highest type of all."[16]) Scopes said he had. The druggist excitedly proclaimed that the book mentioned evolution and everyone agreed that this was sufficient evidence for Scopes to be their defendant.

So right there in the drugstore, Scopes cheerfully admitted to the misdemeanor offense of teaching evolution and a warrant was sworn out for his arrest. The school superintendent delightedly exclaimed, "Something has happened that's going to put Dayton on the map!"

Publicity flyers were immediately sent to New York announcing a trial on evolution. Both the prosecution and the defense were eager to rush the case to trial as quickly as possible—in order to prevent another town from beating Dayton to the punch and getting all the publicity. Each side retained prominent blowhards to assist: populist Democrat William Jennings Bryan for the prosecution and Clarence Darrow for the defense. From beginning to end, the Scopes trial was a scheme cooked up in New York and pawned off on the good citizens of Dayton, much like **Cats.**

Civic leaders formed a Scopes Trial Entertainment Committee to plan activities around the trial. The town erected tents for the show and requested extra trains to accommodate the expected crowds. Pamphlets were prepared, touting the town's virtues. A carnival atmosphere attended the trial, with street performers and bands. Stores in Dayton got into the spirit of things by displaying monkeys in shop windows and selling "simian sodas." The sheriff decorated his motorcycle with a sign that said "Monkeyville Police." The Progressive Club produced a souvenir coin for the trial showing a monkey wearing a straw hat. The drugstore where the plan was hatched displayed a huge banner proudly proclaiming, "Where It Started."

The rest of Tennessee was not so thrilled with Dayton's public relations stunt. Chattanooga Congressman Foster V. Brown summarized the whole affair when he said the trial was "not a fight for evolution or against evolution, but a fight against obscurity."

Hardly a reviled figure by the townspeople, Scopes had to ask his students to testify against him, telling them they would be doing him a favor, and even coached the students on their answers. At least the students knew who Scopes was. When the famous defense attorneys arrived in Dayton for the first day of trial, they didn't recognize their client and handed Scopes their bags. Worried he might be asked if he was a biology teacher at trial, Scopes never took the stand in his own defense.[17]

The defense sought to turn the case into a trial on God, rather than a trial on whether taxpayers could decide what would be taught in the public schools. Defense lawyers repeatedly moved to exclude the court's opening prayer on the grounds that it would prejudice the jury. When those motions failed, the defense demanded opening prayers only from people who believed in a god of nature. The judge turned the matter over to the local pastors' association. Being braying fundamentalist lunatics, the local pastors agreed to alternate prayers between pastors who prayed to God and pastors who prayed to Mother Earth.

In his opening statement, Clarence Darrow compared fundamentalist Christians to dogs, suggesting that the best thing would be to strangle them: "To strangle puppies is good when they grow up into mad dogs." Just a little more than a decade before the rise of monstrous atheistic war machines in Nazi Germany and the Soviet Union, Darrow informed the court, "There is nothing else, Your Honor, that has caused the difference of opinion, of bitterness or hatred, of war, of cruelty that religion has caused."

Despite the defense's religious hysterics, lead prosecutor Tom Stewart repeatedly returned to the dry technicalities of the law, saying the misdemeanor law was "an effort on the part of the legislature to control the expenditure of state funds, which it has the right to do." He denied that anyone's free speech rights were at issue. "Mr. Scopes might have taken his stand on the street corners and expounded until he became hoarse," he said, "but he cannot go into the public schools" and teach evolution.[18] Stewart opposed the defense's request to bring in expert witnesses: "They will say [evolution] was simply the method by which God created man. I don't care. This act says you cannot [teach it]."[19]

The judge largely succeeded in keeping the case confined to the law at issue, but he did allow Darrow a one-day Show Trial on God out of the hearing of the jury. Darrow called Bryan as his only witness and interrogated him about his personal interpretation of the Book of Genesis. The prosecution objected to the sideshow, but keeping Bryan from taking the stand would be like keeping Chuck Schumer from a microphone. For two hours, Darrow asked Bryan such questions as "Do you believe [God] made . . . such a fish and it was big enough to swallow Jonah?"

The atheists had their fun with Bryan, but the jury never heard any of it, inasmuch as it was utterly irrelevant to the misdemeanor statute. The next day, Bryan was champing at the bit to call Darrow as a witness and force him to answer questions, but the prosecutors forbade it. When the jury returned, Darrow said, "We cannot even explain to you that we think you should return a verdict of not guilty. We do not see how you could. We do not ask it." And so the jury did vote to convict Scopes on the misdemeanor offense of teaching evolution. Scopes was given a $100 fine, which Bryan offered to pay.

The Tennessee Supreme Court upheld the misdemeanor law on appeal but threw out Scopes's conviction on a technicality. (The judge, rather than the jury, had levied the $100 fine.) Scopes called the dismissal of his conviction a "disappointment."[20] The ACLU again put out an offer to bring a test case challenging any evolution law, but to no avail. The antievolution laws remained on the books in half a dozen states for another forty years. Still, somehow, the republic survived.

In other words, the movie **Inherit the Wind** portrays the Scopes trial about as accurately as **The Flintstones** portrays prehistoric man. The original play, written in 1955, was intended to be an allegory for McCarthyism. In the fifties, everything was an allegory for McCarthyism. **The Crucible** was an allegory for McCarthyism. **Bad Day at Black Rock** was an allegory for McCarthyism. **Invasion of the Body Snatchers** was an allegory for McCarthyism. McCarthy was an allegory for McCarthyism. For people who were living in abject terror during the McCarthy era, liberals sure churned out a lot of plays, movies, and TV shows about their victimization. When constitutional scholar Gerald Gunther went to see the Broadway play version of **Inherit the Wind,** he stormed out in disgust. "I ended up actually sympathizing with Bryan," he said later, "even though I was and continue to be opposed to his ideas in the case, simply because the playwrights had drawn the character in such comic strip terms."[21]

And yet this fantasy of brave liberals standing up to fascistic Christians has permeated the entire debate over evolution. Liberals act as if they have to maintain a constant vigil against the coming theocracy in America because of what happened in **Inherit the Wind.** But consider that this vicious portrayal of Christians was the first in-flight movie ever shown in a first-class cabin on TWA.[22] Try to imagine a movie that portrayed Muslims as ignorant, backward brutes. Forget it—your mind hasn't yet evolved to the point where you could even conceive of the worldwide chaotic hysteria that would follow the release of such a movie. Today, **Inherit the Wind** is shown in high school and junior high school science classes across the country.[23]

■ ■ ■

THE only religious belief driving opinions about evolution is atheism. God can do anything, including evolution. But the value of Darwinism for atheists is that it is the only way they can explain why we are here. (It's an accident!) If evolution doesn't work out for them, they'll have to expand on theories about extraterrestrials or comets bringing life to Earth. Harvard population biologist Richard Lewontin said, "[T]he tolerance of the scientific community for unsubstantiated just-so stories" of evolution and its willingness to accept "the patent absurdity of some of its constructs" flowed from the scientists' prior commitment to materialism. Materialism is absolute, Lewontin said, "for we cannot allow a divine foot in the door."[24]

Contrary to the cult members' description of science as requiring the exclusion of God, until the last few decades the only reason to do science was to understand God. All the real scientists believed their work was discovering God in the universe—Nicolaus Copernicus, Johannes Kepler, Galileo, René Descartes, Francis Bacon, Isaac Newton, Robert Boyle, Michael Faraday, Gregor Mendel, Louis Pasteur, William Thomson Kelvin, George Gabriel Stokes, James Clerk Maxwell, Max Planck, Albert Einstein, Wolfgang Pauli. I guess they weren't doing real "science."

Louis Pasteur said that "science brings men nearer to God." Pasteur was also, incidentally, one of Darwin's most scathing critics, not on religious grounds but on scientific ones. The inscription over the door to Max Planck's laboratory said, "Let no one enter here who does not have faith."

Sir Isaac Newton, who wrote a book about the prophecies of Daniel, said, "The most beautiful system of the sun, planets, and comets, could only proceed from the counsel and dominion of an intelligent and powerful Being." Wolfgang Pauli, called "the whip of God," believed the greatest problem with science was "the lack of soul in the modern scientific conception of the world." His stated objective was to find the "spirit of matter."

Atheists absurdly try to claim Albert Einstein as one of their own simply because he claimed not to believe in a "personal God." I don't know what that means beyond establishing that he was not a fundamentalist Christian, which I already knew. Einstein described his life's work as trying to uncover God's thoughts: "I am not interested in this phenomenon or that phenomenon. I want to know God's thoughts—the rest are mere details." He said he believed in a God "who reveals himself in the orderly harmony of what exists." He famously said in a letter to Niels Bohr that "an inner voice" told him the theory of quantum mechanics "is not yet the real thing. The theory says a lot, but does not really bring us any closer to the secret of the Old One. I, at any rate, am convinced that He does not throw dice."

Bohr had not kept up his **Scientific American** subscription so he did not know he was supposed to denounce Einstein for "filling the gaps with God." Instead he responded, "Stop telling God what He must do!" If Eugenie Scott had ever found these letters, Bohr and Einstein would have been banned from teaching science at any high school in America.

Evolution cultists come up with crackpot religion, no more scientific than the intergalactic ruler Xenu, and their sole claim to "science" is that they have rigorously excluded God. Liberals have harnessed the language of "science" in order to destroy science. If our goal is to keep religion out of the classroom, evolution has got to go.

11 THE APED CRUSADER

Because though they knew God, they did not glorify Him as God, or thank Him, but rather became vain in their reasonings, and their heart, lacking understanding, was darkened.

Professing to be wise, they became fools;

And changed the glory of the incorruptible God into the likeness of an image of corruptible man and of birds and four-footed animals and reptiles.

—Romans 1:21-23

aving given up on proving evolution scientifically, now the Darwiniacs simply assert that it is true and rush ahead to their main point, which is that God does not exist. On one hand, they're constantly proclaiming that it's possible to believe in God and in evolution, and thereby implying that only a religious belief could

keep anyone from believing in evolution. And then when no one's looking, they announce that evolution has disproved God.

Of course it's possible to believe in God and in evolution. God can wind the clock, however the clock works. But that's not the plan of the Darwiniacs. They hysterically demand that we all pretend their pseudoscience is science and then keep slipping in the fact that evolution shows that belief in God is just a biological compulsion.

Philosophy professor and Darwiniac Daniel Dennett claims to study religion scientifically, saying, "Belief can be explained in much the way that cancer can."[1] He wonders why humans have a "craving" to believe in God. But there is no more scientific evidence for their creation story than for the Biblical creation story—probably less—so how about explaining their "craving" to believe in natural selection? What's that about?

Whether they conceive of themselves as practicing "religion" as such is irrelevant. Darwiniacs have faith in some biological mutation process that dictates a consistent set of beliefs and faiths—among which is the belief that they are not practicing religion, and therefore government advancement of their beliefs is not prohibited by the Constitution.

Compared with their fanciful story of human consciousness developing by random mutation and a bloody battle for survival, the story of Genesis is quantum physics. It's not merely opposable thumbs and a bipedal gait that make us distinct from the other beasts. It is consciousness of our mortality, a moral sense, language, mathematics, art, beauty, music, love, longings for immortality, a sense of symmetry, the soul's ascent, the ability to accessorize, and our fascination with Branson, Missouri—none of which make sense in Darwinian terms. Darwiniacs like Dennett avoid explaining the human soul by calling the soul an illusion. As Dennett says, "[If] mindless evolution could account for the breathtakingly clever artifacts of the biosphere, how could the products of our own 'real' minds be exempt from an evolutionary explanation?"

Genesis posits a simple version of the human story: Adam and Eve are awakened to good and evil by their sin of pride, become aware of their nakedness, and stumble blinking out into the forest. However literal or metaphorical the story is, no one has improved on it in 4,000 years. No Freudian has a clearer image of man's consciousness. We are in God's image, and we're the only ones in God's image, which is why we eat escargot rather than worship them. Whatever your religious persuasion, if you believe we are distinct from the beasts, you're with God.

The Darwiniacs' creationism story is that man

comes from an apelike ancestor and they will accept no other answer. They cling to Darwinism even as the contrary evidence accumulates, because it allows them to ignore God. Liberal secularists will not admit evolution is a crock until they have concocted a new creation myth that also excludes God.

It used to be that Darwiniacs avoided lucid statements of the significance of their religion. That's over. Dennett says it's time to abandon the "taboo" against attacking religion, a taboo similar to the PLO's taboo against attacking Israel. Toward the end of increasing attacks on religion, Dennett has written a book called **Breaking the Spell,** in which he describes religious belief itself as a mere biological quirk in the Darwinian process. In the same book, Dennett attacks religious belief as a malignant force. It seems the miracle mechanism of natural selection has fallen down on the job if it failed to eliminate this harmful mutation. Luckily, Darwinism is a nondisprovable pseudoscience, otherwise, it might be difficult to explain how religion can be an unfit mutation and, at the same time, has won the battle of survival. Everything proves evolution. Good traits, bad traits, inexplicable organs, a tendency to eat poison, half-off sales at Macy's—anything that happens confirms Darwin's theory!

Dennett states as scientific fact that God does not answer prayers: "Certainly the idea of a God that can answer prayers and whom you can talk to, and who intervenes in the world—that's a hopeless idea. There's no such thing."[2] He optimistically refers to Darwinism as a "universal acid," a substance "so corrosive that it will eat through **anything**!" Thus, he says, evolution "eats through just about every traditional concept and leaves in its wake a revolutionized world-view."[3] That's putting it mildly, Professor. Evolution even eats through logic. According to Dennett, the universal acid of Darwinism will "dissolv[e] the illusion of our own authorship, our own divine spark of creativity and understanding."[4] Science has proved it: God is dead.

Richard Dawkins produced a two-part television series for Britain's Channel 4 that is nothing but an all-out attack on religion, titled **Root of All Evil?** He compares Moses to Hitler, says religion is equivalent to child abuse, and calls the New Testament a "sadomasochistic doctrine." In the show titled "The God Delusion," Dawkins stands outside the New Life Church in Colorado Springs, warning his British audience of "Christian fascism" and a growing "American Taliban."[5] (I defy any of my coreligionists to tell me they do not laugh at the idea of Dawkins burning in hell.)

While relentlessly attacking God, the Darwin cult hides behind the claim that they are merely doing "science." The **New York Times** stated unequivocally in an article on evolution that science can say nothing about "why we are here or how we should live." (That's what the **New York Times** op-ed page is for!) Maybe a real science like quantum physics doesn't speak to "why we are here or how we should live,"[6] but evolution's devotees pronounce on those questions all the time.

The theory of gravity has never been invoked to justify mass murder, genocide, or eugenics. Darwin's theory of evolution has. From Marx to Hitler, the men responsible for the greatest mass murders of the twentieth century were avid Darwinists.

Upon first reading **The Origin of Species,** Darwin's mentor from Cambridge, Adam Sedgwick, wrote a letter warning Darwin that he was "deep in the mire of folly" if he was trying to remove the idea of morality from nature. If such a separation between the physical and the moral were ever to occur, Sedgwick said, it would "sink the human race into a lower grade of degradation than any into which it has fallen since its written records tell us of its history."[7]

As Darwinism gained currency, humanity did sink into greater degradation and brutalization than any since written records of human history began. A generation later, the world would witness the rise of the eugenics movement; racial hygiene societies; the first genocide in recorded history; Nazi Germany; Stalinist gulags; and the slaughter of 70 million Chinese at the hands of their exalted chairman. To be sure, other books were published on the eve of the bloody twentieth century. But Hitler and Marx were not citing Louisa May Alcott's **Little Women** for support. They were citing Darwin.

After reading Darwin's **The Origin of Species,** Marx dashed a note to Engels, saying, "This is the book which contains the basis in natural history for our views."**8** While Marx saw the "struggle" as among classes, Hitler conceived of the struggle as among the races. **Mein Kampf** means "My Struggle," which Hitler described in unmistakably Darwinian terms.

The path between Darwinism and Nazism may not be ineluctable, but it is more ineluctable than the evolutionary path from monkey to man. Darwin's theory overturned every aspect of Biblical morality. Instead of honor thy mother and father, the Darwinian ethic was honor thy children. Instead of enshrining moral values, the Darwinian ethic enshrined biological instincts. Instead of transcendent moral values, the Darwinian ethic said all morals are relative. Instead of sanctifying life, the Darwinian ethic sanctified death.

So it should not be surprising that eugenicists, racists, and assorted psychopaths always gravitate to Darwinism. From the most evil dictators to today's antismoking crusaders, sexual profligates, and animal rights nuts, Darwinism has infected the whole culture. And yet small schoolchildren who know that George Washington had slaves are never told of the centrality of Darwin's theory to Nazism, eugenics, abortion, infanticide, "racial hygiene" societies, genocide, and the Soviet gulags.

In his magnificent book **From Darwin to Hitler,** Richard Weikart documents the proliferation of eugenics organizations in Germany around 1900, all of which asserted their "scientific imprimatur by claiming harmony with the laws of evolution."[9] Darwin's theory was quickly and widely accepted among German biologists, a fact Darwin noted with approval, telling a friend, "The support which I receive from Germany is my chief ground for hoping that our views will ultimately prevail."[10] Darwinism provided the lingo for "scientific" racism at the onset of the twentieth century.[11] Not only were all eugenicists Darwinists, but nearly all Darwinists were scientific racists.[12]

The eugenics movement wasn't a wild, irrational perversion of Darwinism. It was a perfectly logical extension. Darwin himself believed the mentally disabled were a reversion to earlier humans—as proof, he cited the superior climbing skills of idiots.[13] The very word **eugenics** was coined by Darwin's half cousin, the famed eugenicist Sir Francis Galton, who conceived his ideas for selective breeding of humans after reading **The Origin of Species.** He hailed Darwin's book for demolishing "dogmatic barriers" and arousing "a spirit of rebellion against all ancient authorities." Galton approvingly noted that the "feeble nations of the world are necessarily giving way before the nobler varieties of mankind." But he despaired that without a program of eugenics, even the noble races were falling behind. Thus, Galton recommended forced sterilization of "unfit" humans, saying they could not be persuaded to stop breeding on their own. Eugenics, he said, "must be introduced into the national consciousness as a new religion."

Ernst Haeckel, the creative genius behind the fake embryo drawings that were cited as proof of evolution for a century, was an influential German Darwinist. Upon reading **The Origin of Species,** Haeckel abandoned his practice as a physician and became a leading proponent of racism and nationalism. He gleefully wrote that

Darwinism had overthrown religion's "anthropocentric fable," which had falsely elevated man above other species. He called politics "applied biology," a phrase later appropriated by the Nazis.

As Haeckel saw it, a "totally different value" must be assigned to "wooly-haired Negroes" from the value assigned to "civilized Europeans." Haeckel pronounced the "lowest" races of man "psychologically nearer to the mammals (apes and dogs)" than to white Europeans. He had phony drawings to prove that, too! In a diagram of six human and six monkey heads, he positioned the European at the beginning, farthest from the apes, and the black and aborigine right next to the apes. Like his fake embryo drawings, the inequality of human races was supposed to prove evolution by demonstrating how man might have evolved from the ape. Haeckel forthrightly stated, "The value of life of these lower wild peoples is equal to that of the anthropoid apes or stands only slightly above them."[14] With Haeckel's encouragement and advice, a Dutch scientist, Bernelot Moens, tried to artificially inseminate a black woman with the sperm from an ape. Haeckel suggested a similar project, using a chimpanzee, to a German "sexologist."

In America, Margaret Sanger, founder of Planned Parenthood and early proponent of "positive eugenics," also cited Darwinism to promote her "religion of birth control." She believed the theory of evolution provided grounds for eliminating the "unfit." In her 1922 book **Pivot of Civilization,** she advocated the elimination of "weeds . . . overrunning the human garden"; the segregation of "morons, misfits, and the maladjusted"; and the sterilization of "genetically inferior races." She was not oblique in identifying the "weeds" of humanity. In a 1939 manifesto titled "Birth Control and the Negro," she noted that "the poorer areas, particularly in the South . . . are producing alarmingly more than their share of future generations." Sanger recommended birth control to lessen the financial burden of caring for such weeds, "destined to become a burden to themselves, to their family, and ultimately to the nation." Undoubtedly, she would be delighted to know that today (1) Planned Parenthood is the leading provider of abortions in the United States, and (2) about 36 percent of our aborted babies are black, almost three times their percentage in the American population. Mission accomplished, Margaret!

Hitler's embrace of Darwinism is not a random fact, unrelated to the reason we know his name. It is impossible to understand Hitler's monstrous views apart from his belief in natural selection applied to races. He believed Darwin's theory of natural selection showed that "science" justified the extermination of the Jews.

In **Mein Kampf,** Hitler wrote:

> [E]veryone who believes in the higher evolution of living organisms must admit that every manifestation of the vital urge and struggle to live must have had a definite beginning in time and that one subject alone must have manifested it for the first time. It was then repeated again and again; and the practice of it spread over a widening area, until finally it passed into the subconscious of every member of the species, where it manifested itself as "instinct."

Hitler said that the "general evolution of things" had indeed "placed the best in the position that it had merited." I guess when you're the dictator, a theory that says the fittest always rise to the top is easy to believe. In **Mein Kampf,** Hitler explained that the races have higher and lower values and that his goal was "to promote the victory of the better, the stronger, and to demand the submission of the worse and weaker." This, he said, was in accordance with "the eternal will that rules this universe."

The Nazis were constantly producing charts to demonstrate how Germany's population was declining, especially compared with the rest of the world. Hitler offered all kinds of monetary awards, Hero Mother medals, and other blandishments as incentives to increase the "Aryan" population. Once the war began, those with large families were promised land in the colonies. But not just any Germans were encouraged to thrive. A big theme of the Nazis—demonstrated in charts, posters, pictures, and even newsreels and movies—was that too much money was being squandered on keeping "idiots" and mental defectives like princes in ivory towers, while healthy, hardworking Germans were starving on the streets.

This is why Hitler hated Christianity: It filled people's heads with silly, sentimental notions about helping the weak and infirm. Like Dawkins and Dennett, Hitler believed that the "heaviest blow that ever struck humanity was the coming of Christianity."**15** He rejected the idea of an ethical idea existing "if this idea is a danger for the racial life of the bearer of a higher ethics." Hitler denounced Christian charity as Jewish propaganda designed to hold the Germans back and help the Jews get an unnatural leg up. Otherwise, he believed, the "Aryans" would easily and naturally win the struggle for survival. The Holocaust was merely rushing along the natural process of evolution. Hitler said, "The Jews formed a sub-human counter race, predestined by their biological heritage to evil, just as the Nordic race was destined for nobility."

Liberals love to cite the fact that Hitler was anti-abortion and antigay, suggesting that he would fit right in with Christian conservatives in America. In an upbeat little piece on "Christian fascists" in **Harper's** magazine, Chris Hedges cited his ethics professor at Harvard Divinity School, James Luther Adams (an official with the Massachusetts ACLU), who "told us to watch closely the Christian right's persecution of homosexuals and lesbians. Hitler, he reminded us, promised to restore moral values not long after he took power in 1933." (One wonders if, in his ninety-three years on earth, the Harvard Divinity professor ever saved one soul.)

In 2004, Gloria Steinem cited Hitler's opposition to abortion in order to compare him to President Bush: "Among the first things [Hitler] did when he came to office was declare abortion a crime against the state."[16] In a column titled "Hitlers Great and Small," Ellen Goodman said pro-lifers "surely know that Hitler was a hard-line opponent of abortion." (Did that make him pro-life?)[17]

Hitler also loved dogs—that doesn't mean we should beat the little creatures. Still, it is puzzling that the author of the Holocaust should have scruples about homosexuality, much less abortion. Hitler's apparent "family values" don't make sense—until you realize that Hitler's worldview was based on Darwinism, not God. He didn't oppose abortion because he believed in the human soul. In fact, and needless to say, he didn't oppose abortion for everyone—only "Aryans." As Weikart explains:

> Hitler's ethical views do not comport well with traditional morality, since he based his morality on an entirely different foundation than did most conservatives. Hitler's morality was not based on traditional Judeo-Christian ethics nor Kant's categorical imperative, but was rather a complete repudiation of them. Instead, Hitler embraced an evolutionary ethic that made Darwinian fitness and health the only criteria for moral standards. The Darwinian struggle for existence, especially the struggle between different races, became the sole arbiter for morality.[18]

With all the books, essays, and Ph.D. theses that have been written promoting various theories on the rise of Nazism—the humiliation Germans felt as a result of the Versailles Treaty (which is the opposite of the truth; the problem was we didn't crush them sufficiently the first time), the weaknesses of the Weimar Republic, the bad economy after World War I, the German character, Hitler's pain at being rejected as an artist, the immense popularity of the "Hitler mustache"—you would think the powerful influence of Darwinism on Hitler, as well as the pervasiveness of Darwinism among the German intellectual class preceding the rise of Nazi Germany, would merit a small mention in college classrooms.

Liberals get upset with people like Hitler and Stalin who apply Darwinism in ways they don't like, but they can't quarrel with the underlying philosophy. Certain patterns of behavior and beliefs flow naturally from the idea that man is an accident with no greater moral significance than a stalk of corn. Eugenics is a logical application of Darwinism. Indeed, if Hitler hadn't given eugenics a bad name, public school students would be taught eugenics as a hard science in high school biology class right after watching **Inherit the Wind.**

Tenured bioethics professor Peter Singer at Princeton University's Center for Human Values represents the contemporary efflorescence of the Darwinian belief that man is just an animal like any other. Recognizing the bad name Marxism acquired in the twentieth century, Singer argues in his book **A Darwinian Left: Politics, Evolu-**

tion, and Cooperation that liberals should drop Marx as their demiurge and make Darwin the center of their cosmology.

Embracing a survival-of-the-fittest ethic, Singer says parents should have the right to kill newborn babies with birth defects, such as Down syndrome and hemophilia, because killing a disabled child, the Princeton professor says, "is not morally equivalent to killing a person." Magnanimously, Singer allows that he "would not require it."[19] Singer says there would be nothing morally wrong with parents conceiving children in order to harvest them for spare parts for an older child—or even for society to breed children on a massive scale for spare parts.[20] It goes without saying that Singer supports abortion rights, explaining in his book **Practical Ethics** that "the life of a fetus is of no greater value than the life of a nonhuman animal at a similar level of rationality, self-consciousness, awareness, capacity to feel, etc., and that since no fetus is a person no fetus has the same claim to life as a person."

While newborn babies are fair game, Singer says it is wrong to kick a mouse, which "does have an interest in not being tormented, because it will suffer if it is." Needless to say, if we can't kick a mouse, Singer also frowns on eating animals.

Singer believes apes deserve a legally protected

right to life, liberty, and due process. He has even issued a demand that the United Nations adopt his "Declaration on Great Apes," which refers to chimpanzees, bonobos, and gorillas as our "community of equals":

> Members of the community of equals are not to be deprived of their liberty, and are entitled to immediate release where there has been no form of due process. The detention of great apes who have not been convicted of any crime or who are not criminally liable should be permitted only where it can be shown that the detention is in their own interests or is necessary to protect the public. In such cases there must be a right of appeal, either directly or through an advocate, to a judicial tribunal.

I vote for "directly." I would like to see a baboon deliver a scorching summation to a jury. If the ape throws his own excrement at the judge, you could sell tickets.

Bringing joy to white supremacists everywhere, Singer compares the liberation of apes to the black liberation movement, saying we must "extend to other species the basic principle of equality that most of us recognize should be extended to all members of our own species." And if you don't understand the trouble apes are having, put on a gorilla suit and try to get a cab to stop for you in Manhattan. Liberals didn't want us to depose a brutal dictator responsible for mass murder, rape rooms, and human torture, but now they want us to protect the entire animal kingdom from assault.

Oh yes—Singer also believes sex with animals is acceptable. That's what gets you tenure at Princeton these days. He has no objections to necrophilia, provided consent was received when the love object was still alive.[21] For pronouncements that ought to land Singer in an institution for the criminally insane, he has been hailed by the liberal clergy at **The New Yorker** as "the most influential living philosopher." The **New York Times** says of Singer, "[N]o other living philosopher has had this kind of influence," and regularly publishes his ramblings. He is also published in the **Los Angeles Times, The Guardian,** and fun-sounding journals with names like **Hypatia: A Journal of Feminist Philosophy**—in other words, all the places that would never publish a conservative. The **New Scientist** credits Singer with creating "a moral framework for the modern animal rights movement."[22] And of course, Singer is rewarded with a prestigious professorship at Princeton, the Ira W. DeCamp Professorship of Bioethics at the university's Center for Human Values. The only accolade more shameful than that would be a Nobel Peace prize.

In **Slate** magazine, William Saletan tried to construct a liberal objection to Singer's argument for bestiality, happily settling on the absence of "consent" from the animal as the missing ingredient. And thus was bestiality narrowly averted as a plank in the Democratic platform!

But this is preposterous. Saletan is still imputing humanity to the animal. It is only through a quirk of its species that the poor mute goat is unable to communicate its consent, and man and beast are forever condemned to being star-crossed lovers, like Tristan and Isolde. I gather if the donkey were somehow able to grunt its permission to a sexual tryst, Saletan's objection would disappear. In the worldview of a liberal, it is wrong to have sex with a donkey because, absent the animal's consent, it would be rape. (Remember: **Whinny** means "no"!) If consent is the only objection to bestiality, then why are animals allowed to have sex with one another? And if sex is permissible between animals because neither one is capable of granting consent, then there is no logical objection to infants having sex with one another. How about this: Any person who wants to have sex with an animal should be in a straitjacket?

Liberals occasionally get huffy with Singer, just as they get huffy with Howard Dean. Like Dean, Singer says out loud what all liberals secretly believe. Liberals may quibble with Singer's conclusions, but his beliefs are logically unassailable if humans are no different from animals. By contrast, Christians are embarrassed by bad Christians, but they never say, "Oh well, adultery, thievery, and murder are perfectly logical extensions of Christianity." This is why liberals make such a big deal out of Christian "hypocrisy"—they can't complain about the underlying theory, only about Christians not living up to it. The worst a Darwinist can say to Peter Singer is "Shame on you for drawing logical conclusions from our shared premises!"

Once man's connection to the divine is denied, you can reason yourself from here to anywhere. As Jean-Paul Sartre said, "If God is dead, everything is permitted." Christians and Jews believe God gave us dominion over the Earth and all the plants and animals. That's not a license to abuse the Earth, but it does mean animals are subordinate to man. Showing mercy doesn't make them our equals. But for liberals, as soon as they conclude it's bad to torture animals, they think they should be able to marry them. Why not? If horses and donkeys can have sex with one another, why not Dick Durbin and his German shepherd?

What's the difference? Why should Dick and his faithful companion be denied the same basic right to marry the rest of us enjoy?

This is why liberals have panic attacks in response to any science that reveals differences in humans—differences in acquiring AIDS, IQ, mathematical abilities, and so on. If there really is a genetic component to IQ, what arguments do atheists have against sterilizing, enslaving, or killing the stupid among us? What if porpoises are as smart as humans? Do they get Senator Dodd's preschool care, too?

No science is ever frightening to Christians. Religious people don't need the science to come out any particular way on IQ or AIDS or sex differences any more than they need the science to come out any particular way on evolution. All humans were created in God's image, and we don't have a right to dominate or kill them even if they are fetuses, have disabilities, can't do math, look like Peter Singer, or have low IQs and refuse to release their SAT scores, like **New York Times** publisher Punch Sulzberger. God exists whether or not archaeopteryx ever evolved into something better. If evolution is true, then God created evolution.

But with the secular crowd, their political ideology keeps shutting off open scientific inquiry. Over and over again, they can only accept one answer: AIDS doesn't discriminate, IQ is an artificially contrived social construct with no genetic component, there are no innate differences between the sexes, and the human soul was created by random mutation and natural selection. Their religion prevents them from engaging in honest discussion because science without God leaves them with no arguments against barbarism—like bestiality, abortion, slavery, and eugenics.

The only lesson liberals learned from Hitler is: Don't discriminate! Not that human life is sacred, but that we must never say people are different. Girls are the same as boys, and homosexuals are the same as heterosexuals, and blacks are the same as whites. That's their plan for nipping any aspiring Hitlers in the bud. Stripped of a belief in God, they have no coherent philosophical argument against genocide. Rather than defending human life, most of the time liberals are manufacturing excuses to kill it. So we all have to waste money and do pointless things—like letting girls try out for the fire department and the Navy SEALs—because the alternative would be to discuss the undiscussable.

If, as Darwin says, humans are just an accident of nature with no greater moral significance than a horsefly, it's perfectly logical to equate owning a pet with slavery and eating a hamburger with murder. And why not treat humans like beasts?

Why not cannibalism? Humans: The New White Meat! Abortion, euthanasia, infanticide, assisted suicide—humans are just animals, so who cares?

Of course, most animal rights kooks would sooner abort an unborn human than an unborn tortoise.[23] After Palestinians strapped explosives to a donkey and sent the donkey to a group of Israelis at a bus stop in Jerusalem, Ingrid Newkirk, the cofounder and president of People for the Ethical Treatment of Animals (PETA), addressed a stern letter to "Your Excellency," Palestinian Authority chairman Yasser Arafat: "We have received many calls and letters from people shocked at the bombing." They were upset that the donkey died. "If you have the opportunity," Newkirk wrote, "will you please add to your burdens my request that you appeal to all those who listen to you to leave the animals out of this conflict?"

Even when liberals are trying to show their moderate, country-music–loving side by claiming to oppose having sex with the family dog, they can't formulate a logical argument to explain why not. The idea of objective truth handed down from the God of Abraham makes them squirm. So they just assert that what they assert is true because they assert it. It's no wonder liberals' default argument is to throw food.

Thanks to people like Peter Singer and the animal rights wackos, these aren't hypotheticals.

PETA posted a slide show on its website with graphic images of blacks being lynched, beaten, and burned alive—and compares their suffering to the treatment of chickens and elephants in a zoo. Another PETA billboard compares Christ to a pig, proclaiming under a giant photo of a pig, "He Died for Your Sins. Go Vegetarian." So at least the folks at PETA aren't a bunch of raving lunatics, like those Methodists Chris Hedges's Harvard professor warned him about.

Stephen R. Dujack, proposed witness for the Senate Democrats during the Supreme Court nomination hearings on Judge Samuel Alito, wrote an entire op-ed in the **Los Angeles Times** elaborating on the similarity of chicken farms to the Holocaust. As Dujack explained it:

> Like the victims of the Holocaust, animals are rounded up, trucked hundreds of miles to the kill floor and slaughtered. Comparisons to the Holocaust are not only appropriate but inescapable because, whether we wish to admit it or not, cows, chickens, pigs and turkeys are as capable of feeling loneliness, fear, pain, joy and affection as we are. To those who defend the modern-day holocaust on animals by saying that animals are slaughtered for food and give us sustenance, I ask: If the victims of the Holocaust had

been eaten, would that have justified the abuse and murder? Did the fact that lampshades, soaps and other "useful" products were made from their bodies excuse the Holocaust? No. Pain is pain.[24]

This is liberalism's real strength: It is no longer susceptible to reductio ad absurdum arguments. Before you can come up with a comical take on their worldview, some college professor has already written an article advancing the idea. With Darwin as their god, everything is just a matter of personal preference. For Singer, the utilitarian ethic is based on "quality of life" and prevention of suffering of living things smart enough to teach at Princeton. For Hitler, it was increasing the population of "Aryans." For liberals, the utilitarian ethic is equality of outcome—which they will enforce with fascistic zeal through confiscatory taxation, abortion on demand, racial quotas, gender-norming strength tests, and "everybody gets an 'A' and a blue ribbon."

But who decides which preference prevails? In October 2005, black activist Kamau Kambon told an audience at Howard University Law School that blacks should wipe "white people off the face of the planet."[25] So I guess that's his personal preference. How does Singer prove him wrong? Does being called "the most influential living philosopher" by **The New Yorker** make Singer more "fit" than Dr. Kambon? Will that make him "fit" enough to withstand a bullet? Whose survival-of-the-fittest regime wins? It's one assertion versus another assertion.

The fundamental difference between our religion and theirs is that theirs always tells them whatever they want to hear. Like the "living Constitution," Darwinism never disappoints liberals. They never say, "Well, I'd like to have cheap, meaningless sex tonight, but that would violate Darwinism." They can't even say, "I'd like to have cheap, meaningless sex tonight with a goat, but that would violate Darwinism." If you have an instinct to do it, it must be an evolved adaptation. Liberals subscribe to Darwinism not because it's "science," which they hate, but out of wishful thinking. Darwinism lets them off the hook morally. Do whatever you feel like doing—screw your secretary, kill Grandma, abort your defective child—Darwin says it will benefit humanity! Nothing is ever wrong as long as you follow your instincts. Just do it—and let Mother Earth sort out the winners and losers.

Religious people have certain rules based on a book about faith with lots of witnesses to that faith. God is not our secret Santa. His commands are not whatever we want them to be, and the Bible is not a "living" document. This is why it's always so disorienting when liberals harangue Christians about Biblical commands. Unlike the liberal religion, morality exists outside our egotistical, materialistic, fickle, megalomaniacal Hillary Clinton, Barbara Boxer, Colin Farrell, Paris Hilton selves. These rules are decreed by a legislator whose opinions are not subject to appeal by the ACLU. We can't discover penumbras that will suddenly allow us to endorse genocide, sex with animals, gay marriage, strip clubs, premarital sex, or whatever the latest liberal fad is. The truth is the truth whether we like it or not. While secularists are constantly comparing conservative Christians to Nazis, somehow it's always the godless doing the genocides.

By their fruits ye shall know them.

Notes

1. ON THE SEVENTH DAY, GOD RESTED AND LIBERALS SCHEMED

1. John Leo, "NEA Teaches Every Culture but Our Own," **Evening Sun** (Hanover, PA), September 4, 2002.
2. Jay Mathews, "In Harmony: Man's Machine," **Washington Post,** August 24, 1982.
3. Elisabeth Rosenthal, "Experts Find Reduced Effects of Chernobyl," **New York Times,** September 6, 2005.
4. Patricia Leigh Brown, "Eco-Privy: Bringing Outdoor Plumbing Indoors," **New York Times,** October 12, 1995.
5. Marc Morano, "Flush Toilets Called 'Environmental Disaster' by Greens," CNSNews.com, June 12, 2003.
6. Ibid.
7. Margalit Fox, "Betty Friedan, Who Ignited Cause

in 'Feminine Mystique,' Dies at 85," **New York Times,** February 5, 2006.

8. Felicity Barringer, "Bitter Division for Sierra Club on Immigration," **New York Times,** March 16, 2004.

9. "When You Break the Big Laws, You Do Not Get Freedom; You Do Not Even Get Anarchy. You Get the Small Laws."—G. K. Chesterton, **Daily News,** New York, July, 29, 1905.

10. Jeannine Stein, "Go Ask Suzi," **Los Angeles Times,** June 6, 1995.

11. **Brown v. Hot, Sexy & Safer Prods., Inc.,** 68 F. 3d 525 at 529 (1st Cir. 1995).

12. See, e.g., Philip Elmer-Dewitt, "Now for the Truth About Americans and Sex," **Time,** October 17, 1994 (citing "the first truly scientific survey" about sex in America by University of Chicago researchers that showed "The women most likely to achieve orgasm each and every time (32%) are, believe it or not, conservative Protestants"; and "Married couples have the most sex and are the most likely to have orgasms when they do").

13. **Brown v. Hot, Sexy & Safer,** 68 F. 3d at 536.

14. "Kansas Senator Says 'Fruits' Comment Not a Joke About Gays," Associated Press, January 31, 2006.

15. Susannah Meadows, "Cut, Thrust and Christ: Why Evangelicals Are Mastering the Art of College Debate," **Newsweek,** February 6, 2006.

16. William Saletan, "The Second Debate: Gore Recovers," **Slate,** October 13, 2000.

17. Terry Mattingly, "Reporters Often Not Prepared to

Write About Religion," Scripps Howard News Service, February 1, 2006.

18. Paul Gilfeather, "Fury Over Dubya Visit: No.10 Ban on Praying," **The Mirror,** November 18, 2003. (A Blair spokesman explained, "[G]iven all the negative publicity after their last prayer session together, Downing Street thought it would be wise to decline.")

19. Chip Berlet, "Religion and Politics in the United States," adapted from **The Public Eye Magazine,** Summer 2003. http://www.publiceye.org/magazine/v17n2/evangelical-demographics.html

20. Joseph Loconte, "Nearer, My God, to the G.O.P.," **New York Times,** January 2, 2006.

21. **Pulpit Politics: Kerry Not Kosher?,** **The Hotline,** June 17, 2004 (quoting Catholic League president William Donohue).

22. Frances Kissling, "Sex & the Clergy," **The Nation,** November 24, 2004.

23. Terry Eastland, "Outreach Goes Only So Far," Opinionjournal.Com, **Wall Street Journal,** August 6, 2004.

24. See, e.g., Matt Bai, "The Framing Wars," **New York Times,** July 17, 2005.

2. THE PASSION OF THE LIBERAL: THOU SHALT NOT PUNISH THE PERP

1. Steven Calebresi is working on a project on American Exceptionalism, which he will eventually turn into a book.

2. Stephen J. Markman and Paul G. Cassell, "Protecting the Innocent: A Response to the Bedau-Radelet Study," 41 **Stanford L. Rev.** 121 (1988) (coauthor with Stephen J. Markman) (reprinted in part in 136 **Cong. Rec.** S6648, May 21, 1990, and in Victor L. Strieb, ed., **A Capital Punishment Anthology** (Cincinnati: Anderson Pub. Co., 1993).

3. See, e.g., Fox Butterfield, "Major Crimes Fell in '95, Early Data by F.B.I. Indicate," **New York Times,** May 6, 1996 (citing Lawrence M. Friedman, a professor of law at Stanford University and an authority on the history of crime in America, noting that crime rates were much lower in the 1940s and 1950s).

4. See, e.g., Raymond Bonner, "Justice Dept. Set to Study Death Penalty in More Depth," **New York Times,** June 14, 2001. In a federal study examining 950 federal cases, begun by the Clinton Justice Department and completed by the Bush Justice Department, it was determined that in all federal prosecutions that could have ended with the death penalty, U.S. attorneys sought the death penalty in 81 percent of the cases when the defendant was white, 79 percent when the defendant was black, and 56 percent when the defendant was Hispanic.

5. After a rape victim spoke at the 1996 Republican National Convention, Brokaw interviewed her, saying, "The Republican Party is dominated by men and this convention is dominated by men. . . . Do you think before tonight they thought very much about what happens in America with rape?"

6. **Brewer v. Williams,** 430 U.S. 387, 392–93 (1977).

7. Paul G. Cassell, "Criminal Law: True Confessions About **Miranda**'s Legacy," **Texas Lawyer,** August 5, 1996 ("Along with Professor Richard Fowles of the University of Utah, I have run multiple regression analyses of this drop, which reveals that, even after controlling for such potentially competing factors of the 1960s as rising crime rates and increasing numbers of 'baby boom' juveniles, clearance rates still dropped significantly at the time of **Miranda**. Our equations suggest that clearance rates for violent crime would be several percentage points higher without **Miranda,** with the result that each year police would solve an additional 100,000-plus violent crimes.")

8. Otto G. Obermaier, "The Warren Court and American Politics," **New York Law Journal,** May 8, 2000 (reviewing Lucas A. Powe Jr., **The Warren Court and American Politics,** 2000).

9. Thomas Sowell, **Vision of the Anointed** (New York: Basic Books, 1995), p. 22.

10. Ibid.

11. Josh Saunders, "Ramsey Clark's Prosecution Complex," **Legal Affairs,** November/December 2003, http://www.legalaffairs.org/issues/November-December-2003/feature_saunders_novdec03.msp (quoting Victor Navasky, Kennedy Justice, New York: Atheneum, 1971).

12. Eleanor Clift, "How to Run Against Cuomo," **Newsweek,** December 9, 1991; Editorial: "Murder

in the Passive Voice," **Washington Times,** January
10, 1990 ("Edward Elwin, executive director of the
State Division of Parole, told us yesterday that New
York law prevents him from revealing the names of
the three board members who voted unanimously
to liberate Shawcross, but he admitted that Gov.
Mario Cuomo appointed all three").

13. Philip Shenon, "Meese Seen as Ready to Challenge
Rule on Telling Suspects of Rights," **New York
Times,** January 22, 1987.

14. James Q. Wilson, "Character and Culture," **Public
Interest,** March 22, 2005.

15. Editorial: "Dickensian Democracy," **New York
Times,** February 27, 2006.

16. Victoria Slind-Flor, "Attorney's Final Frenzy over
Harris," **National Law Journal,** May 4, 1992.

17. **Kreimer v. Bureau of Police for the Town of
Morristown,** 765 F. Supp. 181 (D.N.J. 1991),
Rev'd, 958 F.2D 1242 (3rd Cir. 1992).

18. See, e.g., "3rd Circuit Denies Two Death Row Appeals," **Pennsylvania Law Weekly,** November 6,
1995; Senator Orrin Hatch, Statement Before the
United States Senate, March 29, 1996.

19. See, e.g., Larry Elder, "The 'True Story' of Rubin
'Hurricane' Carter," **Capital Magazine,** February
4, 2000.

20. See e.g., Editorial, "Wrong Judge Pick," **The Au-
gusta Chronicle** (Georgia), October 27, 1993 (citing Paul Gigot of the **Wall Street Journal**).

21. See, e.g., Michael A. Riccardi, "Massiah-Jackson
Made 'Unacceptable' Remarks About HIV," **The**

Legal Intelligencer, February 10, 1998; Anick Jesdanun, "Judicial Nominee Defends Record," Associated Press, March 12, 1998; Chris Mondics, "Judge Answers Her Critics," **Philadelphia Inquirer**, March 12, 1998; Michael Matza, "Some Cases That Fueled Controversy," **Philadelphia Inquirer,** March 17, 1998.

22. Gareth Davis, David B. Muhlhausen, Dexter Ingram, and Ralph A. Rector, "The Facts About COPS: A Performance Overview of the Community Oriented Policing Services Program," The Heritage Foundation Center for Data Analysis, September 25, 2000, http://www.heritage.org/Research/Crime/CDA00-0.cfm.

23. "Building More Prisons and Jails Does Not Seem to Be the Answer to High Rate of Crime in U.S.," CBS News: **60 Minutes,** December 26, 1993.

24. Rebecca Carroll, "Report: Correctional Supervision Rising," Associated Press, November 2, 2005.

25. Fox Butterfield, "Number in Prison Grows Despite Crime Reduction," **New York Times,** August 10, 2000.

26. Laura Mansnerus, "As Crime Rate Drops, the Prison Rate Rises and the Debate Rages," **New York Times,** December 26, 1999.

27. Mike Krause, "Prison Costs Are Running Out of Control: Start with Cutting Drug Sentences," **Denver Post,** June 26, 2005.

28. Susan Williams, "Report: Prison Costs Hurting Education," **Charleston Gazette** (West Virginia), May 15, 2005.

29. Michael P. Jacobson, "Small Jail, Less Crime: Suffolk Is Smart to Reduce the Cost of a New Jail with Alternatives to Incarceration," **Newsday** (New York), March 13, 2005.
30. "Prisons Eat Up Tax Dollars," **Wisconsin State Journal** (Madison), January 27, 2005.
31. Gregory S. Reeves, "More Serving Time as Taxpayers Foot Bill," **Kansas City Star,** January 9, 2005.
32. Jeffrey Hoff, "Prison Overcrowding Poses Tough Issues," **New York Times,** February 24, 1991.
33. Clifford Krauss, "New York City Crime Falls but Just Why Is a Mystery," **New York Times,** January 1, 1995.
34. James Traub, "Giuliani Internalized," **New York Times,** February 11, 2001.
35. Clifford Krauss, "New York City's Gift to Clinton: A Lower National Crime Rate," **New York Times,** September 1, 1996.
36. See, e.g., Editorial: "The Legal Aid Crisis," **New York Times,** October 5, 1994 (mayor's response looked "authoritarian"); Editorial: "Mr. Giuliani's Energetic First Year," **New York Times,** November 25, 1997 (referring to Giuliani's "authoritarian tone"); Editorial: "The Mayor as Uncle Miltie," **New York Times,** November 25, 1997 (referring to the mayor's "authoritarian streak").
37. Ibid.
38. Ibid.
39. See, e.g., Jennifer Loven, "Clinton Says Answer to Terrorism Is Support of Current Administration," Associated Press, October 10, 2001. ("Clinton also

confirmed a failed U.S. attempt in 1996 to have Osama bin Laden arrested in Sudan and placed in Saudi Arabian custody and a CIA-sponsored plan to have Pakistani commandos hunt him down in 1999, abandoned after a military coup there. Bin Laden is the prime suspect in last month's terrorist attacks on New York and Washington.") Michael Ellison, "Attack on Afghanistan," **The Guardian** (London), October 11, 2001. ("Mr Clinton confirmed in a speech to executives at the Kennedy Centre in Washington DC that the US had failed in 1996 to have Bin Laden arrested in Sudan and that a CIA-sponsored initiative to have Pakistani commandos snare him three years later was abandoned because of a military coup in that country. A US cruise missile attack on Bin Laden training camps in Afghanistan in 1998 missed their main target.")

40. CNN: **Paula Zahn Now,** October 25, 2004.
41. Krauss, "New York City's Gift to Clinton."
42. Chris Matthews, "Cheap, Plentiful Gas and an SUV in Every Garage: Do Americans Want It All for Nothing?," MSNBC: **Hardball,** May 18, 2001.
43. Traub, "Giuliani Internalized."
44. Jean O. Pasco, "Sinclair Letter Turns Out to Be Another Exposé," **Los Angeles Times,** December 24, 2005.
45. Ibid.
46. Susan Johns, "Supporters Say Mission Now Unclear," **Sun-Journal** (Maine), May 25, 1992.
47. Gregory D. Kesich, "Supporters Say DNA Bill Not

Just About Dechaine," **Portland Press Herald** (Maine), February 6, 2006 ("Like the new bill, the 2001 legislation was sponsored by state Rep. Rosaire Paradis, D-Frenchville, who has been one of Dechaine's supporters since the early 1990s.")

48. "Lisbon Woman Spends $30,000 on Dechaine's Behalf," Associated Press, August 26, 2004.

3. THE MARTYR: WILLIE HORTON

1. David Bossie, **The Many Faces of John Kerry** (Nashville: Nelson County, 2004), p. 166 (citing Commonwealth of Massachusetts, Executive Office of Public Safety, Fax, May 2, 1996.)
2. Mary McGrory, "Slinging Mud on the Low Road to Office," **Newsday** (New York), November 4, 1988, p. 92.
3. Allan Fotheringham, "Republicans Riding to Victory on Racism," **Financial Post** (Toronto, Canada), October 31, 1988, p. 19.
4. Murray Kempton, "Bush Tactics Turn Ugly," **Newsday** (New York), October 30, 1988, p. 7.
5. Quoted in "Prison Experts Say Bush Attacks Dukakis Unfairly," **Los Angeles Times,** October 12, 1988.
6. Chris Black, "Specialists Defend Furlough Policy: Mass. Program Said to Be in Mainstream," **Boston Globe,** October 15, 1988.
7. Republican Press Conference, Federal News Service, October 25, 1988.
8. Jimmy Breslin, "Bush Used Me to Win: An Inter-

view with Willie Horton," **Newsday** (New York), January 20, 1989.

4. THE HOLIEST SACRAMENT: ABORTION

1. Lesley Stahl and Ed Bradley, "Partial-Birth Abortion: Abortion in the United States," CBS News: **60 Minutes,** June 2, 1996.
2. Ruth Padawer, "The Facts on Partial-Birth Abortion," **Record** (Bergen, NJ), September 15, 1996.
3. Susan Fraker, "Abortion Under Attack," **Newsweek,** June 5, 1978.
4. Laurie Belin, "The Real Issue: Choice," **Washington Post,** November 25, 1989.
5. Jan McReynolds, "The Need for Abortion Information," **Chicago Tribune,** July 11, 1991.
6. Susan A. Farrell, "Reframing Social Justice, Feminism and Abortion: Isn't It Time We Combated the Bishops' Opposition to Reproductive Rights on Our Terms?," **Conscience: Newsjournal of Prochoice Catholic Opinion,** April 30, 2005.
7. "On Abortion, Would Nominee Put Personal Views Aside?" **USA Today,** December 2, 2005.
8. "Schakowsky, Solis, Delauro, Schultz, Advocates Announce Opposition to Nomination of Judge Alito to Supreme Court," **US Fed News,** December 8, 2005.
9. Edward Eichner, director of medicine at a Cleveland abortion facility, statement in 1982, quoted in James Tunstead Burtchaell, **Rachel Weeping and**

Other Essays About Abortion (Kansas City: Andrews McMeel, 1982), p. 43.

10. "Former Governor Howard Dean (D-VT) Holds a News Teleconference on Abortion and Health Care," FDCH Political Transcripts, January 15, 2004.

11. Adam Nagourney, "Democrats Weigh De-emphasizing Abortion as an Issue," **New York Times,** December 24, 2004.

12. David D. Kirkpatrick, "For Democrats, Rethinking Abortion Position Meets with Mix of Reactions in Party," **New York Times,** February 16, 2005.

13. Gloria Febit (President, Planned Parenthood Federation of America), "Doctors' Opinions," **Chicago Tribune,** July 1, 2004 (letter to the editor).

14. Ibid.

15. Bob Woodward and Scott Armstrong, **The Brethren** (New York: Simon and Schuster, 1979), p. 233.

16. Tony Snow, Fox News Network: **Fox News Sunday,** August 9, 1998.

17. Michael Kinsley, "Fool Me Twice, Shame on Me," **Los Angeles Times,** January 16, 2005.

18. Michael Luo, "On Abortion, It's the Bible of Ambiguity," **New York Times,** November 13, 2005.

19. Matt Bai, "The Framing Wars," **New York Times,** July 17, 2005.

20. Ibid.

21. Stuart Taylor Jr., "Glimpses of the Least Pretentious of Men," **Legal Times,** February 8, 1993.

22. Ana Radelat, "Mississippi Judge at Center of Fight over Bush Nominees," Gannett News Service, January 24, 2002.
23. "Judge Pickering Denies Racism," CBS News: **60 Minutes,** March 28, 2004, http://www.cbsnews.com/stories/2004/03/25/60minutes/main608667.shtml.
24. Ibid.
25. Senator John Kerry Interview, ABC News Transcripts, **This Week with George Stephanopoulos,** January 18, 2004. ("On the weekend of Martin Luther King's birthday, this president chooses to appoint a cross-burning defending judge to the court.")

5. LIBERALS' DOCTRINE OF INFALLIBILITY: SOBBING HYSTERICAL WOMEN

1. Joseph Curl, "Spouse of Outed CIA Officer Signs on with Kerry," **Washington Times,** February 14, 2004.
2. Phil Donahue, "9-11: A Day Remembered," MSNBC: **Donahue,** September 10, 2002.
3. This is from the National Geographic website, one of the rare non-nut websites with a detailed timeline for the 9/11 attack, http://channel.nationalgeographic.com/channel/inside911/timeline.html
4. Sheryl Gay Stolberg, "9/11 Widows Skillfully Applied the Power of a Question: Why?," **New York Times,** April 1, 2004.

5. Kimberly Hefling, "9/11 Commission to Look into Atta Claim," Associated Press, August 9, 2005.
6. Douglas Jehl, "9/11 Panel Explains Move on Intelligence Unit," **New York Times,** August 13, 2005.
7. See, e.g., Rowan Scarborough, "Probe Fails to Find Pre-9/11 Atta Data," **Washington Times,** February 16, 2006.
8. Deborah Norville, "Condoleezza Rice Testifies Before the 9/11 Commission: How Was Her Testimony Received?," MSNBC: **Deborah Norville Tonight,** April 8, 2004.
9. Richard Miniter, **Disinformation: 22 Media Myths That Undermine the War on Terror** (Washington, D.C.: Regnery, 2005), pp. 45–47.
10. Ibid.
11. Norville, "Condoleezza Rice Testifies Before the 9/11 Commission."
12. Ibid.
13. **Seattle Times** news services, "Bush Ads with 9–11 Images Stir Controversy," **Seattle Times,** March 5, 2004.
14. David Tirrell-Wysocki, "Former Ambassador Wilson Endorses Kerry," Associated Press, October 23, 2003.
15. Joseph C. Wilson IV, "What I Didn't Find in Africa," **New York Times,** July 6, 2003.
16. Sean Callebs and Dana Bash, "Did Bush Oversell Iraqi Threat?," **CNN Live,** July 6, 2003.
17. Terry Moran, "Bush Administration Deceives America: President Used Known Falsehood to Lead

Americans to War," ABC News: **World News Tonight,** July 6, 2003.

18. "Ambassador Joseph Wilson Discusses Whether the Bush Administration Exaggerated Intelligence on Iraq's Weapons Program in Order to Justify War with Iraq," NBC News: **Meet the Press,** July 6, 2003.

19. Richard Leiby and Walter Pincus, "Retired Envoy: Nuclear Report Ignored," **Washington Post,** July 6, 2003.

20. Ibid.

21. John Distas, "Dean Wants Full Disclosure," **Union Leader** (Manchester, NH), July 11, 2003.

22. David Rennie, "CIA Man Denies Niger-Iraq Uranium Link," **Daily Telegraph** (London), July 7, 2003.

23. Robert Scheer, "A Diplomat's Undiplomatic Truth," **Los Angeles Times,** July 8, 2003.

24. Bianca Jagger, Fox News, **The Big Story with John Gibson,** July 9, 2003.

25. Robert Novak, "The Mission to Niger," **Chicago Sun-Times,** July 14, 2003.

26. Patrick E. Tyler, "Standoff in the Gulf," **New York Times,** December 18, 1990.

27. Ibid.

28. John F. Baker, "Book by Insider Wilson Signed," **Publishers Weekly,** October 20, 2003.

29. Clifford D. May, "Our Man in Niger," **National Review Online,** July 12, 2004, http://www.nationalreview.com/may/may200407121105.asp.

30. Joseph Wilson, **The Politics of Truth: Inside the**

Lies That Led to War and Betrayed My Wife's CIA Identity: A Diplomat's Memoir (New York: Carroll and Graf Publishing, 2004), p. 5.

31. Ibid., p. 346.
32. "Interview with Ambassador Joseph Wilson," CNN: **Paula Zahn Now,** September 29, 2003.
33. Nicholas D. Kristof, "Missing in Action: Truth," **New York Times,** May 6, 2003.
34. Walter Pincus, "CIA Did Not Share Doubt on Iraq Data: Bush Used Report of Uranium Bid," **Washington Post,** June 12, 2003.
35. Andrew Buncombe and Raymond Whitaker, "Ministers Knew War Papers Were Forged, Says Diplomat," **Independent** (London), June 29, 2003.
36. Susan Schmidt, "Plame's Input Is Cited on Niger Mission: Report Disputes Wilson's Claims on Trip, Wife's Role," **Washington Post,** July 10, 2004.
37. Richard Leiby, "Man Behind the Furor," **Washington Post,** October 1, 2003.
38. John Marelius, "Sunday Talk Shows Focus on Vietnam: How It Fits in '04 Contest Debated," **San Diego Union-Tribune,** May 3, 2004.
39. Ed Henry, "Heard on the Hill," **Roll Call,** September 30, 2003.
40. John McCaslin, "Inside the Beltway," **Washington Times,** April 27, 2004.
41. See, e.g., Donald N. Zillman, "108th Congress Lacks Military Veterans," News Releases, University of Maine School of Law, http://www.

usm.maine.edu/mcr/news/releases_02–03/zill-manoped.htm

42. Marc Morano and Randy Hall, "War Hero Status Called into Question," CNSNews.com, January 13, 2006.

43. Kathy Kiely, "Congressman Who Led the Charge in '91 Hangs Back for Now," **USA Today,** September 24, 2002.

44. Weekly Media Availability with House Minority Leader Nancy Pelosi, Federal News Service, May 6, 2004.

45. Jim Abrams, "Murtha Statement on War Being Unwinnable Draws Sharp GOP Response," Associated Press, May 6, 2004.

46. Nedra Pickler, "Bush Has Secret Post-election Plan for Guard Call-ups, Kerry Says," Associated Press, September 18, 2004.

47. Kenneth R. Bazinet and Richard Sisk, "Dems' Hawk Urges Pullout," **Daily News** (New York), November 18, 2005.

48. Dana Milbank, "An Unlikely Lonesome Dove," **Washington Post,** November 18, 2005.

49. Editorial: "The War in Washington," **Chicago Tribune,** November 22, 2005.

50. H.D.S. Greenway, "Bush's Patriotism Smear," **Boston Globe,** November 29, 2005.

51. News Summary, **New York Times,** November 18, 2005.

52. Elisabeth Bumiller, "Cheney Sees 'Shameless' Revisionism on War," **New York Times,** November 22, 2005.

53. Will Dana, "Master of the Game," RollingStone.com, July 13, 2004.
54. Josh Gerstein, "Saudis, Arabs Funneled Millions to President Clinton's Library," **New York Sun,** November 22, 2004.
55. http://clark04.com/moore/
56. Nicholas D. Kristof, "A Challenge for Bill O'Reilly," **New York Times,** December 18, 2005.
57. A. O. Scott, "Where Have All the Howlers Gone?," **New York Times,** December 18, 2005, Section 2, p. 1; Manohla Dargis, "Masculinity and Its Discontents in Marlboro Country," **New York Times,** December 18, 2005, Section 2, p. 13; Frank Rich, "Two Gay Cowboys Hit a Home Run," **New York Times,** December 18, 2005, Section 4, p. 13; Guy Trebay, "Cowboys, Just Like in the Movie," **New York Times,** December 18, 2005, Section 9, p. 1.

6. THE LIBERAL PRIESTHOOD:
SPARE THE ROD, SPOIL THE TEACHER

1. See David Limbaugh, **Persecution: How Liberals Are Waging War Against Christianity** (Washington, D.C., Regnery, 2003).
2. David Salisbury, "Preschool Is No Answer," CATO Institute, Policy Papers, January 10, 2002, http://www.cato.org/pub_display.php?pub_id=5562.
3. Darcy Olsen, "Assessing Proposals for Preschool and Kindergarten: Essential Information for Parents, Taxpayers and Policymakers," Goldwater Institute Policy Report No. 201, Feburary 8, 2005

(citing, inter alia, U.S. Department of Education, National Center for Education Statistics, **International Comparisons in Fourth Grade Reading Literacy: Findings from the Progress in International Reading Literacy Study,** April 2003; Mullis et al., **PIRLS 2001 International Report: Study of Reading Literacy Achievement in Primary Schools,** Boston College, 2003, Chapter 1, avaliable at timss.bc.edu/pirls2001i/pdf/P1_IR_Ch01.pdf; and U.S. Department of Education, National Center for Education Statistics, **Outcomes of Learning: Results from the 2000 Program for International Student Assessment of 15-year-olds in Reading, Mathematics and Science Literacy,** December 2001, Chapter 2, available at nces.ed.gov/pubs2002/2002115.pdf).

4. David Salisbury, "Real Education Reform," **New York Sun,** February 17, 2005. ("According to 1999 data from the National Center for Education Statistics, teachers comprise only 52.2% of all public-school personnel in America. In private schools, the percentage is above 80%.")

5. "Speaker's Corner," **Business/Education Insider** (Heritage Foundation), May 1992 (citing **Congressional Record,** August 1, 1985).

6. Richard Vedder, "Comparable Worth," **Education Next,** 2003.

7. Michael Podgursky, "Fringe Benefits," **Education Next,** 2003,http://www.educationnext.org/20033/71.html

8. Ibid., 63.6 years old for women and 63.7 for men.

9. Roger H. Weaver, "Real Test Is, Did the Kids Learn to Think?," **Los Angeles Times,** November 5, 2003.

10. "Texas-Area Teachers Use Vacations to Work Other Jobs," **San Antonio Express-News,** July 11, 2005.

11. Dave Eggers, Ninive Calegari, and Daniel Moulthrop, "Reading, Writing, Retailing," **New York Times,** June 27, 2005.

12. Saria Carter Saccocio cleans her office toilets herself because she can't afford a cleaning service. After starting in a trailer park, Dr. Carter Saccocio worked her way through medical school, leaving with "only $85,000" in student loans. She began her own practice in 2005. To make it work, she cleans her own toilets and her mother does the bookkeeping. "Dr. Carter's Family Practice: A Fort Lauderdale Doctor Vows to Spend 20 Minutes with Each Patient, Always Has a Hug—and Makes House Calls," Medicine, **Miami Herald,** June 16, 2005.

13. Frederick M. Hess, "Teacher Quality, Teacher Pay," **Policy Review,** April 1, 2004.

14. Ray Sawhill, "Black and Right," **Salon,** November 10, 1999 (interview with Thomas Sowell).

15. Melanie Scarborough, "More Than Money for Teachers," **Washington Post,** July 17, 2001.

16. See FairTest.org http://www.fairtest.org/examarts/winter99/edtestma.html.

17. Fran Schumer, "What She Earns Is Respect," **New York Times,** March 13, 2005.

18. Lizzie Newland, "Getting a Little Respect: Polls on

Prestigious Jobs Favor People Who Help Others; Often Topping the List Are Teachers, Firefighters, and Scientists," **Baltimore Sun,** June 22, 2005.

19. Gordon T. Anderson, "Do Teachers Have It Easy?," **CNN/Money,** July 28, 2003.

20. Margaret Boyd, letter to the editor: "Treat Teachers Better," **Dallas Morning News,** June 4, 2003.

21. Elissa Gootman, "5 Educators Accused of Playing Hooky . . . From Jobs Without Duties," **New York Times,** June 30, 2004.

22. Rocco Parascandola and Wil Cruz, "2 Charged in Slashing of Brooklyn Principal," **Newsday** (New York), January 22, 2005.

23. Julia Levy, "Female Teacher Arrested on Charges of Sexually Abusing a Student, 15," **New York Sun,** April 21, 2005; Joe McGurk, "'Knife-Wield' Teacher Busted," **New York Post,** April 21, 2005.

24. Jennifer Medina, "Former Yonkers Schools Chief Pleads Guilty to Perjury," **New York Times,** September 14, 2005.

25. David M. Herszenhorn, "Skipping Class to Wrestle, Teacher Lands in Trouble," **New York Times,** July 1, 2005.

26. Ellen Yan, "Teacher Turned Pro Wrestler Wants His Job Back," **Newsday** (New York), July 1, 2005.

27. Julia Levy, "Female Teacher Arrested on Charges of Sexually Abusing a Student, 15," **New York Sun,** April 21, 2005. ("The special commissioner of investigation for the city school district, Richard Condon, said his office has received 180 complaints this year about sexual abuse by teachers, and

it has substantiated claims against the teachers in 30 cases.")

28. Domingo Ramirez Jr., "Teacher Sex-Abuse Cases Soar," **Fort Worth Star-Telegram** (Texas), October 29, 2004.

29. Charol Shakeshaft, 2004 U.S. Department of Education Report, "Educator Sexual Misconduct: A Synthesis of Existing Literature," http://www.ed.gov/rschstat/research/pubs/misconductreview/index.html

30. Justin Blum, "Audit Says Union Lost $5 Million to Theft," **Washington Post,** January 17, 2003.

31. Michelle O'Donnell, "Former Auditor of Roslyn, L.I., School District Questions $7 Million Transactions," **New York Times,** June 3, 2004.

32. Michelle O'Donnell, "Shattered Impressions of a School Superintendent," **New York Times,** July 7, 2004.

33. Walter Benn Michaels, "Diversity's False Solace," **New York Times,** April 11, 2004.

7. THE LEFT'S WAR ON SCIENCE: BURNING BOOKS TO ADVANCE "SCIENCE"

1. "The 'Bell Curve' Agenda," **New York Times,** October 24, 1994.

2. Ibid.

3. John Carey, "Clever Arguments, Atrocious Science," **BusinessWeek,** November 7, 1994.

4. "An Angry Book Ignites a New Debate over Race,

Intelligence and Class," **Newsweek,** October 24, 1994.

5. Ellen Goodman, "'Bell Curve' Promotes Pessimism," **Austin American-Statesman** (Texas), October 25, 1994.

6. Robert Reno, "'Bell Curve' Just Gives Ammo to Garbage Carriers," **Newsday** (New York), October 26, 1994.

7. The APA 1996 Intelligence Task Force Report, http://www.indiana.edu/~intell/apa96.shtml.

8. "The 'Bell Curve' Agenda."

9. Thomas Morgan, "At Dartmouth, a Helping Candor," **New York Times,** November 8, 1987.

10. Jonathan Alter, "Press Coverage of AIDS Has Left Some Things Unsaid," **Newsweek,** September 23, 1985.

11. Malcolm Ritter, Today's Focus: "Hudson's AIDS May Dispel Myths of the Disease," Associated Press, July 26, 1985 (quoting Richard Dunne, executive director of the Gay Men's Health Crisis).

12. Bob Greene, "The AIDS Epidemic: Not for Gays Only," **Chicago Tribune,** January 30, 1985.

13. See, e.g., Richard Roeper, "Greene Back to Remind Us of the Good Ol' Days," **Chicago Sun-Times,** November 24, 2004.

14. Abigail Van Buren, "Getting the Facts Straight on AIDS," **Chicago Tribune,** August 12, 1985, p. 3.

15. "Women Living with AIDS," **The Oprah Winfrey Show,** transcript of February 18, 1987, p. 2.

16. Michael Fumento, "Do You Believe in Magic?," **American Spectator,** February 1992.

17. "AIDS in the Shadow of Love: A Teen AIDS Story," WGBH-TV Boston, September 18, 1991 (discussed in Michael Fumento, **The Myth of Heterosexual AIDS** Washington, D.C.: Regnery, 1993).

18. Fumento, **The Myth of Heterosexual AIDS,** p. 361.

19. Text of Surgeon General's AIDS Report, Associated Press, June 2, 1987.

20. Ibid.

21. "Tracking a Killer; Man of Letters; Preserving the Charter," **The MacNeil/Lehrer NewsHour,** February 24, 1987.

22. Thomas Morgan, "At Dartmouth, a Helping Candor," **New York Times,** November 8, 1987.

23. James Barron, "Learning the Facts of Life," **New York Times,** November 8, 1987.

24. Maureen Dowd, "Dr. Koop Defends His Crusade on AIDS," **New York Times,** April 6, 1987.

25. Ibid.

26. Erica E. Goode, "Communicating the Basic Facts Is Hard Enough: AIDS Makes It Even Tougher," **U.S. News & World Report,** November 16, 1987.

27. Dowd, "Dr. Koop Defends His Crusade."

28. Ibid.

29. Ibid.

30. "Koop criticizes **Cosmo,**" United Press International, February 19, 1988.

31. U.S. Health and Human Services and Centers for Disease Control Press Conference Re: AIDS Information and Education Campaign, Washington,

D.C., Federal News Service, October 17, 1988. (The CDC spokesman explained that the prior year's campaign focused on homosexual sex.)

32. Sandra Boodman, "Caution: The Surgeon General of the United States Can Be Hazardous to Your Complacency," **Washington Post,** November 15, 1987.

33. Lynn Simross, "Singles Mull Sexual Behavior as Fears of AIDS Intensify," **Los Angeles Times,** December 13, 1985.

34. Leonard Bernstein, "Shocked by Spread of AIDS, Women Fight Back," **Los Angeles Times,** March 31, 1987.

35. Michael Dobbs, "Harvard Chief's Comments on Women Assailed: Academics Critical of Remarks About Lack of Gender Equality," **Washington Post,** January 19, 2005, p. A2.

36. Marcella Bombardieri, "Summers' Remarks on Women Draw Fire," **Boston Globe,** January 17, 2005, p. A1.

37. "Professor Nancy Hopkins Discusses Why She Walked Out on Harvard President Lawrence Summers' Address," NBC: **Today,** January 18, 2005.

38. Adam Liptak and Michael Moss, The 2004 Campaign: "The North Carolina Senator: In Trial Work, Edwards Left a Trademark," **New York Times,** January 31, 2004.

39. Ibid.

40. John M. Freeman, Letter to the Editor: "A Broken Tort System," **Washington Post,** August 4, 2004.

41. See, e.g., Matthew Mosk, "In Delivery Room,

Baby and Doctor at Risk: Md. Case Highlights Issues in Malpractice Debate," **Washington Post,** November 27, 2004.

42. Connie Chung, "The Dangers of Breast Implants," CBS News: **Face to Face with Connie Chung,** December 10, 1990.

43. See, e.g., Marcia Angell, "Trial by Science," **New York Times,** December 9, 1998; William C. Smith, "No Escape from Science": 86 **A.B.A.J.** 60 (**ABA Journal**), August 2000.

44. Dan Rather, "Experts Confirm This Was the Coldest November–December on Record in the United States," **CBS Evening News,** January 5, 2001.

45. Greta Van Susteren, interview with Laurie David, Fox News Network, **Fox on the Record with Greta Van Susteren,** November 11, 2005.

46. "Aberdeen Sweltered in July 1936 Record Heat," **Aberdeen American News** (South Dakota), July 29, 2005.

47. "John Switzer, 1913 Flood Called Top Ohio Weather Event," **Columbus Dispatch** (Ohio), December 19, 1999, p. C8.

48. James Ivey, "Teeth-Rattling Temperatures Not a Record," **Omaha World Herald** (Nebraska), December 21, 2000, p. 1.

49. Jim Kirksey, "January the City's 5th Driest Ever," **Denver Post,** February 3, 1998, p. B2.

50. Chris Mooney, **The Republican War on Science** (New York: Basic Books, 2005).

51. Anna Quindlen, "A New Look, an Old Battle," **Newsweek,** April 9, 2001.
52. Michael Fumento, "The Adult Answer," **National Review,** December 20, 2004.
53. "The Lame Shall Walk," **Investor's Business Daily,** October 14, 2004.
54. Hankook Ilbo, "Stem Cell Research May Be Money Game," **Korea Times,** July 8, 2005.
55. James Kelly, "The Wrong Path," **National Review Online,** October 21, 2004.
56. Michael Fumento, "Adult Stem Cells Provide New Life for Livers," Scripps Howard News Service, October 20, 2005.
57. Anthony Lewis, "Willie Horton Redux," **New York Times,** February 26, 2000.
58. Gina Kolata, "Parkinson's Research Is Set Back by Failure of Fetal Cell Implants," **New York Times,** March 8, 2001.
59. See generally, Michael Fumento, "Why the Media Miss the Stem-Cell Story," **Citizen Magazine,** May 2005, http://www.fumento.com/sustemcell.html.

8. THE CREATION MYTH: ON THE SIXTH DAY, GOD CREATED FRUIT FLIES

1. Michael Powell, "Doubting Rationalist," **Washington Post,** May 15, 2005; Michael Powell, "'Intelligent Design' Proponent Phillip Johnson, and How

He Came to Be," **Washington Post,** May 15, 2005.

2. Ariel Hart, "Stickers Put in Evolution Text Are the Subject of a Federal Trial," **New York Times,** November 9, 2004.

3. Laurie Goodstein, "California Parents File Suit Over Origins of Life Course," **New York Times,** January 11, 2006.

4. Laurie Goodstein, "Web of Faith: A Law and Science in Evolution Suit," **New York Times,** September 26, 2005.

5. Tom Bethell Replies, **American Spectator,** February 2001.

6. "Talking About Evolution with Richard Dawkins," PBS: **Think Tank with Ben Wattenberg,** October 18, 2001, transcript at http://www.pbs.org/thinktank/transcript410.html. ("Beahy [**sic**] should stop being lazy and should get up and think for himself about how the flagellum evolved instead of this cowardly, lazy copping out by simply saying, oh, I can't think of how it came about, therefore it must have been designed.")

7. Jerry Coyne, "The Case Against Intelligent Design: The Faith That Dare Not Speak Its Name," **New Republic Online,** August 11, 2005.

8. Sharon Begley, "Evolution Critics Are Under Fire for Flaws in 'Intelligent Design,'" **Wall Street Journal,** February 13, 2004.

9. http://www.nsta.org/main/news/stories/college_science.php?news_story_ID=47561.

10. David Berlinski, "A Scientific Scandal," **Commen-**

tary, April 1, 2003; "David Berlinski, A Scientific Scandal?," David Berlinski & Critics; Controversy; letter to the editor, **Commentary,** July 1, 2003.

11. Tom Bethell, **The Politically Incorrect Guide to Science** (Washington, D.C.: Regney, 2005), p. 210.

12. Kenneth Chang, "Study, in a First, Explains Evolution's Molecular Advance," **New York Times,** April 7, 2006.

13. George W. Cornell, "Scientists Say Modern Findings Show Absurdity of Darwinism," Associated Press, December 10, 1982.

14. Stephen C. Meyer, "Not by Chance: From Bacterial Propulsion Systems to Human DNA, Evidence of Intelligent Design Is Everywhere," **National Post** (Canada), December 1, 2005.

15. Carl Zimmer, "The Riddle of the Appendix," **New York Times,** August 9, 2005, p. F5.

16. David M. Raup, "Conflicts Between Darwin and Paleontology," **Bulletin, Field Museum of Natural History,** January 1979, pp. 22–23. More recently, Robert Lynn Carroll, former president of the Society of Vertebrate Paleontology, summarized the evidence this way: "Instead of showing gradual and continuous change through time, the major lineages appear suddenly in the fossil record, already exhibiting many of the features by which their modern representatives are recognized. It must be assumed that evolution occurs much more rapidly **between** groups than **within** groups." Robert Lynn Carroll, **Patterns and Processes of**

Vertebrate Evolution (New York: Cambridge University Press, 1997), pp. 2–4.

17. Raup, "Conflicts Between Darwin and Paleontology," p. 25.

18. Charles Darwin, **The Origin of Species,** reprint of 1st ed. (Cambridge, MA: Harvard University Press, 1964), p. 342.

19. Ironically, Gould was the Alexander Agassiz Professor of Zoology at Harvard, named after the man whose father was among Darwin's most formidable contemporaneous critics. And just to show an example of devolution in the world, the father, Louis Agassiz, wrote that nature shows "not only thought, it shows also premeditation, power, wisdom, greatness, prescience, omniscience, providence. In one word, all these facts in their natural connection proclaim aloud the One God, whom man may know, adore and love." Any Harvard professor who said such a thing today would immediately have his tenure revoked.

20. Carroll, **Patterns and Processes of Vertebrate Evolution,** pp. 2–4.

21. Rick Weiss and David Brown, "New Analyses Bolster Central Tenets of Evolution Theory," Newsbytes, **Washington Post,** September 26, 2005.

22. Stephanie Rosenbloom, "She's So Cool, So Smart, So Beautiful: Must Be a Girl Crush," **New York Times,** August 11, 2005.

23. Coyne, "The Case Against Intelligent Design."

24. John Noble Wilford, "Spectacular Fossils Record

Early Riot of Creation," **New York Times,** April 23, 1991.

25. Ibid.
26. Ibid.
27. Graham Lawton, "Life's Greatest Inventions: The Eye," **New Scientist,** April 9, 2005.
28. Wilford, "Spectacular Fossils."
29. Teresa Watanabe, "Enlisting Science to Find the Fingerprints of a Creator," **Los Angeles Times,** March 25, 2001.
30. Fred Heeren, "Paleontologic Agitprop?," **Insight,** July 24, 2000.

9. PROOF FOR HOW THE WALKMAN EVOLVED INTO THE iPOD BY RANDOM MUTATION

1. Stephen Jay Gould, **Hen's Teeth and Horse's Toes** (New York: Norton, 1993), p. 261.
2. Richard Dawkins, **Climbing Mount Improbable** (New York: Norton, 1996), pp. 118–20.
3. Steven Rose, "Life: The Code That Must Be Cracked," **The Guardian** (London), January 22, 2004.
4. Ibid. (quoting Roger Fouts, **Next of Kin: What Chimpanzees Have Taught Me About Who We Are** [1997]).
5. Paul Raeburn, "The Moth That Failed," **New York Times,** August 25, 2002 (review by Paul Raeburn, senior writer at **BusinessWeek** and president of the

National Association of Science Writers of Judith Hooper, **Of Moths and Men: An Evolutionary Tale: The Untold Story of Science and the Peppered Moth** (W. W. Norton & Company, 2002); see also Nicholas Wade, "Staple of Evolutionary Teaching May Not Be Textbook Case," **New York Times,** June 18, 2002.

6. H. Allen Orr, "Devolution: Why Intelligent Design Isn't," **New Yorker,** May 30, 2005.

7. Jonathan Wells, **Icons of Evolution** (Washington, D.C.: Regney, 2000), pp. 81–82 (quoting Darwin, **The Origin of Species,** p. 346).

8. Wells, **Icons of Evolution,** pp. 81–82 (quoting a September 10, 1860, letter to Asa Gray, in Francis Darwin, ed., **The Life and Letters of Charles Darwin** [1896], vol. 2, p. 131).

9. See Wells, **Icons of Evolution,** pp. 108–9.

10. Quoted in David Berlinski, "On the Origins of Life," **Commentary,** February 2006.

11. Jim Holt, "Supernatural Selection," **New York Times,** April 14, 2002.

10. THE SCIENTIFIC METHOD OF STONING AND BURNING

1. Fred Heeren, "Update: The Deed Is Done," **American Spectator,** December, 2000 ("Though few of the opposing faculty had the training or knowledge even to understand Dembski's mathematical methods . . ."); see also Lauren Kern, "Monkey Business," **Dallas Observer** (Texas), January 11, 2001

(noting that the committee assembled to investigate Dembski consisted of "nine biologists, philosophers, science historians, and theologians—primarily from other universities" and that Dembski remarked that the school was risking "his academic reputation with a very public review by scholars he wasn't even sure were qualified to assess his work.")

2. Kenneth Chang, "In Explaining Life's Complexity, Darwinists and Doubters Clash," **New York Times,** August 22, 2005. ("Dr. Dembski says designed objects, like Mount Rushmore, show complex, purposeful patterns that evince the existence of intelligence. Mathematical calculations like those he has developed, he argues, could detect those patterns, for example, distinguishing Mount Rushmore from Mount St. Helens. But other mathematicians have said that Dr. Dembski's calculations do not work and cannot be applied in the real world.")

3. David Silverstone, letter to the editor: "Factual Relativism," **New York Times,** June 15, 2005 ("Is it any wonder that the theory of evolution is under siege, or that many Americans still believe in a link between Iraq and 9/11, when facts and evidence can be dismissed as matters of opinion?")

4. Mary K. Crow, M.D., letter to the editor: "Did Belief Win Out Over Reason?," **New York Times,** November 8, 2004.

5. Dana Mack, "What the Sex Educators Teach," **Commentary,** August 1993 (citing Planned Parenthood's "Teaching Safer Sex," "in which Peggy

Brick matter-of-factly lists brachiopractic inter-course among 30 sexual acts evaluated for HIV-in-fection risk").

6. See, e.g., Melissa Ludwig, "New Force in the Fray on State's Textbooks," **Austin American-Statesman** (Texas), July 9, 2003. ("But Eugenie Scott, Executive Director of the National Center for Science Education, says scientists such as William Dembski, Michael Behe and Jonathan Wells, all senior fellows at the institute, are not taken seriously by mainstream scientists. Scott and Maguire say work on intelligent design is not published in scientific, peer-reviewed journals.")

7. Bill O'Reilly, "Editor Ousted for Intelligent Design," Fox News Channel: **The O'Reilly Factor,** August 24, 2005.

8. Michael Powell, "Editor Explains Reasons for 'Intelligent Design' Article," **Washington Post,** August 19, 2005.

9. David Klinghoffer, "The Branding of a Heretic," **Wall Street Journal,** opinionjournal.com, January 28, 2005.

10. Powell, "Editor Explains Reasons for 'Intelligent Design' Article."

11. Ibid.

12. Ibid.

13. Paul J. Gough, "Emotional Rather Blasts 'New Journalism Order,'" Reuters, September 19, 2005.

14. Edward J. Larson, **Summer for the Gods** (New York: Basic Books, 1997).

15. Ibid., pp. 200–201.
16. George William Hunter, **A Civic Biology** (1914), p. 196, http://www.law.umkc.edu/faculty/projects/ftrials/scopes/hunt196.htm
17. Larson, **Summer for the Gods,** p. 174.
18. Ibid., pp. 161–162.
19. Ibid., p. 179.
20. Ibid., p. 221.
21. Ibid., p. 242.
22. Jack Schnedler, "The Real Scopes Trial: 'Inherit the Wind' Is Seared into the American Public Consciousness," **Arkansas Democrat-Gazette** (Little Rock), July 10, 2005.
23. See, e.g., Diane Carroll, "Evolution Debate Enters 'Round Two,'" **Kansas City Star,** January 30, 2005, http://www.kansascity.com/mld/kansascity/news/politics/10768962.htm. ("Celtie Johnson said her 10th-grade daughter felt appalled and humiliated two years ago when her biology teacher in the Shawnee Mission School District showed 'Inherit the Wind,' a film that depicted the 1925 Scopes 'monkey trial.' The film ridiculed the conservative Christians in it who criticized evolution, Johnson said. "That's hardly an unbiased view, she said."); "Drama on Scopes Trial Is Barred from Class," **New York Times,** February 21, 1984 ("Teachers Association demanded arbitration of principal's decision not to allow an Earth science teacher to show the 1960 movie **Inherit the Wind** to 300 students during class time"). See also Deb-

orah Robiglio, "Real Tool or Reel Copout?," **News and Observer** (Raleigh, NC), May 23, 1999 ("And, as an extra-credit option for his 10th-grade U.S. history students, he recently showed 'Inherit the Wind' after school. The movie is about a teacher who is tried for teaching the theory of evolution.")

24. J. Budziszewski, "The Second Tablet Project," **First Things,** June 1, 2002 (citing Harvard population biologist Richard Lewontin in the **New York Review of Books** [January 9, 1997]).

11. THE APED CRUSADER

1. Questions for Daniel C. Dennett, "The Nonbeliever," **New York Times,** January 22, 2006.
2. Ibid.
3. Daniel C. Dennett, **Darwin's Dangerous Idea: Evolution and the Meanings of Life** (New York: Simon and Schuster, 1995), p. 63.
4. Ibid.
5. "Dawkins: Religion Equals 'Child Abuse,'" WorldNetDaily.com, January 8, 2006.
6. Kenneth Chang, "A Debate Over Darwin: Evolution or Design?," **New York Times,** August 22, 2005.
7. Richard Weikart, **From Darwin to Hitler: Evolutionary Ethics, Eugenics, and Racism in Germany** (New York: Palgrave MacMillan, 2004), p. 1.

8. J. D. Bernal, **Marx & Science** (New York: International Publishers, 1952), p. 17.
9. **From Darwin to Hitler,** p. 70.
10. Ibid., p. 10.
11. Ibid., p. 126.
12. Ibid., p. 114.
13. Ibid., p. 95.
14. Ibid., p. 109.
15. Adolf Hitler, **Hitler's Table Talk** (New York: Enigma Books, 2000), pp. 6, 7 (night of July 11–12, 1941).
16. Burt Constable, "Steinem Says Another Bush Term Will Make Abortion a Crime," **Chicago Daily Herald,** May 27, 2004.
17. Ellen Goodman, "Hitlers Great and Small," **Baltimore Sun,** June 6, 1995.
18. Weikart, **From Darwin to Hitler,** p. 210.
19. Ronald Bailey, "The Pursuit of Happiness: Controversial Philosopher Peter Singer Argues for Animal Rights, Utilitarian Ethics, and a Darwinian Left," **Reason,** December 2000.
20. Marvin Olasky, "Blue-State Philosopher," **World Magazine,** November 27, 2004.
21. See, e.g., ibid., and Bailey, "The Pursuit of Happiness."
22. Nell Boyce, "Only Human," **New Scientist,** January 8, 2000.
23. Florida made it illegal to "take, possess, transport or sell"—they don't even mention "kill"—unborn gopher tortoises. Terry Brady, "Housing Project

Draws Fire," **News-Press** (Fort Myers, FL), November 12, 2005.

24. Stephen R. Dujack, "Animals Suffer a Perpetual 'Holocaust,'" **Los Angeles Times,** April 21, 2003.

25. See, e.g., Editorial: "Nobles and Knaves," **Washington Times,** October 22, 2005.

Acknowledgments

All my long-suffering, magnificent friends will be happier than I am when this book is finally finished so that I will stop pestering them to read chapters and can resume pestering them to read only my columns. The ones I bother the most are: Robert Caplain, Steve Gilbert, Melanie Graham, James Higgins, Jim Moody, and Ned Rice. Also, Hans Bader, Trish Baker, Jon Caldera, Mallory and Thomas Danaher, John Harrison, Gary Lawson, Jim Hughes, Mark Joseph, Mark Kielb, Merrill Kinstler, Jon Ledecky, David Limbaugh, Gene Meyer, Dan Travers, Jon Tukel, Joe Sobran, Jeff Schwartz, Rich Signorelli, Edward Sisson, Suzy Vasillov, and Bill Zachary. So many of my friends have helped me, I apologize now for the seven I've forgotten.

I am eternally indebted to Ned Rice, who gives me more jokes than I will ever admit. Jim Downey gives me enough ideas in a single phone call for an entire chapter, several of which are included here.

I couldn't have written about evolution without the generous tutoring of Michael Behe, David Berlinski, and William Dembski, all of whom are fabulous at translating complex ideas, unlike liberal arts types, who constantly force me to the dictionary to relearn the meaning of **quotidian.** Michael Fumento has been cheerfully exposing scientific frauds for decades and consequently gave me a lot of help with chapter 7—and anything else I could slip into his in-box. Doug Johnson and everyone at National Right to Life are a font of information and can always be counted on for the truth.

I owe an enormous debt of gratitude to the people I've tortured by getting my book in many months late: my publisher, Steve Ross; my editors, Doug Pepper and Jed Donahue; David Tran for his always brilliant book covers; my now-exhausted copy editor, Toni Rachiele; my sainted agent-for-life, Joni Evans; and my fabulous new agents, Suzanne Gluck and Mel Berger. Thanks in advance to my book publicists, Diana Banister and Anne Tyrrell.

And thanks always to my family, especially my mother and father, to whom all my books should be dedicated.

Index